SYMBOLS
Their Migration
and Universality

PLATE I.

APOLLO AND THE GAMMADION.

(From a vase in the *Kunsthistorisches Museum* of Vienna.)

SYMBOLS
Their Migration and Universality

Count Eugene Goblet d'Alviella

with an Introduction by
Sir George Birdwood, M.D., K.C.I.E.

DOVER PUBLICATIONS, INC.
Mineola, New York

Bibliographical Note

This Dover edition, first published in 2000, is an unabridged republication of the work originally published in 1894 under the title *The Migration of Symbols* by Messrs. Archibald Constable and Company, Westminster.

Library of Congress Cataloging-in-Publication Data

Goblet d'Alviella, Eugène, comte, 1846–1925.
    [Migration of symbols]
    Symbols : their migration and universality / Count Eugene Goblet d'Alviella ; with an introduction by George Birdwood.
        p. cm.
    Originally published: The migration of symbols. Westminster : A. Constable, 1894.
    ISBN 0-486-41437-X (pbk.)
    1. Symbolism. I. Title.

BL603 .G6 2000
302.2'223—dc21

00-024042

Manufactured in the United States of America
Dover Publications, Inc., 31 East 2nd Street, Mineola, N.Y. 11501

INTRODUCTION.

THOSE familiar with the delightful papers contributed in recent years by the Count Goblet
d'Alviella to the *Bulletin de l'Académie royale de
Belgique* on "le Triçûla, ou Vardhamâna des
Bouddhistes," "l'histoire du Globe Ailée," "la Croix
Gammée ou Svastika," "les Arbres Paradisiaques,"
and other allusive types of the ancient religions of
the Old World, warmly welcomed the publication,
at Paris, in 1892, of his collective work on *La Migration des Symboles,* setting forth on a more systematic plan, and with fuller references to original
authorities and illustrations from authentic examples, the matured and permanent results of the
learned and accomplished author's examination of
the enigmatic subject of which he is now everywhere
recognized as the greatest living exponent. It had
been treated by others in a similar comprehensive
spirit, but never before in the same thoroughly
scientific manner ; and thus, while the writings of
Dupuis and Creuzer have, in spite of their immense
erudition, but served to discredit it, and are already
obsolete, the Count Goblet d'Alviella, by pursuing
his investigations on a severely inductive basis, at
once, and, so to say, single handed, raised the
inquiry to its proper position as a department of
archæological research, producing a work destined
to exert an abiding influence on the whole future
of the study of symbolism, and also, I would fain
hope, on that of the decorative designs of the artistic
industries of the West. One, indeed, of Messrs.

Archibald Constable and Company's special objects in publishing the present English translation of the Count Goblet d'Alviella's alluring book has been to bring it within the reach of the Schools of Art throughout the United Kingdom : the other being to make it as widely accessible as possible to archæological students in India, where so much of the symbolism of antiquity still survives as a quickening religious and æsthetic force, permeating the entire mass of the Hindu populations,—like that idealizing thread of scarlet which runs through the ropes used in the British Royal Navy, "from the strongest to the weakest,"—elevating it by the constantly felt presence of the unseen realities of human life, and the diffusion throughout it of a popular spiritual culture ; and where, consequently, the clues to the mystery of so many historical emblems may be successfully followed up on every hand, even among the humblest and the most illiterate.

Of course, the way had been prepared for the Count Goblet d'Alviella by the remarkable discoveries made during the passing generation of the rich remains of ancient art in Egypt, Phœnicia, Mesopotamia, Syria, Phrygia, and Greece, and by the wide interest created on the continent of Europe in the ancient arts of India by the French International Exhibition of 1878. All this the Count Goblet d'Alviella frankly and generously acknowledges; but none the less is his merit in having applied the true Baconian principles of observation and comparison to the classification of the bewildering mass of materials thus placed at his disposal, and elaborating therefrom, in the laborious processes of his most patient analysis, a volume that will always remain the *locus classicus* on the various transcendental types constituting the materials of its seductive theme.

The general conclusion arrived at by the Count

Goblet d'Alviella is, as the superscription of the volume indicates, that the religious symbols common to the different historical races of mankind have not originated independently among them, but have, for the most part, been carried from one to the other, in the course of their migrations, conquests, and commerce; and his specific achievement is to have demonstrated the fact by an overwhelming induction of ancient and modern instances. The imprint of "the Feet of Buddha" on the title-page further indicates the Count Goblet d'Alviella's tentative opinion that the more notable of these symbols were carried over the world in the footsteps of Buddhism, or rather of that commerce of the East and West with Babylonia and Egypt, promoted by Nebuchadnezzar III. and Psammetichus I., respectively, out of which, through the internationalization of Hinduism, Buddhism arose in India, as later on, under the influence of the continued intercourse thus initiated between the countries of the Indian Ocean and the Mediterranean Sea, Christianity and Islam were successively developed from Judaism.

One of the most remarkable instances of the migration of a symbolical type is that afforded by the *triskelion* ["tripes"], or, as we more familiarly know it, "the Three Legs of Man." It first appears on the coins of Lycia, *circa* B.C. 480; and then on those of Sicily, where it was adopted by Agathocles, B.C. 317-7, but not as a symbol of the Morning, Mid-day and Afternoon Sun [the "Three Steps of Vishnu"], but of the "three-sided," or rather "three-ended," or "three-pointed" ["triquetrous"], land of Trin-akria, *i.e.*, "Three Capes," the ancient name of Sicily; and, finally, from the seventeenth century, on the coins of the Isle of Man; where, as Mr. John Newton has shown, in the *Athenæum* of the 10th of September, 1892, it was introduced by Alexander III. of Scotland, when,

in 1266, that prince took over the island from
the Norwegians; he having become familiar with
the device at the English Court of Henry III.
[1216-72], who for a short time was the nominal
sovereign of Sicily.[1] The *triskelion* of Lycia is
made up of three cocks' heads, a proof added to
that presented by the cock sculptured on the
"Harpy Monument" at Xanthus, that in the fifth
century B. C.[2] this exclusively Indian bird had
already reached the Mediterranean Sea. But on
the coins of Sicily and the Isle of Man the *triskelion* consists of three human legs of an identical
type, excepting that those of the latter island are
spurred. This form of *triskelion* is borne on the
armorial coats of several old English families, and

[1] Cæsar, *De Bello Gallico*, v. 13, describes Britannia as:
"Insula natura triquetra;" and one of the coins of Edward I.
has the king's head in a triangle, such as is seen on the Irish
money of the time, but here its symbolism, if there be any, is
probably Christian: yet some coins of Henry III. have the
Persian sun and moon, "Crescent and Star," above the king's
head. Beside the instances of the classical *triskelion* given
by the Count Goblet D'Alviella, I may here add that it occurs
on the shield of Memnon in the scene of his contest with
Achilles, painted, in black, on an archaic Attic vase, figured
in James Millengen's *Peintures antiques et inédites des vases
grecs* [Rome, 1813]; and that a similar triquetrous cognizance,
resembling a triple-headed hammer, is seen on the shield of one
of the warriors in the well-known sea fight painted by Aris-
tonophos, in the seventh century B.C., on a crater from Cervetri
[Cære, Agylla], now in the Museo Etrusco Capitolino, Rome.

[2] We find the cock also blazoned on the shield of one of the
young men assisting Herakles in capturing the herd of Geryones,
as the myth is painted by Euphronios on a cylex by Chachry-
lion, now in the Munich Pinakothek; and two cocks fighting
furiously in the scene representing Amphiaraus with Euriphyle
and her child [Alcmaeon] on another Attic vase of the same
period, now in the Berlin Antiquarium; and if the Corinthian
vase painted, in black, with fighting heroes, of whom one bears
a cock on his shield, figured in the *Monumenti inediti dell'
Instituto Correspondenza Archæologica* [Rome], is correctly
dated by Arthur Schneider [*Der troische Sagenkreis*, Leipzig,
1886], the Indian cock was familiarly known in Greece even
so early as the seventh century B.C.

it was in all probability first introduced throughout this country between the eleventh and thirteenth centuries by Crusaders returning from the East by way of Sicily.

The *triskelion* is but a modification of the *gammadion*, or "fylfot-cross," a type formally identical with the *swastika* of the Hindus. The latter was long ago suspected by Edward Thomas to be a sun symbol; but this was not positively proved until Percy Gardner found a coin of the ancient city of Mesembria, struck with a *gammadion* bearing within its opened centre an image of the sun,—"Mes-embria" meaning the city of the "Mid-day" sun, this name being stamped on some of its coins by the decisive legend ΜΕΣ 卐. Such a discovery makes one of "the fairy tales of science," and inspires the sequestered student of "the days of old, the years of ancient times," with the perennial enthusiasm that is the true end and highest recreation of all labour.[1]

The *gammadion* or *swastika*, for we may now absolutely identify them, has travelled farther afield than any other sacred type of antiquity; and from Iceland, which it reached in the ninth century A.D., and Thibet and Japan, between the third and eighth, and China, Persia, North Africa, France, Germany, Scandinavia, and the British Isles, between the second century A.D. and the second B.C., and India[2] and Sicily between the

[1] "Das Beste, was wir von der Geschichte haben, is der Enthusiasmus, den sie erregt."—GOETHE.

"Omnia quæ gerebam ad aliquam animi mei partem pertinebunt."—CICERO.

This last is a distinct reflection of the Buddhist doctrine of *karma*, with the hope of immortality for a difference.

[2] At the close of Chapter III. the Count Goblet d'Alviella would seem to imply that the *swastika* had now almost disappeared from the symbolism of India. But this is by no means the case. It is universally found worked into the mats, and cotton rugs, and finer textile fabrics of Assam; and in Western India always appears on the wooden ladles used in

third and fourth centuries B.C., and Asia Minor
and Greece between the sixth and twelfth centuries
B.C., the Count Goblet d'Alviella traces it back
on the monuments to the Troad, some time
anterior to the thirteenth century B.C.

Then there is the strange eventful history of
the migration of the imperial type of the " Double-
headed Eagle." It is now borne on the arms of
Austria and Russia; and as a form of the *Garuda*
bird [cf: the Assyrian Nisroch, and Etruscan
Tuchulcha] is to be found everywhere in Southern
India,—on the temple sculptures, in wood carvings,
on embroidered, printed, and woven cloths, and
on amulets. Also the cherubim guarding the
" Tree of Life," on the modern Syrian amulet
presented by me to the Count Goblet d'Alviella,
and figured by him at page 249 of his original
volume, and page 202 of the present translation,
are distinctly modelled on the traditional type of
the " Double-headed Eagle." It first appears on
the so-called Hittite sculptures at Eyuk, the ancient
Pteria, in Phrygia. In 1217 it is seen on the
coins and standards of the Turkman conquerors of
Asia Minor; and H. de Hell, in his *Voyage en
Turquie et en Perse*, reproduces [Plate XII.] a
variant of it from the walls of their old fortress at
Diarbekr. Now it was in 1227-28 that the
Emperor Frederick II. set out on the sixth
Crusade, landing at Acre on September 7th in
the latter year, and being crowned King in the
Church of the Holy Sepulchre at Jerusalem on
March 18th, 1229; and within thirty years from
these dates we find the type struck on the coins of
the Flemish princes, Otho, Count of Gueldres,

the worship of Agni, and at the head of every Hindu invoice
of goods and book of accounts. The fact of its being carved
on the ladles with which the libations of *ghi* [clarified butter]
are offered to Agni is surely some proof of at least a congenital
connection between the *swastika* and the *arani*.

Arnold, Count of Looz, Robert de Thourette, Bishop of Liège, and others. In 1345 it for the first time replaced the Single-headed Eagle on the armorial bearings of the Holy Roman Empire, represented, since 1806, by the dual state known, since 1868, as the Austro-Hungarian Monarchy. It first appeared as the cognizance of the Russian Empire in 1497, on a seal of Ivan [John] III. [1462-1505], the first of the Grand Dukes of Moscow who took the title of Czar of Muscovy, ten years after his marriage [1472] with Sophia, niece of the last Byzantine Cæsar, Constantine Palæologus.

The "Winged Globe," "the Sun of Righteousness with healing on its wings" of Malachi iv. 2, is another sacred type that has wandered under various modifications into every part of the Old World, until it appears over the doors of the Secretary of State's rooms at the India Office, reduced to a meaningless circle, with two appended flowing ribbons, representing the two *uræus* snakes of the original Egyptian "Winged Globe," the *urimthummim* jewel, attached to the divining zodiacal "breastplate of Aaron."[1]

One of the most unexpected results of the critical study of these symbols is the establishment of their essential paucity. They undergo, alike by

[1] See my remarks on the "Breastplate of Aaron," in the *Journal of the Society of Arts* for March 18th, 1887 ; and with reference to "the Hand of Providence" sometimes associated with the Winged Globe, see my letters on "*The tughra of the Turks*" in the *Journal of the Society of Arts* for September 4th and 25th and October 9th, 1891. This "Hand" is represented on the reverse of some of the coins of Eadweard the Elder, A.D. 901-25, appearing out of a cloud in the formula of benediction ; and again on a "St. Peter's coin" of the same period, A.D. 900-50, but so rudely that numismatists have never yet identified it, and, indeed, it is only identifiable by the representation on others of these "St. Peter's coins" of the bow [with an arrow here] seen in the Hand associated with the Winged Globe of the Persians.

devolution and evolution, and a sort of ceaseless interfusion also, infinite permutations of both type and meaning, but in their earliest monumental forms they are found to be remarkably few.

They were at first but the obvious ideographs of the phenomena of nature that made the deepest religious impression on archaic man, such as the outstretched heavens above him, and the outspread earth beneath; both of which he naturally divided into four quarters, the east "fronting" him as he watched anxiously for the returning sun, the south on his "right" hand, the west "backing" him, and the north on his "left" hand; and this four-fold heaven and earth he signified by a circle, or a square, divided cross-ways; from which he was led to conceive of a "heavenly garden," watered by four rivers, and of a foursquare "heavenly city" with its four went ways; and gradually to model more and more in their similitude the four-square cities of antiquity, and those four-square well watered "paradises" ["far —*i.e.*, heavenly—country"], the ground plans of which yet survive in every part of India. Then came the observation of the daily renewed miracle of the phenomena of vegetable, animal, and human reproduction, expressed at first, as still in India, by the most directly realistic types, and afterwards by the lotus bud and flower, the date palm, and other conspicuously phallic flowers and trees: and that the symbolical "Tree of Life" of the Chaldæans, Assyrians and Babylonians, is indeed but a conventional representation of the date palm is sufficiently proved by the description given of the adorning of King Solomon's temple in 1 Kings, vii. 29-35 :—"And he carved all the walls . . . round about with carved figures of cherubims and palm trees [*tamar*, the 'date palm']. . . . And for the entering of the oracle he made doors of olive tree . . . and he carved upon them carvings of cherubims and palm trees and open flowers, and overlaid them with gold, and spread gold upon the cherubims and upon the palm trees. . . . And the two doors of fir tree . . . he carved thereon cherubims and palm trees and open flowers : " and, again, of the adorning of the visionary temple of Ezekiel, chapter xli. 18 :—" And it was made with cherubims and palm trees, so that a palm tree was between a cherub and a cherub ; " and chapter xl. 26 :—" And there were seven steps to go up to it, and the arches [" propylons," *toruns* or *gopuras* of the four cardinal points] thereof were before them, and it had palm trees, one on this side, and another on that, upon the posts thereof." These are exact descriptions of the architectural decoration of the temples and palaces of Nineveh and Babylon, and they should satisfy anyone of, at least, the proximate botanical source of the Sacred Tree of the " Nineveh marbles." The Syrian brasses which have recently become articles of regular import into Europe, however, place the question beyond dispute. The so-called Saibis, the people who make these articles, call themselves *mando Yahya*, or " disciples of St. John," and are generally referred to by western writers as " Christians of St. John," and Mendæans. By their neighbours they are called *sabiun*, literally, " washers," *i.e.*, in the ritualistic sense, " Baptists." They are, and they are not, confoundable with the Sabæans,—not the people of that name in ancient South Arabia, but the Chaldæan wor- shippers of the " Host [*saba*] of Heaven." [1] The Saibis of Mahomet were not idolaters in any form, but their modern representatives com- bine with pseudo-Christian and pseudo-Zoroas- trian doctrines, the whole remaining body of ancient Chaldæan astrolatry ; and how this came

[1] The name of the Joktanite Sabæans is spelt with the letter *samech*, and that of the Cushite Sabæans with a *sin*.

about is a matter of the utmost importance to the students of the history of the arts of the East, and of their applied symbolism. The Saibis of Mahomet's time were recognized by him as believers in a revealed religion, and were always treated by his followers with toleration. But their sword was unsparing against the still surviving star worshippers of Syria and Mesopotamia, and particularly against the handicraftsmen among them, who, in their several ritualistic arts, perpetuated the familiar "types" and "motives" of the obsolescent idolatry of Nineveh and Babylon. These Sabæans of the Haran and Valley of the Tigris and Euphrates, to escape extermination, sheltered themselves under the name of the Saibis, and introduced all their own pagan practices among the latter sect, which is now really idolatrous. Its members are nearly all artizans, and most of the metal-work from the neighbourhood of Mosul, and Damascus, and Hillah, sold in Alexandria and Cairo, and now largely imported into Paris and London, is fabricated by these "Saibis." The "Tree of Life" appears everywhere on their brass dishes and bowls, and on a dish presented to me by the Count Goblet d'Alviella, and figured in his original volume and in the present translation on Plate V., letter l, the Sacred Tree is realistically rendered by the date palm. The conventional "Tree of Life," under the name of *satarvan* is an object of still living adoration among them, and as its worship has been traditionally handed down by them from the remotest Chaldæan period, the dish figured by the Count Goblet d'Alviella conclusively proves, so it seems to me, that the ancient Mesopotamian "Tree of Life"

"Encinctured with a twine of leaves,"

was indeed none other than the date palm of "the

waters of Babylon,"—associated, at times, with the half mythical *homa* plant of the Iranian Aryas, the *soma* of the Vedic Hindus, as the source of the earliest intoxicating sap known in Persia and India.[1] In *The Industrial Arts of India* [Chap-

[1] It is difficult to determine the ultimate botanical source of the *homa* of the ancient Persians, the *soma* of the Hindus. The proximate source of *homa* in Persia was the vine, and, later, the date palm. In India the plants identified with the *soma* plant are *Sarcostemma brevistigma*, and other species of *Sarcostemma*, but it may be questioned whether these plants were the ultimate sources of the Vedic *soma* juice, or the Indian substitutes for the grape and date palm. The Parsis of Bombay import from Persia as *homa* the stems of the jointed fir, *Ephedra vulgaris*, and they use also the twigs of the spurge-wort, *Euphorbia Neriifolia*. It has been argued against the identification of any *Sarcostemma* as the source of *homa* or *soma* that the juice of no *Asclepiad* could be voluntarily drunken as an intoxicant by man; but in Western India an intoxicating beverage, called *bar*, is prepared from the juice of *Calotropis gigantea*, and drunk with relish by the hill people about Mahabaleshwur; and we know from Pliny, xiv. 19, that the ancients made intoxicating drinks from the juice of all sorts of unlikely plants. Beside this the *homa* or *soma* twigs may have been added, like hops, merely as an adjuvant to the intoxicant prepared with it. They were gathered by moonlight, and carried home in carts drawn by rams, and mixed, after fermentation, and straining through a sieve of goat's hair, with barley wort and *ghi* [or clarified butter]; and the enjoyment of the brew was sacramental:

"We've quaff'd the *soma* bright,
And are immortal grown;
We've entered into light,
And all the gods have known."

As a libation to Agni, *soma* is now superseded in India by *ghi*.

Soma means not only the juice of the *soma* plant, *Sarcostemma brevistigma*, and Siva, as identified with its intoxicating juice, but the moon, as in *somvara*, Monday, which gave its name to the *soma* plant and juice. *Soma-yaga* is the rite, in Vedic times the sacrificial rite, in the celebration of which *soma* was drunk; *soma-yagi* and *soma-devi* are the celebrants of the rite; *soma-pa* are "*soma* drinkers," *i.e.*, Brahmans; *soma-varga-tilt* are a caste of oil millers, the members of which worship Siva as *Soma*; and *soma-vati*, the ceremony observed by the women of Maharashtra by circumambulating the sacred fig-tree [*Urostigma religiosum*] whenever the new moon falls on a Monday.

man and Hall, 1880], I traced this type through
all its marvellous metamorphoses in the arts of the
ancient Greeks and Romans, and of the Islamite
Saracens, and the mediæval and modern Europeans;
and that it was received by the latter not only through
the intermediation of the Greeks and Romans and
Arabs, and as modified by them, but also, at different unascertained dates, in its crude forms directly
from Mesopotamia and Syria, is suggested by a
silver coin of Ceolwlf II., King of Mercia, A.D.
874, bearing on its reverse a nine-branched "Tree
of Life," standing among the "Host of Heaven,"
or "Host of God," between two cherubim, or other
acolytes, the whole overshadowed by the "Winged
Globe," with wings as of palm branches, and the
globe marked like a face.   The coin is figured
[580] in Edward Hawkins' *Silver Coins of England* [Quaritch, 1887], and its reverse type is
there described as follows :—" Two figures seated,
holding a globe between them ; above Victory
with expanded wings ; unique."

But beside the sun and moon the others of " the
seven planets" of the ancient astronomers came
slowly into the observation of archaic man, and the
whole universe was perceived to be full of moving
life, and was now symbolized by a " Holy Mountain," with its cosmical palm, deep rooted in the
earth, the " Garden of Eden " of the Semitic races,
and lifting up its laden branches of clustered dates
to the highest heavens; and again by a "Virgin
Mother." Everywhere he saw creative force in
operation, and everywhere adopted the most
homely and personal implements of that force as
the visible and material symbols of the invisible
and spiritual Creator, or Creators, in whose express
image he postulated that the worlds were made.
It was in this ingenuous unaffected spirit that the
Semite nations named their phallic stone, or phallic
tree, *beth-El*, the "house of God," or simply *El*,

the Godhead's self. Ashtoreth was symbolized by the phallic *Cupressus sempervirens*, one of the original "arbores vitæ" [*asherim*] of Anterior Asia; and from it are derived not only the pyramidal images of the goddess in Phœnician sculptures, but the stiff cypress-like representations on the talismanic jewelry of Southern Europe of the Blessed Virgin Mary; to whom we have also consecrated, since the sixteenth century, the American "Arbor Vitæ," *Thuja occidentale.* It is under the impulse of the same naïve and artless temper of mind that the Hindus everywhere set up the *lingam*, and the *yoni*, and combined *lingam* and *yoni* images, and bow down to them and worship them as the supreme symbols of creative deity; and the inability of English people, and of Europeans generally, to enter into their mental disposition in this matter is a most pertinent illustration of that ubiquitous antagonism between Eastern and Western ideas, or between the ancient pagan world still left to us in Southern and Eastern Asia and the modern world of Christendom and Islam, which constitutes one of the greatest difficulties besetting British rule in India.

Only three years ago I recorded in the *Times*[1] the flogging, by order of the Police Magistrate of Black Town, Madras, of a Hindu boy "for exhibiting an indecent figure in public view." What he had explicitly done was to set up, in accordance with universal custom, a phallic image before a house that was in course of erection by a Mr. K. Streevanasa, who was first tried under the indictment, but was acquitted, he, the owner, not having been the person who had actually exhibited the image. It is the fact that the image referred to is often very naturally fashioned in Southern India, a most fortunate fact in relation to the

[1] Of Sept. 3rd, 1891.

history of art; but even so it conveys no more idea of indecency to a Hindu, than do the words "fascination," "testimony" [cf. Genesis xxiv., 2, 3, 9; xxxii., 25; and xlvii., 29], "Lord and Lady" [*Arum sps:*], "orchid," *et-cætera*, to ourselves. It has indeed for the Hindus a significance of the highest sanctity, of which only the remotest trace remains in the words "fascination" and "testimony," and of which there is no trace in the word "orchid" or "orchis," the "testiculus" of the Romans, unless possibly through its Greek synonym σατύριον. The image was indeed set up before Mr. Streevanasa's house as a symbol of the Deity in whose strength alone can any work of man be surely established, and as a devout and public acknowledgment that, in the words of the Hebrew Psalmist:—"Except the Lord build the house they labour in vain that build it." The pillars Jachin and Boaz set up by king Solomon before the porch of his temple at Jerusalem [1 Kings vii., 21] had exactly the same significance, and their restorations by Chipiez and Perrot, although they disclose none of the offensive realism sometimes observed in similar phallic presentments in the Madras Presidency, are not nearly so severely conventional as those to be everywhere seen in Northern and Western India.[1] The ultimate

---

[1] These closely resemble the *omphalos* of Apollo Pythius at Delphi, which, as we learn from the accounts of Pausanias [X. 16] and Strabo [IX. iii. 6], and various Greek coins and fictile paintings, was simply a *beth-El* or *lingam*. In the same way in India "the navel of Vishnu" is identical with "the *lingam* of Siva;" and it is a Brahmanical saying that "those who think they differ err." On the marble bas-relief from Sparta, figured in the *Mittheilungen der Deutschen Archaologischen Instituts in Athen* [vol. xiii. plate xii.], and on a stater of Cyzicus, figured by Canon Greenwell in the *Numismatic Chronicle* [3rd series, vol. viii., plate i., No. 23], the Pythian *omphalos* is represented between two eagles, of which Strabo relates: "A fable, referred to by Pindar, was invented, according to which two eagles or, as others say, two crows, set free by

artistic form of the symbol, as I have been able to trace it, step by step, from India to Greece and Italy, is the conventional "Tree of Life," or "Symbolical Tree," guarded by affronted beasts or cherubim, that is, "the Two Witnesses." [1]

At every page we have similar exemplifications of "the long results of time," [2] worked out with rare

---

Jupiter, one from the east, the other from the west, alighted together at Delphi. In the temple is seen a sort of navel wrapped in bands, surmounted by figures representing the birds of the fable."

These "bands" are none other than the rosaries and garlands with which the *lingam* in India is hung on high Saivite holidays, while the "supporters" of the naturalistic *lingams* to be sometimes seen in Southern India leave no doubt as to the significance of the "two eagles" or "two crows," which in the Spartan bas-relief point as clearly as these Southern Indian *lingams* to the ultimate origin of the symbolical "Tree of Life" :—

"The Tree of Life,
The middle tree, and highest there that grew,"

Delphi itself providing the counterpart of the *yoni*, [δελφύς, cf. : ἀδελφός, ὁμογάστριος, ἐκ νηδύος], the ultimate "Garden of Eden."

In the scene of the murder of Neoptolemos, figured in red on an amphora of the fourth century B.C., found at Ruvo in Apulia, and now in the Caputi Collection, the elaborately garlanded *omphalos* is represented rising up from an eight-divided base, closely resembling the eight-petalled "Lotus Throne" of some of the Saivite combined *lingam yoni* images: the *yoni* and the symbolical Lotus being in India one and the same matrical emblem.

[1] One of the most interesting of the Mediæval Christian Trees of Life was the "Arbor Perindex," known also as the *arbre de Judée.* The legend was that it grew in India, and typified the Catholic Roman Church, the doves, cooing among its branches, being the Congregation of the Faithful, and the Serpent, which sought to entice them away from their healing habitation, to destroy them, "that ancient worm the Devil." Not the least interesting point in connection with this Tree of Life is its name, "Arbor Perindex," *parinda* being the Hindustani and Persian for "bird."

[2] The reader will have understood from the first that the Count Goblet d'Alviella here treats of symbols only after they

scholarship, conscientiousness, and enthusiasm, and with that lucidity of literary expression for which the Count Goblet d'Alviella is distinguished. His book is, therefore, likely to be as welcome to the general reader as to the specialist in archæology. I wish, however, to emphatically recommend it to the earnest·attention of the students of ornamental art, for it is a book which, like Husenbeth's *Emblems of the Saints in Art,* should ever be with them. Beauty in decoration ought not to be sacrificed to symbolism, but it is always enhanced by being symbolical; while to employ

have become historical, and indeed monumental, and that the symbolism of pantomime, the gesture language of primæval, and primitive or savage man, which survives among civilized men in the current formulæ of salutation and clerical benediction, in thumb "biting" and pointing, making "long-noses," *et cætera,* is beyond the sphere of his work ; as is also the symbolism of colours, numbers, and purely geometrical figures, such as the Pythagorean talisman, known by the various names of *pentalpha,* Signum Solomonis, Fuga Dæmonorum, Druid's Foot, pentangle, *et cætera.** A very piquant form of the archaic, and probably primitive, or, it may even be, primæval practices in which the Greek word symbol originated still widely survives in India ; where, when " our Mr. Thomas Atkins " arranges a tryst with a casual Indian sweetheart, the latter breaks a piece of pottery in two with him, each keeping the fragment left in their respective right hands, to be fitted together again when they next meet,—and thus make sure that they are the same couple as met before. In this simple *súm-bolon,* or "tally," we have the actual *chirs-aelychoth,* or "sherd of good fellowship," of the Phœnicians, corresponding with the " tessera hospitalis" of the Romans. When I was at school at Plymouth fifty years ago the boys in pledging themselves to any secrecy invariably did so by holding a potsherd between them. If it was a very dark and direful conspiracy to which we bound ourselves we spat on the ṣherd.

---

* It is sometimes identified with the Scutum Davidis, which appears to me to rather be the figure formed by the intersection of two equilateral triangles, one of the symbols of supreme Deity. It is also sometimes denominated the "pentacle," a symbolical headdress, the form of which I have never been able to accurately determine.

these sacred ancient types irrespective of their significance is to make nonsense of an artistic composition, and is, in reality, as distressing a solecism as the use of fine words by pretentious people ignorant of their etymological derivation and full meaning.

I am in no way responsible for the present translation; but having read it through from beginning to end I have found that, although it cannot be said to in any degree reflect the literary quality of the original French, it is perfectly accurate, and this is what would above all else be desired of the translation of so strictly a scientific work as *La Migration des Symboles*, alike by its English readers, and its author,—who, I have, in conclusion, to gratefully add, has been good enough to completely revise the text where it has occasionally been found necessary to adapt it to the discoveries made since the first publication of the Count Goblet d'Alviella's profoundly fascinating volume.

GEORGE BIRDWOOD.

7, APSLEY TERRACE, ACTON, NEAR LONDON, W.
Saturday, 7th July, 1894.

POSTSCRIPTUM.

At the last moment of going to press I have chanced upon three remarkable variants of the *swastika* which the Count Goblet d'Alviella wishes me to reproduce here. The first is from a sepulchral stone at Meigle in Perthshire, and the second, which is a sinister *swastika*, from a Cross at St. Vigeans in Forfarshire.

Both these are illustrated in Stuart's *Sculptured Stones* of Scotland. The third is from one of the old Mahometan buildings of the Mo(n)gol period at Lahore.

This is also ignorantly rendered as the inauspicious *suwastika*; and twisted into a legend, which I read as, *ya Fattah*, "O Opener," "Beginner," "Leader," "Victorious," "Conqueror," and so forth.

GEO. B.

CONTENTS.

LIST OF PLATES.

THE AUTHOR'S PREFACE.

FEW words have acquired such a wide signification as the word symbol.[1] Originally applied, amongst the Greeks, to the two halves of the tablet they divided between themselves as a pledge of hospitality—in the manner of our contract forms, detached along a line of perforations from the counterfoil record—it was gradually extended to the engraved shells by which those initiated in the mysteries made themselves known to each other ; and even to the more or less esoteric formulas and sacramental rites that may be said to have constituted the visible bond of their fellowship. At the same time its meaning was so amplified as to include on the one hand oracles, omens, and every extraordinary phenomenon that could be passed off as a warning from the gods, and on the other, military pass-words, badges of corporate bodies, tokens of attendance, and pledges of every kind, from the wedding ring, to the ring deposited before partaking of a banquet as an earnest for the due payment of one's share of it. In short the term came to gradually mean everything that, whether by general agreement or by analogy, conventionally represented something or somebody.

A symbol might be defined as a representation which does not aim at being a reproduction. A reproduction implies if not identity with, at least

---

[1] Σύμβολον, from σύν and βάλλειν, to throw together.

similitude to, the original; but a symbol only requires that it shall have certain features in common with the object represented, so that, by its presence alone, it may evoke the conception of the latter, as is the case with a missile weapon and lightning, a sickle and harvest-time, a ring and marriage, a pair of scales and the idea of justice, kneeling and the sentiment of submission, and so forth.

By symbolism the simplest, the commonest objects are transformed, idealized, and acquire a new and, so to say, an illimitable value. In the Eleusinian mysteries, the author of *Philosophoumena* relates that, at the initiation to the higher degree, "there was exhibited as the great, the admirable, the most perfect object of mystic contemplation, an ear of corn that had been reaped in silence." [1] The scrap of cloth which, in ordinary circumstances, we discard as a rag, at the top of a staff sums up all the aspirations included in the idea of one's country; and two crossed lines suffice to recall to millions of Christians the redemption of the world by the voluntary sacrifice of a god.

We live in the midst of symbolical representations, from the ceremonies celebrating a birth to the funereal emblems adorning the tomb; from the shaking of hands all round of a morning to the applause with which we gratify the actor, or lecturer, of the evening; from the impressions figuring on the seal of our letters to the bank notes in our pocket-book. The pictorial and plastic arts are naught else but symbolism, even when they claim to adhere to the servile imitation of reality. We write, as we speak, in symbols; and it is in symbols again that we think, if those schools of philosophy are to be believed which affirm our powerlessness to perceive things in themselves. The philo-

[1] *Philosophoumena*, v. i., ed. Cruyce. Paris, 1860, p. 171.

sophy of evolution goes the length of proclaim-
ing, through the organ of its founder, that the
conception of force, to which it refers all phenomena, is simply the symbol of an unknown and
unknowable Reality. Herbert Spencer even adds,
in the most explicit terms, that it will always be
permissible for us to picture to ourselves that
Reality by concrete symbols, so long as we do
not regard them as resemblances of that for
which they stand.[1]

In this sense we may apply to the symbol what
Professor Sabatier has written of the myth :—
" To create a myth, that is to say, to catch a
glimpse of a higher truth behind a palpable
reality, is the most manifest sign of the greatness
of the human soul, and the proof of its faculty of
infinite growth and development."[2] Without
doubt the symbols that have attracted in the
highest degree the veneration of the multitude
have been the representative signs of gods, often
uncouth and indecent; but what have the gods
themselves ever been, except the more or less
imperfect symbols of the Being transcending all
definition Whom the human conscience has more
and more clearly divined through and above all
these gods ?

It is sentiment, and above all, religious sentiment, that resorts largely to symbolism; and in
order to place itself in more intimate communication with the being, or abstraction, it desires to
approach. To that end men are everywhere
seen either choosing natural, or artificial, objects
to remind them of the Great Hidden One,
or themselves imitating in a systematic manner
the acts and deeds they attribute to Him
—which is a way of participating in His life—

---

[1] *First Principles.* Lond. 1862, § 32.
[2] A. SABATIER. *Mémoire sur la notion hébraïque de l'esprit.*
Paris, 1879.

or again rendering objective by acts, as various as they are significant, all the gradations of the sentiments with which He inspires them, from the most profound humility to the most ardent love. Hence the extreme diversity of symbols; which may be divided into two classes, according as they consist of acts or rites, and of objects or emblems. We will here occupy ourselves exclusively with this second category, or rather with the figured representations it suggests, and which past generations have transmitted to us as so many material vestiges of their beliefs. Even thus restricted, the field of investigation is vast enough to make one fearful of wandering from the right way.

Studies in comparative symbolism have fallen, during the latter half of this century, into a discredit which their former vicissitudes sufficiently explain. To the syntheses no less premature than brilliant, constructed with insufficient and imperfect materials by the rationalistic school, whose most illustrious representative was the French Dupuis, there succeeded, more than fifty years ago, the system, more philosophical than historical, of Creuzer and his followers, who claimed to discover in all the religious practices of antiquity the disguised or disfigured reflection of a profound primitive wisdom. All these theories, after having successively captivated the learned, have been slowly overthrown by the accumulated objections afforded by later discoveries in archæology, ethnography, philology, and history; and, as so often happens, the reaction against them has been in proportion to the first infatuation in their favour.

Even the more recent attempts of MM. Lajard and Emile Burnouf, although keeping more closely to facts, were not of such a nature as to cause us to retrace our steps. It seemed as if comparative archæology must definitely sacrifice all imagination that could profit critical research, and to-day certain scientists would even attempt nothing less than the proscription of all hypothesis in investigations relating to the origin and signification of symbolism ; as if hypothesis was not in every sort of study a necessary factor of scientific progress, provided it be not enunciated as an ascertained fact.

Meanwhile, for anyone who would wish to resume this kind of investigation, the situation has greatly changed within the last thirty-five years. Documents which allow us to compare, under all the desirable conditions of authenticity, the symbolic representations of different nations, have accumulated to such a degree, that henceforth the principal bar to their utilization lies in their number and their dissemination. It is not so many years ago that the transactions of the Academies founded in the principal capitals of Europe, and the new-born annals of a few archæological societies, constituted, together with certain great publications relating to the monuments of classical antiquity and of Egypt, the only collections to which the historian of symbolism could turn. To-day we have everywhere at hand, in publications which will never be surpassed in importance and in accuracy, the result of excavations carried on simultaneously in Chaldæa, Assyria, Persia, Asia Minor, Phœnicia, Egypt and Libya, not forgetting the reproduction of memorials discovered or studied anew in Greece, Italy, India, the extreme East, and even in the two Americas. Archæological reviews and special collections, which have rendered so much service to the study of ancient art, have multiplied even in the smallest states of Europe. There is no branch of archæology, from the study of seals to numismatics, which has not its organs and societies. Thanks specially to the liberality of the different governments, not only have museums been enriched in proportion to the discoveries made, but the more important collections form the subject of descriptive catalogues which allow of the utilization of materials at a distance.   Lastly, the joint labours of many workers, planned from the most various points of view, are centralizing all these documents, thus lightening the task of those who desire to restore the traces and eluci- date the meaning of the principal symbols of the world.

Moreover the deciphering of inscriptions, the classification and interpretation of written docu- ments, the general advancement of the study of history, more especially religious history, whilst enlightening us on the creeds of nations, enable us the better to establish the connection between their symbols and their myths; at the same time that a more exact knowledge of the social and geographical centres whence these symbols origi- nated aids us to discover in many cases the origins of the image which has furnished a body to the idea.

Henceforth there is no longer any reason why in the study of symbols we may not arrive at results as positive as in the study of myths.   The comparative examination of myths long ago en- tered upon a scientific phase, whether, with Pro- fessor Max Müller and the philological school, we are content to compare the traditions of nations speaking allied languages; or, with Mr. Andrew Lang and the majority of ethnographers, we do not scruple to compare the mythology of all known peoples.   Now, the myth, which may be de- fined as a dramatization of natural phenomena, or of abstract events, offers more than one feature in common with the symbol.   Both depend upon reasoning by analogy, which in the one case creates an imaginary tale, in the other a material image.

Doubtless there is this difference, somewhat ignored by those who have obscured the idea of religious symbolism by blending it with mythology, that in the symbol we must be conscious of a distinction between the image and the object, or being, thus represented, whilst an essential feature of the myth is to believe the narration to be in conformity with the reality. But it is easy to understand that both are frequently formed by the help of the same mental operations, and above all are transmitted through the same channels.

In any case, there are religions which we cannot understand if we do not endeavour to supplement the insufficiency of the texts by the study of the monuments. A significant symptom in this connection is the growing tendency among savants to utilize, in the study of particular religions, the texts to verify the symbols, and the symbols to verify the texts; as may be seen in the recent works of Senart on the history of Buddhism, Gaidoz and Bertrand on the symbols of ancient Gaul, J. Menant on the sculptured stones of Central Asia, and Fr. Lenormant, Clermont-Ganneau, Ledrain, and Ph. Berger on the symbols of the Semitic religions. These works are the best proofs of the services which the interpretation of symbols can render to the history of religions when strictly scientific methods are rigidly followed.

It is not merely a question of avoiding preconceived ideas and hasty generalizations. What is needed above all is to provisionally substitute analysis for synthesis, the history of symbols for the history of symbolism; in other words, to take the principal symbolical figures one by one, in order to establish their respective history, first among each people, and then over the whole area of countries where they are found. It may happen that we may succeed, after repeated and patient investigations of this kind, if not in establishing the laws of symbolism, as has been done for comparative grammar, at least in collecting together the materials for a general history of symbolism, as has been already accomplished for almost every other branch of knowledge.

My aim, is simply to furnish a contribution to this history, by investigating the limits within which certain symbolical representations have been transmitted from people to people, and how far in the course of their migrations their meaning and their form may have been modified. I have here applied myself particularly to figures which, by the importance and the very complexity of their rôle, have seemed to me the most capable of throwing some light on the general conditions of symbolical transmission, such as the *gammadion* or *tétrascèle* and the *triscèle*, the Paradisaical Tree, or rather the special type it assumed amongst the Assyrians, the Sacred Cone of the western Semitic nations, the Winged Globe of Egypt, the Caduceus of the Phœnicians, and the *trisula* of the Buddhists. This selection will further permit me to bring into prominence one of the most curious and perhaps least explored sides of comparative symbolism. I speak here of the attraction which analogous symbols exercise on one another, or rather of the tendency they display to coalesce and lose themselves in intermediate types.

Most of the observations which I have brought together in the following chapters have already appeared during the last three years in the *Bulletins de l'Académie royale de Belgique*, the *Revue des Deux-Mondes*, and in the *Revue de l'Histoire des Religions*. In recasting them as a whole I have fully considered the remarks which their first publication elicited from sympathetic critics, as well as the modifications produced in my own views by subsequent researches. I have also added a variety of illustrations calculated to show more strongly the cases of symbolical filiation and fusion of which I have endeavoured to verify the existence and elucidate the theory.

GOBLET D'ALVIELLA.

COURT SAINT ETIENNE, BRABANT,
March, 1891.

THE MIGRATION OF SYMBOLS.

CHAPTER I.

ON SYMBOLS COMMON TO DIFFERENT RACES.

Identity of certain images in the symbolism of different races.—On spontaneous coincidences in the applications of the symbolical faculty.—The Cross apart from Christianity.—St. Anthony's Cross *potencée*.—The fight between the eagle and the serpent.—Readiness with which symbols are transmitted from nation to nation.—Principal causes of their diffusion.—The complexity and singularity of identical symbols is a presumption in favour of their unity of origin.—The *triscèle*.—The Double-headed Eagle.—The Hand of Providence.—Information supplied by identity of meaning and use.—The Lotus-flower.

THE variety of symbols seems at first to be as boundless as the combinations of the human imagination. It is not uncommon, however, to discover the same symbolical figures amongst races the furthest apart. These coincidences can hardly be explained by chance, like the combinations of the kaleidoscope. Except in the case of symbols found amongst peoples who belong to the same race, and who, consequently, may have carried away from their common cradle certain elements of their respective symbolism, there are only two possible solutions : either these analogous images have been conceived independently, in virtue of a law of the human mind, or else they have passed from one country to another by a process of borrowing.

There exists a symbolism so natural that, after
the manner of certain implements peculiar to the
stone ages, it does not belong to any definite
region or race, but constitutes a characteristic
feature of humanity in a certain phase of development.

To this category belong, for example, the representations of the sun by a disc or radiating face,
of the moon by a crescent, of the air by birds, of
the water by fishes, also by a wavy line, and so
forth.

Perhaps certain more complicated analogies
should be added to these, such as the symbolizing
of the different phases of human existence by the
life of the tree, the generative forces of nature by
phallic emblems, the divine triads, and generally
every triple combination whose members are equal,
by the equilateral triangle, and, lastly, the four
main directions of space by a cross.

What theories have not been built upon the
existence of the equilateral cross as an object of
veneration amongst nearly all the races of the Old
and the New World! Of late years orthodox writers
have protested with good reason against the claim
of attributing a pagan origin to the Cross of the
Christians because earlier creeds had included
cruciform signs in their symbolism. And the same
objection might be urged against those who seek
for Christian infiltrations in certain other religions
under the pretext that they possess the sign of
the Redemption.

When the Spaniards took possession of Central
America, they found in the native temples real
Crosses, which were regarded as the symbol, sometimes of a divinity at once terrible and beneficent
—Tlaloc, sometimes of a civilizing hero, white
and bearded—Quetzacoalt, stated by tradition to
have come from the East. They concluded from
this that the Cross had reached the Toltecs through

Christian missions of which all trace was lost ; and, as legend must always fix upon a name, they gave the honour to St. Thomas, the legendary apostle of all the Indies. Although this proposition has again found defenders in recent congresses of Americanists, it may be regarded as irrevocably condemned. It has been ascertained beyond all possibility of future doubt that the Cross of pre-Columbian America is a kind of compass card, that it represents the four quarters whence comes the rain, or rather the four main winds which bring rain, and that it thus became the symbol of the god Tlaloc, the dispenser of the celestial waters, and, lastly, of the mythical personage known by the name of Quetzacoalt.[1]

By a similar process of reasoning the Assyrians

FIG. 1. IDEOGRAM OF ANU.
(RAWLINSON. *Western Asia Inscriptions*, vol. ii. pl. 48, fig. 30 obv.)

were led to represent by an equilateral cross their god of the sky, Anu. The ideogram of this god is formed by four cruciform characters which radiate at right angles from the circle or lozenge denoting the sun in the cuneiform inscriptions. Is

[1] ALBERT REVILLE, *Religions du Mexique, de l'Amérique centrale et du Pérou*. Paris, 1885.—It appears that in South America also the Cross was a wind-rose. A Belgian traveller, M. E. Peterken, relates that he saw in the Argentine Republic a monolith in the form of a Latin Cross, called by the natives "the Father of the four winds." (*Congress of Americanists* of 1877, Paris and Luxemburg, 1888. Vol. i. p. 57.)—In North America the Cross symbolizes both the sun and the sky. Among the Blackfeet Indians, according to Mrs. Murray Aynsley (*Transactions of the Quatuor Coronati*, vol. v. p. 82), it represents the "old man in the sun who rules the winds."

not the sky indeed the space in which light radiates?

It is proper to remark that amongst the Assyrians themselves the equilateral cross, as denoting the main directions in which the sun shines, became also the symbol of that luminary, and consequently, here again, of the god who governs it. It was the same with the Chaldæans, the Hindus, the Greeks, the Persians, and perhaps with the Gauls, and the ancient civilizers of Northern America (fig. 2).

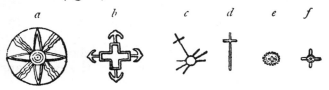

FIG. 2.   SOLAR CROSSES.[1]

In China, the equilateral cross inscribed in a square ⊞ represents the earth, and according to Mr. Samuel Beal, a saying is met with there to the effect that "God made the earth in the form of a cross."[2]

Egyptian writing utilizes among its signs the Greek and even the Latin Cross.   In connection

[1]   *a*. Within a Disc in Assyrian bas-reliefs. J. MENANT, *Pierres gravées de la Haute-Asie*, Paris, 1886, vol. ii. p. 71.—*b*. Alternating with the radiated Disc, on ancient Indian coins. A. CUNNINGHAM, *The Bhilsa Topes*, pl. xxxi., figs. 8 and 9. —*c*. Surmounting the solar Disc, on a whorl, from Troy. SCHLIEMANN, *Ilios, ville et pays des Troyens*, Paris, 1885, No. 1954.—*d*. Sceptre in the hand of Apollo on a coin of Gallienus. VICT. DURUY, *Histoire des Romains*, Paris, 1885, vol. viii. p. 42 —*e*. In a Mithriatic scene on an engraved stone. LAJARD, *Introduction à l'étude du culte de Mithra, Atlas*, pl. cii., fig. 7.—*f*. Above a lion, on a Gallic coin. ED. FLOUEST, *Deux stèles de Laraire*, Paris, 1885, pl. xvii.—For the American solar Cross, see further on, fig. 29, the engraving on a shell found in the mounds of the Mississippi.

[2]   *The Indian Antiquary*, 1880, p. 67, *et seq*.

with this we find in a recent article by the Abbe Ansault a characteristic example of the readiness with which one may go astray in the identification of symbols, if satisfied with a merely superficial resemblance. On the famous Damietta stone, the Greek words Πτολεμαῖος Σωτήρ, "Ptolemy the Saviour," are rendered by the demotic characters forming the equivalent of Πτολεμαῖος, followed by the sign † ; from which the author concludes that the term Saviour being rendered by a cross, this sign was with the Egyptians, an allusion to the future coming of the Redeemer.[1] Unhappily for this ingenious interpretation, M. de Harlez, who has taken the trouble to refute M. Ansault's article, points out to him that in

FIG. 3. HIEROGLYPH OF THE HAMMER.

(E. COEMANS, *Manuel de langue égyptienne*, p. 47, § xviii.)

demotic the sign † is the simplest form of a hieroglyph representing a hammer, or a boring tool, and is usually employed to express the idea of grinding, avenging, and by amplification, "the Grinder," "the Avenger," a not uncommon epithet of Horus, and some other gods.[2]

Even in the presence of an analogy of signification combined with a resemblance of forms, it is well to look twice before identifying symbols. The St. Anthony's Cross (*croix potencée*, literally "*gibbet-cross*") T is found, with almost the same symbolical signification, in Palestine, in Gaul, and in ancient Germany, in the Christian Catacombs, and amongst the ancient inhabitants of Central

[1] *Le culte de la croix avant Jésus-Christ*, in the French periodical, *le Correspondant* of the 25th October, 1889.

[2] *Le culte de la croix avant le christianisme*, in *La Science catholique* of the 15th February, 1890, p. 163.

America. Among the Phœnicians and their kindred races, it was the character known by the name of *tau*, and from an oft quoted passage in Ezekiel [1] we learn that it was accounted a sign of life and health. Among the Celts and the ancient Germans it was the representation of the celestial Two-headed Mallet which was accounted an instrument of life and of fecundity. Amongst the early Christians it was a form sometimes given to the Cross of Christ, itself called the Tree of Life.[2] In Central America where, according to M. Albert Réville, the Cross was surnamed the Tree of Plenty,[3] it assumed also the form of the *tau*.

Are we to conclude from this that all these *gibbet-crosses* have the same origin and the same aim ? That would be a rather hasty conclusion. The symbolical signification of the *tau* is explained by its resemblance to the *Key of Life* or *crux ansata* of Egypt, so widely diffused throughout all Western Asia. The Double Hammer of Thor and of Tarann is a symbol of the lightning, and, for this reason, could not fail to represent the vivifying forces of the storm, according to the tradition common among the Indo-European nations.[4] Similarly, if in pre-Columbian America, the Cross became an emblem of fertility, it is, as we have seen, because it represents the rain-god. As for the early Christians, if they made of the Cross a symbol of life, it is especially in the spiritual

---

[1] Ezek. ix. 4-6.

[2] A. DE GUBERNATIS, *Mythologie des Plantes*. Paris, 1878, vol. i., p. 6.

[3] *Religions du Mexique*, etc., p. 91.

[4] A. KUHN, *Herabkunft des Feuers*. Berlin, 1889.—A Germanic tradition, related by M. Karl Blind, shows to what an extent the old Pagan beliefs have been fused, in the popular imagination, with the dogmas of Christianity. The Virgin Mary, in order to explain the mystery of her conception, says that "the Smith from above" threw the Hammer into her breast. (*Antiquary*, 1884, p. 200.)

sense ; and, if they sometimes gave it the form of the *patibulum*, it was because such was the instrument employed among the Romans in the punishment by crucifixion.

In the mythology of primitive nations the contest between the sky, or sun, and the clouds is frequently represented by a fight between an eagle and a serpent. This subject has been treated more than once in ancient art.[1] Already in the Homeric ages it had become a symbol of victory, for we are told in the Iliad that the Trojans were on the point of abandoning the assault on the Greek entrenchments through having seen an eagle which held a serpent in its claws take flight, being wounded by its prey.[2] Now according to the tradition of the Aztecs, the founding of Mexico is said to have been resolved on owing to the apparition of an eagle which, perched upon an agave, and with wings outstretched towards the rising sun, held a serpent in its talons.[3] The first conquerors of Mexico saw therein an emblem of future greatness, and to the present day this emblem figures in the arms of the capital. Yet it is unlikely that the Aztecs had read Homer.

On the other hand, the ease with which symbols are borrowed is indisputable. Represented on the ordinary productions of industry, favourite subjects with artists, they pass unceasingly from one country to another, with commodities of commerce and articles of ornament ; as witness the specimens of Hindu, Chinese, and Japanese symbolism and pictorial art which have penetrated

[1] Particularly on the coins of Elis. (BARCLAY V. HEAD, *Historia Numorum*, p. 353.)
[2] *Iliad*, book xii., l. 200, *et seq.*
[3] ALB. REVILLE, *Religions du Mexique*, etc., p. 29.

among us with the vases, the fabrics, and all the curiosities of the far East. The centres of artistic culture have always been foci of symbolic exportation. Have there not been found even among the "treasures" of our mediæval churches on the one hand, and among those of Chinese and Japanese temples on the other, masterpieces of Sassanian art, which themselves reproduce the symbols of classic paganism?[1]

In olden times soldiers and sailors and travellers of every profession never left home without taking with them, under some form or another, their symbols and gods, a knowledge of which they thus spread in remote parts—bringing back from abroad others in return. Slavery, so largely known in the ancient world, must likewise have favoured the importation of symbols through the medium of those innumerable captives whom the fortune of war, or the chances of piracy, brought everywhere from the most distant regions, without depriving them of the memory of their gods and the forms of their worship. Lastly, coins have never failed to propagate through immense distances the symbols of the nations who put them into circulation. Gallic coins are nothing but counterfeits of the Greek coinage of Phillip or Alexander, and even in the *tumuli* of Scandinavia native coins have been found which roughly imitated the coinage of Bactria.[2]

Now nothing is so contagious as a symbol unless perhaps a superstition; they are all the more so when combined together, as they generally were among the nations of antiquity, who scarcely

[1] M. Louis Gonse, *L'Art japonais*, p. 143, draws particular attention to a Sassanian vase, decorated with winged horses recalling the Greek Pegasus, among the treasures in the temple of Horiouji at Nara.

[2] C. A. Holmboe, *Traces de bouddhisme en Norvége*. Paris, 1857, p. 30, *et seq.*

adopted a symbol without attaching a talismanic value to it. Even to-day there are tourists who return from Naples with a coral horn, suspended, according to the sex of the traveller, from the bracelet, or the watchchain. Do they really believe that they have found a preservative against the evil eye in this Italian survival of an old Chaldæan symbol? To many of them it is assuredly only a local curiosity, a trinket, a souvenir of travel. But there are some amongst the number who let themselves be influenced, even unconsciously, by the Neapolitan superstition. " It can do no harm and may perhaps do good " they would be tempted to reply, in imitation of certain gamblers when bantered about their *fetiches*.

We have here an argument which is almost universal among polytheistic populations, where everyone thinks it safe to render homage not only to his own gods, but also to those of others, and even to unknown divinities, for do we ever know of whom we may have need in this world, or in the next? Egyptian *scarabæi* have been found by the thousand from Mesopotamia to Sardinia, wherever either the armies of the Pharaohs or the ships of the Phœnicians penetrated. Everywhere too in these latitudes there have been found native *scarabæi* made in imitation of those of Egypt, and reproducing with more or less exactness the symbols which the engravers of the valley of the Nile displayed so lavishly on the flat side of these amulets. It is thus again that, long before the diffusion of coins, the pottery, the jewels, the statuettes of Greece and of Etruria, furnished Central and Western Europe with divine types and symbolic figures.

Are there any indications which enable us to determine whether analogous symbols have been produced independently, or were derived from the same source?

Intricacy and singularity of forms when they exceed certain limits may justify the second of these propositions.

We may well suppose that in the desire to symbolize the strength or activity of superhuman beings, the Egyptians, the Aztecs, the Hindus, and the Chinese, have been separately led to enrich by several pairs of arms and legs, or even by several heads, certain figured representations of their superhuman beings.[1] But does this hypothesis of an independent origin hold good when, for example, we see both on the ancient coins of Lycia and in the feudal coat of arms of the Isle of Man, a figure at once so precise as the *triscèle* or *triquetra*, those three legs, joined together at the thigh, which radiate from a central point?

FIG. 4. TRISCÈLE ON THE SHIELD OF ENCELADUS.
(DE WITTE and LENORMANT. *Monuments Céramographiques*, vol. i., pl. viii.)

There is nothing for it but to ask one's self how this ancient solar symbol can have passed from one country to the other. The intermediate stage may perhaps be found in Sicily, where the *triscèle* was used in the coinage, from the time of Agathocles, to symbolize the configuration of the island with three promontories. As the Isle of Man also presents this geographical peculiarity, it is very possible that, at the commencement of the

[1] Captain Becker saw once in Central Africa an idol with many heads; it was explained to him that the *fetiche* was able therefore to better detect criminals. *La vie en Afrique.* Bruxelles, 1888, vol. ii. p. 304.

middle ages, a Norman baron, or even a Crusader, or simple adventurer, returning to his home after a sojourn in Sicily, applied to his native country a symbol still living in the classic traditions of the ancient Trinacria, save that in order to suit the age he added spurs to the heels.[1]

We are familiar with the Double-headed Eagle of the old German empire, still blazoned on the armorial bearings of Austria and of Russia. What was the surprise of the English travellers Barth and Hamilton, when, in exploring Asia

FIG. 5. BAS-RELIEF OF EYUK.
(PERROT and CHIPIEZ. *L'Art dans l'antiquité*, vol. iv., fig. 343.)

Minor about fifty years ago, they discovered a Double-headed Eagle of the same type sculptured in the midst of religious scenes on Pterian bas-reliefs dating back to the civilisation of the Hittites?

[1] It is from the thirteenth century that the *triscèle* figures in the coat-of-arms of the Isle of Man. According to a letter from Mr. John Newton, published in *The Athenæum* of the 10th September, 1892, it had been introduced there by Alexander III. of Scotland, when that Prince took over the Island of Man from the Norwegians in 1266, he himself having become familiar with that emblem at the English Court during the reign of Henry III. This king had been appointed by the favour of Pope Innocent IV. the nominal sovereign of Sicily, with which country, however, his connection was but short-lived.—The *triquetra* is likewise met with in the armorial bear-

It is difficult to admit that, on both sides, there
was conceived spontaneously, on identical lines, a
representation of the eagle so contrary to the laws
of nature.   M. de Longpérier has solved the
enigma by reminding us that it was only about
1345 that the Eagle with Two Heads replaced the
monocephalous one on the armorial bearings of
the Western Empire.   It would seem to have
been Flemish princes who, during the Crusades,
appropriated the device from the coins and standards of the Turkomans, then the masters of Asia
Minor.   The latter had adopted it as the symbol
of omnipotence, perhaps the *hamka*, the fabulous
bird of Moslem tradition, which carries off the
buffalo and the elephant, as the kite carries off the
mouse.   " Thus," observes M. Perrot, " there
would seem to have been transplanted into our
modern Europe a symbol belonging originally to
an Asiatic creed of the highest antiquity ; and by
a singular turn of fortune the Turks saw, at Bel-
grade and at Lepanto, their advance towards the
West barred by that same eagle which had conducted them triumphantly along the banks of the
Euphrates and the shores of the Bosphorus."[1]

Perchance the Turkomans themselves had borrowed this symbol from the sculptures carved by
their mysterious predecessors on the rocks of
Eyuk and of Iasili-Kaïa.   But it is equally
possible that they acquired it through the medium
of the Persians.   We find in the collection of
M. de Gobineau an intaglio, attributed by him to
the time of the Arsacidæ, on which is engraved
the traditional type of the Double-headed Eagle
holding, as at Eyuk, a hare in each claw.

ings of several noble families in England, Germany, Switzerland, and Poland. (MICHEL DE SMIGRODZKI. *Geschichte der
Suastika.*   Braunschwlig, 1890, pl. ii. fig. 155.)

[1] PERROT and CHIPIEZ. *L'Art dans l'antiquité,* vol. iv.
p. 683.

M. de Longpérier observes that if the stem of certain ferns (*Pteris aquilina*) be cut transversely a fairly accurate image of the Double-headed Eagle

FIG. 6. ARSACIAN INTAGLIO.
(*Revue Archéologique* of 1874, vol. xxvii., pl. v., No. 371.)

is obtained. Now the fern is named in Greek πτέρις or πτερία, as is the province where the bas-reliefs of Eyuk are found. The learned archæologist wondered if it was not this similarity which caused the Double-headed Eagle to be chosen as the symbol of Pteria :[1] but we know now that the bas-reliefs in question date from a period far earlier than that of the appearance of the Greeks in this part of the world, and, besides, it is probable that the Greeks had given a name to the fern before knowing Pteria. The most that can be admitted is that the resemblance of the Hittite symbol to the bicephalous figure obtained from the fern led the Greeks to name the country after the plant.

The Greeks, whom we have seen adopting as a symbol of victory the figure of an eagle holding a serpent between its talons, sometimes replaced the serpent by a hare which corresponded with the Hittite scheme. Only they rejected anything monstrous that the latter might offer, and contented themselves with faithfully copying nature.[2] India on the contrary seems to have accepted without hesitation the bicephalous type which Persia probably transmitted to it. We there find the Double-headed Eagle on ancient coins, where

[1] *Revue archéologique* of 1845, vol. ii. p. 82.
[2] *The coins of Elis.* (BARCLAY V. HEAD. *Loc. cit.*)

it holds an elephant instead of a hare, not only in
each talon, but also in each beak.   Moor saw in
this a representation of Garuda the solar Eagle
which Vishnu rode.   In any case we here draw
singularly near the *hamka* of the Turks ; and it may
even be that the latter derived their legend of the
fabulous bird from some representation of this
kind, where the part of the hare was taken by an
elephant, or buffalo.

FIG. 7. ANCIENT INDIAN COIN.
(MOOR.   *Hindoo Pantheon*, pl. 103, fig. 3.)

It cannot, however, be said that Greece had
nothing to do with the production of this emblem.

M. Clermont-Ganneau has shown how, in the
popular iconography, complex monsters were frequently produced by a false interpretation of
groups formed of separate individuals.   There is,
for example, an image of Phœnician origin which
shows us Orthros in the form of two dogs distinctly apart. " Hellenic image makers," he goes on
to say, "unite the two animals, while fable goes still
further and endows the imaginary creature with a
third head which it does not always possess in
ancient art." [1]   Thus again the Chimæra originates
in the group, so widespread in Lycian art, of a
lion devouring a goat; the two animals having been
taken for one by the Greek copyist.   In the same
manner the triple Geryon slain by Herakles owes
its existence to a wrong interpretation of the scene,
taken originally from Egypt, in which a king is
seen raising his club as if to strike three barbarians,
who are grouped in such a manner as to give the

[1] CLERMONT - GANNEAU.   *L'imagerie phénicienne*.   Paris,
vol. i. p. 15-19.

illusion of a single body with three heads, six arms, and six legs.

I had long since surmised a similar origin in the Double-headed Eagle, when, turning over once more the pages of Schliemann's *Mykenæ*, I discovered the solution of the problem in some golden *fibulæ* dug up by the famous archæologist among the tombs of the ancient Mycenæ (fig. 8 and 9). We there find two eagles, as Schliemann says, "leaning against each other with their whole bodies and even with their claws while turning their heads in opposite directions."

At Eyuk the two eagles are fused in one. In this instance it is not Greek mythology which has clumsily interpreted a Phœnician image, but the Asiatic sculptor who has misunderstood the real meaning of the Mycenian image.

When, therefore, the Double-headed Eagle changed sides in the thirteenth century of our era, during the struggle which has waged for more than thirty centuries between Europe and Asia, it did nothing else than return, after many wanderings, to its original home.

FIG. 8.   FIG. 9.
JEWELS FROM MYKENÆ.
(SCHLIEMANN, *Mykenæ*.)

I will cite yet another symbol, come from afar, the Semitic origin of which is not to be gainsaid; even when we cannot identify all the stages of the route it followed in order to reach us.

Christian symbolism has often represented God the Father, or Providence, "the Hand of God," by a hand emerging from a cloud.   In some of these figures the finger-tips emit rays of light, " as if it were a living sun," observes M. Didron in his *Histoire de Dieu;* and a miniature of the ninth century in the Bibliothèque Nationale of Paris, shows the Divine Hand in the middle of a *nimbus* encircling a Cross.

FIG. 10.   THE HAND OF GOD.
(DIDRON.   *Histoire de Dieu*, p. 32.)

M. Gaidoz has compared this figure with certain Gallic amulets, the solar Wheels formed of four rays through which a hand passes.[1]

Might not the two symbols have their prototype upon an Assyrian obelisk, where two hands are shown to issue from a solar Disk, the right open and exhibiting the palm, the left closed and holding a bow ?

FIG. 11.   ASSYRIAN SYMBOL.
(G. RAWLINSON.   *The Five Great Monarchies*, vol. ii. p. 233.)

The representation of the open, or uplifted, hand, intended to typify the divine might, is, moreover,

[1] H. GAIDOZ.   *Le dieu gaulois du soleil et le symbolisme de la roue.*   Paris, 1886, p. 64.

common to all branches of the Semitic race; it appears already amongst the Chaldæans, for a cylinder, of Babylonian origin, exhibits an uplifted hand, which emerges from a pyramidal base, between persons in an attitude of adoration; this is precisely the type of our " Hand of Justice."

FIG. 12. CHALDÆAN CYLINDER.
(LAJARD. *Mithra*, pl. xxvii., fig. 5.)

According to M. François Lenormant, the celebrated pyramid of Borsippa was called "the Temple of the Right Hand," and one of the names of Babylon was that of "the city of the Hand of Anu," or, what amounts to the same thing, of "the Celestial Hand."[1]

The hand uplifted towards the sky is an oft repeated image on the *ex voto* of Carthage, and even at the present time it is figured on native houses in Palestine and Marocco to ward off evil spirits from the dwellers therein.[2] Moreover this symbol passed also to India, where it decorates the

[1] *Gazette archéologique* of, 1877, p. 31.

[2] PH. BERGER in the *Gazette archéologique* of 1876, pp. 119-120.—It is remarkable that certain of the aborigines of Australia attribute similar power to their chiefs' or ancestors' hands, which they detach from the corpse and carefully preserve in their tribe. An English traveller, Mr. Howitt, states that at the sight of an *aurora australis* all the Kurnai in the camp began to swing one of these dried hands towards the portent, shouting out, "Send it away! send it away! do not let it burn us up!" (*Jour. Anthropological Institute*. London, 1883-1884, p. 189.)

pedestal of the Holy Tree in a bas-relief at Bharhut (see pl. iv., fig. *h*).

In default of adequate proofs drawn from singularity of form, identity of meaning and of use may afford strong presumptions in favour of the relationship of symbols.

There would be nothing surprising in Hindus and Egyptians having independently adopted, as a symbol of the sun, the lotus-flower, which every morning opens under the first rays of that luminary to close again at eventide, and which seems to spring up of itself on the surface of the placid waters. However, the hypothesis of a transmission becomes very plausible when, in the iconography of the two nations, we see this flower serving both as a support to the solar gods, Horus and Vishnu, and figuring in the hand of the goddesses associated with these gods, Hathor and Lukshmi, the Venuses of Egypt and India. Lastly, this plausibility becomes a sort of certainty when, on both sides, we find the lotus employed to interpret the same shade of thought in some indirect and subtle enough applications of solar symbolism.

It must indeed be remarked that on either side the Lotus-flower symbolizes less the sun itself than the solar Matrix, the mysterious sanctuary into which the sun retires every evening, there to acquire fresh life.

This miracle, which was believed to be renewed every day, was regarded as the origin of whatever exists. The Egyptians, who believed that the world had sprung from the liquid element, made the sun to proceed from a Lotus which one day had emerged from the primordial waters;[1] this they rendered in their iconography by represent-

---

[1] G. MASPERO, in the *Revue de l'histoire des religions*, vol. xviii., 1889, p. 21.

ing Horus as springing forth from a lotus-shaped calyx held by Hathor.[1] In the same way the Indian sacred books constantly speak of gods as sprung from the lotus; it is on a golden Lotus that Brahma appears in the beginning of time, and it is with the different parts of this plant that he created the world.[2] A Hindu legend, related by Father Vincenzo de Santa Catarina, states that Brahma keeps watch six months of the year and sleeps the other six in a Lotus-flower of extraordinary size and beauty.[3]

Hence a fresh enlargement given to the figurative meaning of the lotus. The symbol of solar renascence, it became, with the Egyptians, the symbol of human renascence and, generally, of life in its eternal and unceasingly renewed essence. On a sarcophagus in the Louvre there is depicted a *scarabæus* emerging from a Lotus between Isis and Nephthys in their characteristic attitude of guardians and protectresses of the dead.[4] Thus were represented both the sun and the deceased passing through the tomb to renew their existence in the luminous fields of space. The lotus was even adopted with this signification in the funeral symbolism of Europe. It is met with again, not only in the Greek traditions relating to the Lotophagi, those fabulous people who partook of the lotus in order to forget life and its troubles, but even in the inscriptions on tombstones which are met with, dating from the latter centuries of Paganism, from Libya to Belgium.[5]

Renascence has but few attractions for the

[1] G. LAFAYE. *Histoire des divinités d'Alexandrie hors de l'Égypte.* Paris, 1884, p. 247.
[2] JAMES DARMESTETER. *Essais orientaux.* Paris, 1883, p. 148.
[3] DE GUBERNATIS. *Mythologie des plantes,* vol. i. p. 206.
[4] This painting is reproduced by M. Ledrain in the *Gazette archéologique* of 1878, p. 192.
[5] See further fig. 16 and 17.

Brahmans, and still fewer for the Bhuddists.   The
latter adopted the ancient Flower of Life but to symbolize, according to their different schools, nature
in the sum of her manifestations—the eternally
active matter—the innumerable worlds which fill
space—the Buddha dwelling in each of them—
lastly, the teaching of the Master, that is to say, the
means of escaping from that chain of causes and
effects which engenders personal existence. It is thus
that they carried to the confines of Asia *the Lotus
of the Good Law;* and even to-day in the Himalayas
there is no valley so remote that the traveller does
not hear everywhere on his approach, as an utter-
ance of sanctification and of welcome, the mystic
formula : *om mani padmi om,--" Oh! the Jewel
in the Lotus."*

However, popular traditions and engraved monuments would suffice to remind us of the ties which
unite the Lotus of Buddhism to that of Egypt. A
legend relates that, when the Buddhisattva appears,
a miraculous Lotus springs out of the earth, and he
seats himself thereon, and takes in all the worlds at
a glance.[1]   Buddha, besides, is everywhere represented seated on the Lotus-flower like Vishnu and
Horus.   It is perhaps not impossible to fix the
intermediate stages of this symbolism. The Lotus
passed from Egypt to the monuments of Phœnicia
and, towards the eighth century before our era, to
those of Assyria,[2] which in their turn transmitted
it to Persia.   Thus, in the sculptures of Phœnicia
goddesses are found who hold in the hand a Lotus-
flower, and, in the Sassanian bas-reliefs at Tagh-i-
Bostan, the solar god Mithras stands upon a Lotus-

[1] SENART. *La légende du Bouddha* in the *Journal asiatique.*
Paris, 1874, 347.
[2] At least this is the date assigned by Layard, who gives
the epoch of the building of Khorsabad as the date of the first
appearance of the Egyptian lotus in Assyria as a symbol or
subject for ornament. (*Nineveh and its Remains,* vol ii.
p. 213.)

flower.[1] Lastly, among the Mesopotamians and the Persians it is not uncommon to find the Lotus blossoming on shrubs in which may be recognized either the Sacred Tree of the Semitic religions, or the Iranian tree which secretes the Elixir of Immortality.[2]

Nowadays the beautiful rose-blossomed lotus, *Nymphæa Nelumbo*, observed on the monuments of Egypt, no longer grows in that country in its wild state, but by a curious coincidence, it has remained in the *flora*, as in the symbolism, of India.[3]

FIG. 13. CAVES OF KANERKI.
(FERGUSSON and BURGESS. *Cave Temples of India*, pl. x., fig. 35.)

We may add that it has been imported from India to China and Japan, so that it is still one of the principal symbolical figures by which at the present day we recognize the sacred vases and other objects employed in religious services by the Buddhists of these countries.[4]

---

[1] FLANDIN and COSTE. *Voyage en Perse*, vol. i., pl. iii. and xiv.

[2] See further on, chap. iv.

[3] PERROT and CHIPIEZ. *Histoire de l'art dans l'antiquité*, vol. i. p. 578.

[4] MICHEL PALÉOLOGUE. *L'art chinois*. Paris, 1887, p. 45.

CHAPTER II.

ON THE GAMMADION OR SWASTIKA.

I. Geographical distribution of the *gammadion*.—Different patterns of the *gammadion*.—Its common occurrence amongst all the nations of the Old World, with the exception of the Egyptians, the Phœnicians, the Mesopotamians, and the Persians.—The *fylfot*.—The *swastika*.

II. Previous interpretations of the *gammadion*.—Opinions of Messrs. George Birdwood, Alexander Cunningham, Waring, W. Schwartz, Emile Burnouf, R. P. Greg, Ludwig Müller, and others.

III. Probable meaning of the *gammadion*.—The *gammadion* a charm.—The *gammadion* symbolical of the solar movement, and, by analogy, of the heavenly bodies in general.—The arms of the *gammadion* are rays which move.—Connection between the *tétrascèle* and the *triscèle*. — Figures connected with the *gammadion*.—Equivalence of the *gammadion* and certain solar images.—The Three Steps of Vishnu.—Lunar *tétrascèles*.

IV. Cradle of the *gammadion*.—Was it conceived simultaneously in several places?—Uniformity of its meaning and use.—Discussion as to its Aryan or Pelasgic origin.—Information furnished by the "whorls" of Hissarlik and the prehistoric pottery of Northern Italy.—The question is archæological, not ethnical.—Conclusions.

I. GEOGRAPHICAL DISTRIBUTION OF THE GAMMADION.

a   *b*

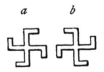

FIG. 14. GAMMADIONS.

THE name *gammadion* is given to that form of cross whose extremities are bent back at right angles, as if to form four *gammas* joined together at the base (fig. 14).

It may be called a cross *pattée* when the bent parts end in a point so as to form a sort of foot (fig. 15*a*), and a cross with hooks when the arms after being bent a first time are again twisted either inwards (15*b*), or outwards (15*c*). Lastly, it takes the name of *tétrascèle* when the arms are rounded off whilst curving backwards (15*d*).

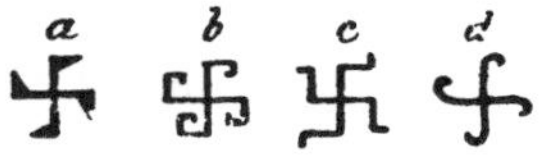

FIG. 15. VARIETIES OF THE GAMMADION.

With the exception of the solar Disk and the Greek Cross there are few symbolical marks so widely distributed.

Dr. Schliemann, exploring the *débris* of the towns piled upon the plateau of Hissarlik, beginning with the second or "burnt city," which the learned explorer identifies with the Ilium of Priam,[1] found innumerable *gammadions*, especially amongst the decorations of those terra cotta disks which have been thought to be "whorls," and which served perhaps as *ex voto*.[2] It likewise ornaments certain idols of feminine shape, which recall roughly the appearance of the Chaldæan Ishtar; in one of these statuettes, a leaden one, it occupies the centre of the triangle denoting the belly.[3]

In Greece, as in Cyprus and at Rhodes, it first appears on that pottery with geometrical ornamentation which constitutes the second period of

[1] SCHLIEMANN. *Ilios, ville et pays des Troyens.* Paris, 1885, pp. 507 *et seq.*
[2] SCHLIEMANN. *Troja.* London, 1884, p. 39.—See below fig. 22, 23*a*, 30, also plate ii., etc.
[3] SCHLIEMANN. *Ilios*, fig. 226. See also *Troja* (English ed.) on an "owl headed" vase of the most recent prehistoric city.

Grecian ceramics;[1] it then passes to those vases with decorations taken from living objects, whose appearance seems to coincide with the development of Phœnician influences on the shores of Greece.[2]

It is seen on the archaic pottery of Cyprus, and of Rhodes, and of Athens, on both sides of the conventional Tree, so frequently reproduced on the inscribed monuments of Hither Asia between two monsters facing each other (see further on, pl. iv.). It appears on an Athenian vase in a burial scene, three times repeated in front of the funeral car.[3] On a vase from Thera several *gammadions* are reproduced round an image of the Persian Artemis.[4] At Mycenæ it figures on ornaments collected during Dr. Schliemann's excavations.[5]   At Pergamus it adorns the balustrade of the portico which surrounded the temple of Athene, and at Orchomenus the sculptured roof of the so-called nuptial chamber in the palace of the Treasury.[6]   Lastly, when the introduction of money disclosed a new outlet for the symbolic forms of religion and of art, it became a favourite emblem in the coinage, not only of the Archipelago and of Greece Proper, but also of Macedon, Thrace, Crete, Lycia, and Paphlagonia.

From Corinth, where it figures amongst the most ancient mint marks, it passed to Syracuse under Timoleon, to be afterwards spread abroad on the

---

[1] ALB. DUMONT. *Peintures céramiques de la Grèce propre.* Paris, 1873, vol, i., pl. xv., fig. 17.

[2] PERROT and CHIPIEZ. *Histoire de l'art dans l'antiquité.* Paris, 1885, vol. iii., figs. 513, 515, 518.

[3] VICTOR DURUY. *Histoire des Grecs.* Paris, 1888, vol. i., fig. 729.

[4] DAREMBERG and SAGLIO. *Dictionnaire des antiquités des grecques et romaines.* Fasc. 12. Paris, 1888. *S. v. Diane,* p. 153, fig. 2389.

[5] SCHLIEMANN. *Mycènes.* Paris, 1879, p. 193.

[6] SCHLIEMANN. *Troja,* p. 123.

coins of Sicily and of Magna Græcia.[1] In Northern Italy it was known even before the advent of the Etruscans, for it has been met with on pottery dating from the terramare civilization.[2] It appears also on the roof of those ossuaries, in the form of a hut, which reproduce on a small scale the wicker hovels of the people of that epoch.[3] In the Villanova period it adorns vases with geometrical decorations found at Cære, Chiusi, Albano, and at Cumæ,[4] and when Etruria became accessible to oriental influences it appears on *fibulæ* and other golden ornaments.[5]

At a still later period it is found on the breasts of personages decorating the walls of a Samnite tomb near Capua ;[6] lastly it appears as a *motif* for decoration in the Roman mosaics.   It is singular that at Rome itself it has not been met with on any monument prior to the third, or perhaps the fourth, century of our era.   About that period the Christians of the Catacombs had no hesitation in including it amongst their representations of the Cross of Christ.   Not only did they carve it upon the tombs, but they also used it to ornament the garments of certain priestly personages, such as the *fossores*, and even the tunic of the Good Shepherd.[7] At Milan it forms a row of curved Crosses round the pulpit of St. Ambrose.

On the other hand, it appears to have been

---

[1] *Numismatic Chronicle.*   London, vol. viii. (3rd series), p. 103.

[2] DE MORTILLET.   *Musée préhistorique*, pl. xcix.

[3] J. MARTHA.   *Archéologie étrusque et romaine*, fig. 1.

[4] ALEXANDRE BERTRAND.   *Archéologie celtique et gauloise.* Paris, 2nd ed., 1889, figs. 65-68.

[5] ALEXANDRE BERTRAND.   *La Gaule avant les Gaulois.* Paris, 1884, fig. 77.

[6] TH. ROLLER.   *Les catacombes de Rome.*   Paris, vol. ii. p. 32.

[7] TH. ROLLER.   *Les catacombes de Rome*, vol. i., pl. vi. 1 ; pl. x., 29, 30, 31 ; pl. xxxii., 15 ; pl. xxxix., 19 ; vol. ii., pl. lv., 2 ; pl. lxxxviii., 13, and pl. xciv., 2.

widely distributed throughout the provinces of the Roman empire, especially among the Celts, where in many cases it is difficult to decide whether it is connected with imported civilization, or with indigenous tradition. From Switzerland, and even from the Danubian countries, to the most remote parts of Great Britain, it has been found on vases, on metal plates, on *fibulæ*, on sword belts, and on arms.[1] In England it adorns fragments of mosaics collected from the ruins of several villas,[2] as well as a funeral urn unearthed in a mound of the bronze age.[3] In Gaul it is observed frequently enough on coins ranging from the third century B.C. to the third century of our era, and even later, for it is met with on a Merovingian piece.[4] We may add that it already figures on fragments of pottery and even on terra cotta matrices found in a lacustrine city in Lake Bourget.[5]

In Belgium, we meet with it at Estinnes (Hainault) and at Anthée (Province of Namur) in tile *débris* dating back to the Roman epoch.[6] It is also seen repeated several times, in association with the Lotus-flower, among the inscriptions on tombstones discovered, some years ago, in the Belgo-Roman cemetery of Juslenville, near Pepinster (fig. 16).

An interesting discussion, arose in the *Institut archéologique liégeois* as to whether—in spite of the invocation D[iis] M[anibus]—the presence of the *gammadion* did not imply the Christian

---

[1] MORTILLET. *Musée préhistorique*, pl. xciii., xcviii. and c.

[2] ROB. SEWELL, in the *Jour. Rl. As. Soc.*, vol. xviii. (new series), p. 383.

[3] G. DE MORTILLET. *Le signe de la croix avant le christianisme.* Paris, 1866, fig. 76.

[4] LELEWEL. *Numismatique du moyen âge.* Atlas, pl. iv., No. 57.

[5] ERN. CHANTRE. *L'âge du Bronze.* Paris, 1876, 2nd part, pp. 194, 195.

[6] *Bulletins de l'Institut archéologique liégeois*, vol. x. p. 106.

character of this sepulchral monument.[1] To the arguments brought forward to refute this theory we may add that a sepulchral *stele* of an unques-

FIG. 16. TOMBSTONE FROM JUSLENVILLE.
(*Institut archéologique liégeois*, vol. x. (1870), pl. xiii.)

tionably pagan character, discovered in Algeria, offers an analogous combination of two *gammadions* placed over a Wheel.

FIG. 17. LIBYAN SEPULCHRAL STELE.
(Proceedings of the *Soc. franç. de numism. et d'archéol.*, vol. ii., pl. iii. 3.)

The fact may be mentioned that in the middle of the Christian era, eleven or twelve centuries later, the *gammadion* reappears on a sepulchre in

---

[1] It was maintained that these letters signified :—*DoMus æterna* or *D*[*eo*] *M*[*aximo*], so that instead of reading, *Diis manibus Primus Marci Filius*, M. Buckens, formerly Professor at the Academy of the Fine Arts at Liege, did not hesitate, by a free interpretation of the *gammadions*, the floral ornamentation, the triangle, the niche, and the lotus leaves, to translate them textually as follows : "The last abode of the son of Marcus in Jesus Christ, God, baptized in the name of the Father and of the Holy Ghost"! (*Bulletins de l'Institut archéologique liégeois*, vol. x. (1870), p. 55.)

the same Belgian province. On a tombstone of the fourteenth century, discovered in 1871, during the construction of a tunnel at Huy, three personages are sculptured, one of whom is a priest clothed in a chasuble, and on this chasuble three bands of *gammadions* can be distinctly seen.[1]

The *gammadion*, associated with the Wheel, as well as with the Thunderbolt, likewise adorns votive altars found, in England, and near the Pyrenees, on the site of Roman encampments.[2]

FIG. 18. ALTAR IN THE TOULOUSE MUSEUM.
(*Reveu archéologique de* 1880, vol. xl. p. 17.)

At Velaux, in the Bouches-du-Rhône department, there has been found the headless statue of a god sitting cross-legged, who bore on its breast a row of crocketed crosses surmounting another row of equilateral crosses.[3]

In Ireland, however, and in Scotland, the *gammadion* seems really to have marked Christian sepulchres, for it is met with on tombstones associated with Latin Crosses.[4]

The Rev. Charles Graves, Bishop of Limerick, has described an ogham stone found in an aban-

---

[1] The stone is now in the " Musée du Parc du Cinquantenaire " at Brussels.

[2] LUD. MÜLLER. *Det saakaldte Hagekors.* Copenhagen, 1877, pp. 21, 22.

[3] ALEX. BERTRAND. *L'autel de Saintes et les triades gauloises,* in the *Revue archéologique* of 1880, vol. xxxix. p. 343.

[4] LUD. MÜLLER. *Op. cit.,* p. 114.

doned cemetery in Kerry, which he believes to belong to the sixth century; it bears an arrow between two *gammadions*.[1]

The Anglo-Saxons gave to the *gammadion* the name of *fylfot*, from the Norse *fiöl* (full, *viel* = "numerous"), and *fot* (foot).[2] It has been observed on pottery and funeral urns of the bronze age in Silesia, in Pomerania, and the eastern islands of Denmark. In the following ages it is met with on ornaments, on sword-hilts, on golden brackets, on sculptured rocks, and on tombstones.[3] Amongst the Scandinavians it ended by combining, doubt-

FIG. 19. CROSS ON A RUNIC STONE FROM SWEDEN.
(LUDWIG MÜLLER, p. 94, fig. *a*.)

lessly under the influence of Christianity, with the Latin Cross.

In an old Danish church it ornaments baptismal fonts which date from the early times of Christianity.[4] In Iceland, according to Mr. Hjaltalin, it is still in use at the present day as a magic sign.[5]

Amongst the Slavs and Finns it has not yet been found, save in a sporadic state, and about the period of their conversion to Christianity only. We may remark, by the way, that it is very diffi-

---

[1] *Transactions of the Royal Irish Academy*, vol xxvii., Feb., 1879. See also the same vol., April, 1879, *On the Croix gammée* or *Swastika*.

[2] R. P. GREG. *The Fylfot* and *Swastika*, in *Archæologia*. London, vol. xlviii., part ii., 1885, p. 298.

[3] LUD. MÜLLER. *Op. cit., passim.*—R. P. GREG. *Loc. cit.*, pl. xix., fig. 27, 31, 32, 33.—C. A. HOLMBOE. *Traces du bouddhisme en Norvège.* Paris, 1857, pp. 34 *et seq.*

[4] LUD. MÜLLER. *Op. cit.*, p. 113.

[5] *Nineteenth Century* for June, 1879, p. 1098.

cult to determine the age and nationality of the terra cotta or bronze objects on which it has been observed in countries of mixed or superposed races, such as Hungary, Poland, Lithuania and Bohemia.

In the Caucasus, M. Chantre has met with it on ear-drops, ornamental plates, sword-hilts, and other objects found in burial-places dating back to the bronze period and the first iron age.[1]

Amongst the Persians its presence has been pointed out on some Arsacian and Sassanian coins only.[2]

The Hittites introduced it on a bas-relief at Ibriz, in Lycaonia, where it forms a border on the dress of a king, or priest, who offers up a sacrifice to a god.[3]

The Phœnicians do not seem to have known or, at least, to have used it, except on some of the coins which they struck in Sicily in imitation of Greek pieces. A coin of Byzacium on which it is figured, near the head of Astarte, dates from the reign of Augustus.[4]

It is not met with either in Egypt, in Assyria, or in Chaldæa.

In India it bears the name of *swastika*, when its arms are bent towards the right (fig. 14*a*), and *sauwastika* when they are turned in the other direction (fig. 14*b*). The word *swastika* is a derivative of *swasti*, which again comes from *su* = well, and the verb *asti* = it is; the expression would seem therefore to correspond with a Greek formula—εὖ εστὶ, and, in fact, amongst the Hindus

[1] ERN. CHANTRE. *Recherches archéologiques dans le Caucase.* Paris, 1886, vol. ii., atlas, pl. xi., xv., etc.

[2] LUD. MÜLLER. *Op. cit.*, fig. 3.

[3] PERROT and CHIPIEZ. *Histoire de l'art dans l'antiquité*, vol. iv., fig. 354.

[4] *Numismatique de l'ancienne Afrique.* Copenhagen, 1860-1862, vol. ii. p. 40, No. 4.

as amongst the Buddhists, its representation has always passed for a propitious sign.[1]

The grammarian Panini mentions it as a character used for earmarking cattle. We see in the *Ramayana* that the ships of the fleet, on which Bharata embarked for Ceylon, bore, doubtlessly on their bows, the sign of the *swastika*.[2] Passing now to inscribed monuments we find the *gammadion* on the bars of silver, shaped like dominos, which, in certain parts of India, preceded the use of money proper.[3]

It even appears upon a coin of Krananda, which is held to be the oldest Indian coin, and which is

FIG. 20. ANCIENT INDIAN COIN.
(*Archæological Survey of India*, vol. x., pl. ii., fig. 8.)

likewise remarkable as exhibiting the first representation of the *trisula*.[4]

Occurring frequently at the beginning and the end of the most ancient Buddhist inscriptions, several examples of it are to be seen on the Foot-Prints of Buddha sculptured at Amravati.[5] The *swastika* represents, moreover, according to Buddhist tradition, the first of the sixty-five marks which distinguished the Master's feet, whilst the

[1] See Prof. Max Müller's letter, in SCHLIEMANN. *Ilios*, pp. 517-521.
[2] *Ramayana*.
[3] EDW. B. THOMAS. *The early Indian Coinage*, in the *Numismatic Chronicle*, vol. iv. (new series), pl. xi.
[4] See our fig. 146.
[5] JAMES FERGUSSON. *History of Indian and Eastern Architecture*. London. Murray, 1876, p, 184. See our title-page.

fourth is formed by the *sauwastika*, and the third
by the *nandyavarta*, a kind of labyrinth, which, in
the manner of the Greek *meander*, may be connected with the *gammadion*.[1]

FIG. 21. THE NANDYAVARTA.

It must be observed that amongst the Jains,
the *gammadion* is regarded as the emblem of
Suparsva, the seventh of the twenty-four *Tirthankaras*, whilst the *nandyavarta* is that of the eighteenth.[2]

Even at the present day, according to Mr.
Taylor, the Hindus, at the time of the new year,
paint a *gammadion* in red at the commencement
of their account books, and, in their weddings and
other ceremonies, they sketch it in flour on the
floors of their houses.[3]   It also figures at the end
of manuscripts of a recent period, at least under
a form which, according to M. Kern, is a development of the *tétrascèle*.[4]

The *gammadion* has been likewise preserved to
the present time amongst the Buddhists of Tibet,
where the women make use of it in the ornamentation of their skirts, and where it is placed on the

---

[1] EUG. BURNOUF.   *Le Lotus de la Bonne-Loi.*   Paris, 1852,
p. 626.

[2] COLEBROOKE.   *Observations on the Jainas*, vol. ix., *Asiatic
Researches*, p. 308.

[3] EUG. BURNOUF.   *Op. cit.*, p. 626.

[4] KERN.   *Der Buddhismus.*   Leipzig, 1884, vol. ii. p. 239,
note 3.—Colebrooke gives to this sign the name of *srivatsa*, and
makes it out to be the distinctive mark of the tenth Tirthan-
kara of the Jains.   M. Schwartz has compared it to the four-
leaved clover, which also " brings luck."

breasts of the dead.[1] In China—where it bears
the name of *ouan*—and in Japan it adorns vases,
caskets, and the representations of divinities, as
may be seen in the Musée Guimet at Paris; it is
even figured upon the breasts of certain statues of
Buddha and the Buddhisattvas, where, according
to M. Paléologue, it would seem to symbolize the
heart.[2] According to another interpretation, given
by the Annamite bonzes, it might be the cicatrice
of a spear-thrust received by Buddha; but these
bonzes, according to M. G. Dumoutier, continue
to venerate this symbol without understanding it.[3]

In the Woolwich Arsenal the *gammadion* may
be seen upon a cannon captured at the Taku forts
by the English. According to M. G. Dumoutier
it is nothing else than the ancient Chinese character *che*, which implies the idea of perfection, of
excellence, and would seem to signify the renewal
and the endless duration of life.[4] In Japan, according to M. de Milloué, it represents the number
10,000, which symbolizes that which is infinite,
perfect, excellent, and is employed as a sign of
felicity.[5] A statue of the Buddhisattva Jiso, in the
Musée Guimet, rests upon a pedestal ornamented
with *swastikas*.

Lastly let us conclude this long recital, which
is in danger of becoming tedious without hope of
being complete, by mentioning the presence of the
gammadion in Africa, on bronzes brought from
Coomassie by the last English Ashantee ex-

[1] *Journal Asiatique*, 2nd series, vol. iv. p. 245. PALLAS.
*Samlungen historischer Nachrichten über die mongolischen Volker-
schaften*, vol. i. p. 277.
[2] MICHEL PALÉOLOGUE. *L'Art chinois*, p. 47.
[3] G. DUMOUTIER. *Les Symboles, les Emblèmes et les Accessoires
du culte chez les Annamites*. Paris, 1891, pp. 19-20.
[4] G. DUMOUTIER. *Le svastika et la roue solaire en Chine*, in
the *Revue d'Ethnographie*. Paris, 1885, p. 331.
[5] DE MILLOUÉ. *Le svastika*, in the *Bulletins de la Société
d'Anthropologie* of Lyons, 1881, v. i. pp. 191 *et seq.*

pedition;[1] in South America, on a calabash from
the Lenguas tribe; in North America, on pottery
from the mounds and from Yucatan, as also on
the rattles made from a gourd which the Pueblos
Indians use in their religious dances.[2]

II. DIFFERENT INTERPRETATIONS OF THE GAMMADION.

That a great number of *gammadions* have been
mere ornaments, monetary signs, or trade-marks,
is a fact which it would be idle to dispute.   But
the uses which have been made of this figure in
all the countries which I have just instanced, the
nature of the symbols with which it is found associated, its constant presence on altars, tombstones,
sepulchral urns, idols, and priestly vestments, besides the testimony of written documents and
popular superstitions, afford more than sufficient
proof that in Europe as in Asia it partook everywhere of the nature of the amulet, the talisman,
and the phylactery.[3]   Moreover, for the *gammadion* to have thus become a charm, it must first of
all have been brought into contact with a being, or
a phenomenon, more or less concrete and distinct,
invested, rightly or wrongly, with some sort of
influence on the destiny of mankind.   Might it
not be possible to find out this original meaning
of the *gammadion* by laying stress on the indications provided by the monuments themselves?

[1] SCHLIEMANN. *Ilios*, figs. 248, 249, and 250.
[2] T. LAMY. *Le svastika et la roue solaire en Amérique*, in
the *Revue d'Ethnographie*.   Paris, 1885, p. 15.
[3] M. Michel de Smigrodzki, who in his recent essay, *Zur
Geschichte der Svastika* (Braunschwig, 1890, extracted from
the *Archiv für Anthropologie*), has classified chronologically a
considerable number of *gammadions* belonging to monuments
of the most different periods and nations, has made it his
special study to show that this cross has everywhere had a
symbolical, and not merely an ornamental value.

Many archæologists have thought so, whilst however arriving at different solutions. There is hardly a symbol which has given rise to more varied interpretatious—not even the *trisula* of the Buddhists, which is saying a great deal.

I will confine myself to mentioning the opinion of those who have confounded the *gammadion* with the *crux ansata* of the Egyptians, the *tau* of the Phœnicians, the *vajra* of India, the Hammer of Thor, or the Arrow of Perkun—all of which are signs having a form and meaning too clearly defined for this identification to be maintained without corroborative evidence. If even the *gammadion* ever replaced one of them—as in the Catacombs it sometimes takes the place of the Cross of Christ—it only did so as a substitute, as the symbol of a symbol.

Several writers have ascribed a phallic import to the *gammadion*, some, like M. J. Hoffman, seeing therein the union of the male with the female principle ;[1] others, as Sir George Birdwood, believing that they recognize in it especially the symbol of the female sex.[2] The latter supposition would seem to be sufficiently justified by the position assigned to the *gammadion* on some female idols from the Troad, as also by its association with the image of certain goddesses, the Persian Artemis, Here, Demeter, Astarte. But the *gammadion* may very well have furnished a symbol of fecundity, as elsewhere a common symbol of prosperity and of salvation, without therefore being necessarily a phallic sign. In the one case, as in the other, the point in question is to ascertain if this is not a secondary meaning, connected with a less abstract conception.

General Cunningham believes that he found in

---

[1] *Das Buddha Pantheon von Nippon*, quoted by M. LUDVIG MÜLLER, *Op. cit.*, p. 103.
[2] *Jour. R. As. Soc.*, v. xviii. (n. s.), p. 408.

the *swastika* a Pali monogram formed of four
characters corresponding to our letters S. U. T. I.[1]
But Professor Max Müller maintains that the likeness is hardly striking, and seems to be purely
accidental.[2] In any case, the explanation would
apply only to the Indian *gammadion ;* an objection
which may likewise be urged against Mr. Frederic
Pincott's hypothesis, that the *swastika* is the
emblem of the four castes united in the same
symbolical combination.[3]

Waring held that the *gammadion* was a figurative represention of water, on account of its
resemblance to the *meander*, and also of its
frequent occurrence in combination with the
wavy line, a well-known symbol for water in
motion.[4] However, as we shall see further on,
this combination is far from being invariable, and
certainly the form of the *gammadion* has, in itself,
nothing which conjures up the idea of running
water, or of rain.

Others have discerned in it a symbol of the
storm, or lightning, because it can be separated
into two zigzags or interlaced Z's. W. Schwartz,
who, with his usual ability, has upheld this theory,
—which conforms with his general views on the
meteorological origin of myths and symbols,—
draws attention to the numerous points of contact
existing between the lightning and the different
forms of the Cross not only in the symbolism of
many religions, but also in popular language.[5]
This agrees with the practice, so common in
Catholic countries, of making the sign of the Cross,
on the appearance of lightning, to prevent being

---

[1] *The Bhilsa Topes.* London, 1884, p. 386.
[2] Letter to Schliemann in *Ilios*, p. 520.
[3] *Journal of the Royal Asiatic Society*, vol. xix. (n.s.), p. 245.
[4] *Ceramic Art in Remote Ages.* London, 1875, p. 13, *et seq.*
[5] *Der Blitz als geometrisches Gebild*, in the *Jubiläumschrift
der Posener Naturwissenchaft. Verein*, 1887, pp. 221-234.

struck, as also with the custom spread amongst
our peasantry, especially in Flemish Brabant, of
tracing a Cross in whitewash on their houses to
preserve them from the same calamity. But it
may be questioned if these customs are not owing
to the general talismanic value which the Christian
symbol receives in the popular beliefs : the sign
of the Cross, in fact, is reputed to drive away evil
spirits and to call in divine protection. As for
Crosses painted on the outer walls, they seem to be
held of use not only against lightning, but also
against fires, epidemics amongst cattle, and, generally, against all the unforeseen accidents which
threaten the dwelling-place.

In any case there is here no question of the
gammadion, and the popular talk about the flashes
of lightning "which cross" is not sufficient to
account for the derivation of the form of the *fylfot*.
I am well aware that amongst the ancient Germans,
and even amongst the Celts, the *gammadion* is
sometimes met side by side with the symbols of
thunder on weapons, amulets, ornaments, and even
on altars. But these objects present also to our
view the image of the Disk, the Crescent, the
triscèle, and many other symbolical figures.[1] It
would seem as if the engraver had simply wished
to bring together all the symbols possessing, to
his knowledge, a phylacteric, or talismanic character ; by a process of reasoning analogous to
that which, in the latter period of Greek paganism,
prompted the manufacture of pantheian figures.

M. Emile Burnouf makes the *gammadion* the
symbol of fire, or rather of the mystical twofold
arani, that is to say of the fire-drill, which was
used to produce fire amongst the early Aryans.
" This sign," he writes, "represents the two pieces
of wood forming the *arani*, whose extremities were

---

[1] R. P. GREG, *in Archæologia*, 1885, pl. xix. fig. 31, 32, 23 ;
pl. xx., fig. 2.

curved, or else enlarged, so that they could be
firmly kept in place by four nails. At the point
where they joined there was a small hole in which
was placed the piece of wood, shaped like a spear,
whose violent rotation, produced by whipping,
made Agni to appear." [1]

Up till now it has been by no means proved
that the lower part of the *arani* ever had the form
of the *swastika* or even of the Cross. On the contrary there are reasons for supposing that it was
usually a mere log of wood in which the point of
the *pramantha* was made to turn.[2] Perhaps, in
some cases, it had a circular form ; the fire was
then produced by making it revolve round a nave.
If, as has been maintained, it really assumed, in
some Indian temples, the appearance of the *gammadion*, it had doubtlessly been given this form to
imitate the *swastika*.[3] As for the four points
which are placed between the arms of certain
gammadions, there is nothing to prove that they
represent nails (see our plate II., *litt.* B, Nos. 19,
20, 21, 22, and 23), and in most cases they do not
even touch the branches of the cross which,
according to M. Burnouf, they are intended to
fasten. Schliemann, who seems not unwilling
to subscribe to M. Emile Burnouf's theory, observes that in Troas the *gammadion* accompanies
the linear drawings of burning altars,[4] but—admitting that these are altars—can they not blaze in
the honour of some other god than the fire itself ?
Further, nothing prevents us from supposing that
the sun itself has been represented as a blazing
altar.

[1] EMILE BURNOUF. *La science des Religions.* Paris, 1876,
p. 240.

[2] J. C. NESFIELD. *Mythology of Fire* in the *Calcutta Review*
of April, 1884, p. 375.

[3] It is thus the Buddhists have even erected *stoupas* in the
form of the *gammadion*. (Cf. SCHLIEMANN. *Ilios*, p. 520.)

[4] SCHLIEMANN. *Ilios*, figs. 1872, 1911, 1914, 1916.

In support of M. Burnouf's theory, attention might further be called to the fact that the *swastika* with branches turned towards the right is, amongst the Hindus, accounted of the feminine gender, which would make it agree with the symbolism of the *arani*. But it must be remarked that the *swastika* turned in the other direction passes as masculine. Moreover, according to Sir George Birdwood, it is a common custom in modern India to divide into the two sexes all objects occurring in interdependent pairs.

Mr. R.-P. Greg has written, in the Memoirs published by the *Society of Antiquaries*, London, a very interesting study on the *gammadion*, in which, whilst striving to deal impartially with the other explanations of this sign, he contends it is especially a symbol of the air, or rather of the god who rules the phenomena of the atmosphere, Indra with the Hindus, Thor with the ancient Germans and the Scandinavians, Perkun with the Slavs, Zeus with the Pelasgians and Greeks, Jupiter *tonans* and *pluvius* with the Latin race.[1] Unfortunately, the proofs which he adduces are neither numerous nor conclusive. The fact that in India the bull is sacred to Indra, and that on certain monetary ingots the *gammadion* surmounts an image of this animal, is hardly sufficient to prove that the *swastika* is a symbol of Indra.[2] It is likewise difficult to admit that the *gammadion* represents the god of the atmosphere amongst the Greeks because on some pottery from Cyprus there are *gammadions* which recall the image of birds flying in the air.

The above-named writer makes much of the fact that on many incised monuments the *gammadion* is placed above images representing the earth,

[1] R.-P. GREG. *The Fylfot and Swastika*, in *Archæologia*, 1885, p. 293 *et seq.*

[2] ID., *ibid.*, p. 302.

or terrestrial creatures, and below other images symbolizing the sky, or the sun. But this arrangement is far from being invariable or even predominant. Frequently the *gammadion* is found on the same level with astronomical symbols; sometimes even it occupies the upper place. Mr. Greg, it is true, gets over the difficulty by asserting that in this case it must represent the god of the ether in the capacity of supreme God.[1]

The only example I am acquainted with of a *gammadion* consecrated to Zeus, or to Jupiter, is on a votive altar, where it is incised above the letters I. O. M.[2] But this is a Celto-Roman altar, erected, to all appearance, by Dacians garrisoned in Ambloganna, a town in Great Britain; that is to say, that here again we may be in the presence of a strange god, assimilated to the supreme divinity of the empire, the *Jupiter Optimus Maximus* of the Romans. Moreover, the *gammadion* is here flanked by two four-rayed Wheels, symbols which M. Gaidoz has clearly proved to have been, amongst the Gauls, of a solar character.[3]

Lastly, Ludvig Müller, Percy Gardner, S. Beal, Edward B. Thomas, Max Müller, H. Gaidoz, and others, have succeeded, by their studies of Hindu, Greek, Celtic, and ancient German monuments, in establishing the fact that the *gammadion* has been, among all these nations a symbolical representation of the sun, or of a solar god. I should like here to sum up the respective conclusions of these authors, setting forth, at the same time, the other reasons which have led me, not only to accept, but also to develop their interpretation. This attempt may perhaps be the less superfluous since, judging by the comparatively recent works of M. M. Greg

---

[1] R.-P. GREG. *Loc. cit.*, pp. 307 and 309.
[2] LUDVIG MÜLLER. *Op. cit.*, fig. 29.
[3] H. GAIDOZ. *Le dieu gaulois du Soleil et le symbolisme de la roue.* Paris. 1886.

and Schwartz, the solar, or even the astronomical character of the *gammadion* is not yet beyond dispute.

III. PROBABLE MEANING OF THE GAMMADION.

We have seen that most nations represented the sun by a circle. Some, also, have depicted it by a cruciform sign, more particularly the Assyrians, the Hindus, the Greeks, the Celts, etc. (see fig. 2).

This symbolism doubtlessly renders the idea of the solar radiation in the four directions of space. But the sun does not restrict itself to darting its rays in all directions, it seems, further, animated by a circular movement from east to west. The latter action may have been symbolized, sometimes by changing the Disk into a Wheel, sometimes by adding to the four extremities of the solar Cross feet, or broken lines, usually turned in the same direction.

Sometimes the curve of the rays was rounded off, perhaps either to accentuate still further the idea of a rotary motion by a figure borrowed from the elementary laws of mechanics, or else by an effect of that tendency, which, in primitive writings, has everywhere substituted the cursive for the angular. Thus was obtained the *tétrascèle* (*cf.* fig. 15*d*), which, as I have said above, is simply a variety of the *gammadion*.

M. Gaidoz has defined the *gammadion* as a graphic doublet of the Wheel.[1] The expression is exact, and is even a very happy one, provided it means, not that the *gammadion* is derived from the Wheel by the suppression of a part of the felloe, but that it is, like the Wheel, a symbolical representation of the solar movement.

For the very reason that the *gammadion* represents the sun in its apparent course it has readily

---

[1] H. GAIDOZ. *Op. cit.*, p. 113.

become a symbol of prosperity, of fecundity, of blessing, and—with the help of superstition—it has everywhere received the meaning of a charm, as in India the very name *swastika* implies.

Moreover, after having figured the sun in motion, it may have become a symbol of the astronomical movement in general, applied to certain celestial bodies, the moon, for example—or even to everything which seems to move of itself, the air, water, lightning, fire—in as far as it really served as a sign of these different phenomena, which fact has still to be made good.[1]—This, in brief, is the whole theory of the *gammadion*.

This theory is not the outcome of any *à priori* reasoning; it is founded on the following considerations :

A. The form of the *gammadion*.

B. The connection between the *tétrascèle* and *triscèle*.

C. The association of the *gammadion* with the images, symbols, and divinities of the sun.

D. The part it plays in certain symbolical combinations, where it sometimes accompanies and sometimes replaces the representation of the solar Disk.

A. *The branches of the gammadion are rays in motion.*

To be convinced of this, it is only necessary to cast one's eyes on the manner in which, at all times, the idea of solar movement has been graphically expressed (fig. 22).

The first of these figures (*a*) is an ancient *fibula* found in Italy. At the top is seen a Disk from which radiate small rays, bent at right angles ; these rays seem to have been modelled on the

---

[1] " On a terra-cotta from Salamine, representing a *tethrippos* or four-wheeled chariot, a *gammadion* is painted on each quarter of the wheel."—CESNOLA, *Salamina*, London, 1832, fig. 226.

branches of the *gammadions* sketched immediately beneath.

The second (*b*) is taken from the "whorls" of Troy. Crooked rays, turned towards the right, alternate with straight and undulating rays, all of which proceed from the same Disk.

The third (*c*) comes from a reliquary of the

a   b   c   d   e

FIG. 22.[1]

thirteenth century, on which it forms a pendant to the lunar crescent, with an image of Christ between them. That this is a representation of the solar Disk results not only from its parallelism with the Crescent, but also from the fact that on a number of mediæval Christian monuments Christ is thus represented between the sun and moon.[2]

The same image—a Disk with five inflected rays—is met with on coins of Macedon (*d*), where it alternates sometimes with the *tétrascèle* (*e*).

Mr. Samuel Beal, who distinguishes two parts in the *gammadion*,—an equilateral cross and four hooks,—thinks that the purpose of the former is to symbolize the earth ; as for the hooks, they might serve to indicate the direction of the solar movement round our planet.[3] But the figures which

[1] *a. Congrès international d'anthropologie et d'archéologie préhistoriques.* Reports of the Copenhagen Session, 1875, p. 486. *b.* SCHLIEMANN. *Ilios*, No. 1993. *c.* On a reliquary from Maestricht in the Museum of Antiquities in Brussels, No. 24 in catalogue. *d* and *e.* On coins from Macedon. *Numism. Chronicle*, vol. xx. (N. S.), pl. iv., Nos. 6 and 9.

[2] The same figure, separated from the lunar crescent by the cross, is met with on a sculpture at Kelloe in Durham. (*On a sculptured cross of Kelloe*, in *Archæologia*, vol. lii., part i., p. 74.)

[3] *Indian Antiquary*, 1880, p. 67 *et seq.*

we have reproduced here give more than sufficient proof that the arms of the *gammadion*, if they are solar rays, are so in their whole length; besides, the Disk which sometimes forms their point of intersection is certainly an image of the sun; lastly, there is no indication that, either in classic antiquity, or in India, the earth was ever symbolized by an equilateral cross.

B. *The triscèle, formed by the same process as the tétraskèle, was an undeniable representation of the solar movement.*

This assertion is especially obvious in the case of *triskèles* formed of three legs bent, as in the

a   b   c   d

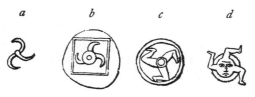

FIG. 23. VARIETIES OF THE TRISCÈLE.[1]

act of running, so frequently seen on coins of Asia Minor.

On Celtiberian coins the face of the sun appears between the legs. The same combination is found, above the image of a bull, on a votive *stele* of Carthage, reproduced by Gesenius.[2]

Is it possible to better interpret the idea of motion, and of its application to the image of the sun?

I will further instance the coins of Aspendus, in Pamphylia, where the three legs, ranged round a

---

[1] *a.* On a coin from Megara (PERCY GARDNER, *Numismatic Chronicle*, vol. xx. (N. S.), p. 60). *b.* On a Lycian coin (FELLOWS, *Coins of Ancient Lycia.* London, 1855, pl. x.). *c.* On a Lycian coin (*Numism. Chron.*, vol. viii. (3rd series), pl. v., No. 1). *d.* On a Celtiberian coin (LUD. MÜLLER, fig. 46).

[2] GESENIUS. *Scripturæ linguæque Phœnicæ monumenta.* Leipsic, tab. 23.

central disk, are literally combined with animal representations of the sun, the eagle, the wild boar, and the lion.[1] Lastly, on certain coins of Syracuse the *triscèle* permutes with the solar Disk above the *quadriga* and the winged horse.[2]

Moreover, the connection between the *triscèle* and the *tétrascèle* is manifest from their very shape. The transition from one to the other is visible on the "whorls" of Troy as well as on coins of Macedon and Lycia.

FIG. 24. SYMBOLS ON LYCIAN COINS.
(LUDVIG MÜLLER, figs. 48 and 49.)

C. *The images oftenest associated with the gammadion are representations of the sun and the solar divinities.*

Greek coins often show, side by side with the *gammadion*, the head of Apollo, or the reproduction of his attributes. On a piece from Damastion, in Epirus, the *gammadion* is engraved between the supports of the Delphic tripod;[3] on painted vases from Rhodes and Athens it figures beside the *omphalos*.[4] A crater in the Museum of Ancient Art in Vienna shows an image of Apollo bearing it on his breast (see our Plate I.); on a vase from Melos it precedes the chariot of the god.[5] Even amongst the Gauls it accompanies, on coins, the laurelled and *nimbus*-encompassed head of

[1] BARCLAY V. HEAD. *Hist. num.*, p. 581.
[2] *Numismatic Chronicle*, vol. xx. (new series), pl. iii., figs. 1 and 3.
[3] *Numismata cimelii regii Austriaci.* Vienna, 1755, part i., tab. viii., No. 3.
[4] J. B. WARING. *Ceramic Art in remote Ages.* London, 1875, pl. xxvii., f. 9.
[5] J. OVERBECK. *Atlas der griechischen Mythologie, Apollon,* pl. xix., fig. 7.

Apollo Belenus.[1] To be sure, it is also found on Greek medals associated with the images of Dionysos, Hercules, Hermes, and of several goddesses. But, in addition to the explanations of this peculiarity which I have given, it must be borne in mind how readily polytheistic nations and cities assign to their principal god the emblems as well as the attributes of other divinities—witness, in classic antiquity, the use of the Caduceus, the Thunderbolt, the Cornucopia, and so forth.

Amongst the symbols accompanying the *gammadion* there is none nearly so frequent as the solar Disk. The two signs are, in a manner, counterparts, not only amongst the Greeks, the Romans, and the Celts, but also with the Hindus, the Japanese, and the Chinese. I have already given some examples (figs. 17, 18, 20). On a "whorl"

FIG. 25. WHORL FROM HISSARLIK.
(SCHLIEMANN. *Ilios*, No. 1990.)

from Hissarlik this parallel order is repeated three times.

FIG. 26.[2]

Sometimes, as if to accentuate this juxtaposition, the *gammadion* is inscribed in the disk itself.

[1] LUD. MÜLLER. *Op. cit.*, fig. 27.
[2] *a.* On a "fusaïole" from Hissarlik. SCHLIEMANN. *Ilios*.

Sometimes, on the contrary, it is the solar Disk which is inscribed in the centre of the *gammadion*, as may be verified particularly on a Tibetan symbol reproduced by Hodgson,[1] and also on a coin from Gnossus, in Crete, where, perhaps, it depicts the Labyrinth.

FIG. 27. CRETAN COIN.

(*Numismatic Chronicle*, vol. xx. (new series), pl. iii., No. 6.)

On a Gallic coin, of which numerous specimens have been found in the Belgian province of Limburg and in the Namur country, a *tétrascèle* is visible, formed by four horses' heads ranged in a circle round a Disk.

FIG. 28. GALLO-BELGIAN COIN.

(HUCHER. *L'art gaulois*, p. 169.)

It is impossible not to recognize here an application of solar symbolism, as M. Eug. Hucher has so frankly admitted, in language whose terms exclude all preconceived ideas upon the solar nature of the *tétrascèle*, or even on the affinity existing between the Gallic symbol and the *gammadion* : " These four busts of horses," he writes,

No. 1987. *b.* On a Celtic stone of Scotland. R.-P. GREG, *Archæologia*, 1885, pl. xix., fig. 27. *c.* On an ex voto of clay in the sanctuary at Barhut. *Numism. Chron.*, vol. xx. (new series), pl. ii., fig. 24. See also below, pl. ii., *litt.* B, No. 16.

[1] See below, No. 18, *litt.* B of pl. ii.

"are evidently the rudiments of the four fiery
steeds which draw the chariot of Helios in Etruscan and Greek antiquity.   But the fact cannot
be ignored that the gyratory arrangement, *not
in use amongst the Greeks*, is a product of the
Celtic imagination."[1]

What, perhaps, is the product of the Celtic
imagination, is the ingenious transformation of
the arms of the *gammadion* into horses' busts.
Would it not be possible to find in Greek symbolism precedents, and even models for this metamorphosis?—witness the cocks' heads and lions'
busts which take the place of the rays of the
triscèle on Lycian coins.[2]

We may observe, by the way, that the horse,
and the cock, as well as the eagle, and the lion, are
essentially solar animals.

It is interesting to verify the fact that the same
combination has been produced, doubtlessly through
the spontaneous agency of similar factors, in
Northern America.   There have been found,

Fig. 29. Engraved Shell from the Mississippi Mounds.
(Holmes.   *Bureau of Ethnology*, vol. ii., p. 282.)

amongst the engraved shells of the mounds or
tumuli of the Mississippi, several specimens of
solar Crosses inscribed in circles, or squares, each
side forming a support to a bird's head turned in

[1] Eug. Hucher.   *L'art gaulois*.   Paris, 1868, vol. ii.,
p. 169.
[2] See below, chap. v., figs. 89, 90, 91.

the same direction—which, as a whole, forms a veritable *gammadion*.

D. *In certain symbolical combinations the gammadion alternates with the representation of the sun.*

Edward Thomas has pointed out the fact that, amongst the Jains of modern India, the sun, although held in great honour, does not appear amongst the respective signs of the twenty-four *Tirthankaras*, the saints or mythological founders of the sect. But, whilst the eighth of these personages has the half-moon as an emblem, the seventh has the *swastika* for a distinctive sign.[1] Moreover, as the same writer remarks, the *swastika* and the Disk replace constantly each other on the ancient coins of Ujain and Andhra.

Another proof of the equivalence between the *gammadion* and the image, or, at least, the light of the sun, is found amongst the coins of Mesembria in Thrace. The very name of this town, Μεσημβρία, may be translated as " mid-day," that is, the " town of noon," as Mr. Percy Gardner calls it.[2] Now, on some coins, this name is figured by a legend which speaks for itself : ΜΕΣⴄ.

It is impossible to show more clearly the identity of the *gammadion* with the idea of light or of the day.—" But," objects Mr. Greg, " the day is not necessarily the sun."—In addition to this distinction being rather subtle, how can one continue to doubt, in face of the facility with which in Greece, as in India and elsewhere, the *gammadion* interchanges with the Solar Disk and *vice versâ* ?[3]

I will take the liberty of calling attention to the

---

[1] *Indian Antiquary*, 1881, pp. 67, 68.

[2] PERCY GARDNER. *Solar Symbols on the Coins of Macedon and Thrace*, in the *Numismatic Chronicle*, vol. xx. (N. S.), p. 59.

[3] IBID. *Loc. cit.*, pp. 55-58.—On coins from Segesta the *gammadion*, which surmounts the image of a dog, alternates with a four-spoked wheel. (*Hunter*, pl. xlviii., 4, and lvii., 5.)

adjoining plate (II.), where I have brought together
several peculiar examples of those transpositions.
They are arranged in two classes of combinations,
which, by their regularity no less than by their
frequency, seem to imply a symbolical intention.
In the first is visible a grouping together of three
signs *gammadions*, or Disks, round the one central
Disk ; in the second it is these same signs, to the
number of four, which are arranged in a square or
lozenge, either round a fifth analogous sign, or else,
between the branches of an equilateral cross. I
should here like to attempt, in connection with the
general meaning of the *gammadion*, an explanation
of these symbolical arrangements—in so far, of
course, as on certain Disks these signs are not
merely ornaments, intended to fill up the empty
spaces.

The three first numbers of the first combination
(*litt.* A) are taken from the "whorls" of Hissarlik ;[1]
the fourth from a sepulchral vase from Denmark ;[2]
the fifth from Silesian pottery ;[3] the sixth, which
represents a foot-print of Buddha, from the bas-
reliefs of Amaravati ;[4] the seventh, a curious
example of the *trisula*, from the Græco-Buddhist
sculptures of Yusufzaï, in North-western India.[5]
To these must be added, on the following page,
the image taken from Hindu symbols and reproduced by Guignaut, after Nicolas Müller.

It is this latter figure which will assist us in
explaining the others, or, at least, in formulating a
conjecture as to their signification.

The subject is a tree, standing apparently for
the Cosmic Tree of Hindu mythology, which sprang

---

[1] SCHLIEMANN. *Ilios*, Nos. 1951, 1947, and 1861.

[2] LUD. MÜLLER. *Op. cit.*, fig. 31.

[3] IBID. *Op. cit.*, fig. 30.

[4] JAMES FERGUSSON. *Eastern and Indian Architecture.*
London, p. 184.

[5] *Græco-Buddhist sculptures of Yusufzaï*, in the publication
Preservation of National Monuments of India, pl. xxi.

PLATE II.

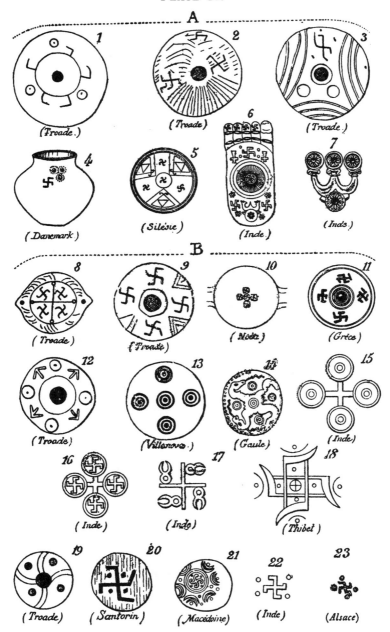

A

1 (Troade.) 2 (Troade) 3 (Troade.)
4 (Danemark) 5 (Silésie) 6 (Inde) 7 (Inds.)

B

8 (Troade) 9 (Troade) 10 (Noёn) 11 (Grèce)
12 (Troade) 13 (Villanova.) 14 (Gaule) 15 (Inde)
16 (Inde) 17 (Inde) 18 (Thibet)
19 (Troade) 20 (Santorin) 21 (Macédoine) 22 (Inde) 23 (Alsace)

from the primordial egg in the bosom of the
chaotic ocean. It spreads out into three branches,
each of which supports a sun, whilst a fourth and

FIG. 30. HINDU SYMBOL.
(GUIGNAUT, vol. iv., 2nd part, pl. ii., fig. 16.)

larger sun is placed at the bifurcation of the
branches.

Guignaut informs us, in his translation of Creuzer, that this image was a symbol of the *trimurti*,
the Hindu Trinity. We need not here investigate
this very questionable proposition. I think, however, that the learned Frenchman was right when
he added, in a foot-note :—" There are here three
suns, and yet it is always the same sun." [1]

In reality might not the object of this combination be to represent the sun in the three points or
positions which circumscribe its apparent daily
course, its rising, its zenith, and its setting; which
the figurative language of Vedic mythology has
rendered by the Three Steps of Vishnu ?

We know that at all times popular imagery, in
order to represent movements, or changes of position, has resorted to the artifice of multiplying the
image of the same personage, or object, whilst
assigning to it a different attitude each time. It
is the process of juxtaposition applied to the idea
of succession, or, as M. Clermont Ganneau has
expressed it : " The reappearance of the actors to
mark the succession of the acts." [2] Do we our-

[1] GUIGNAUT. *Les religions de l'antiquité.* Paris, 1841, vol. iv.,
first part, p. 4.
[2] See CLERMONT-GANNEAU. *L'imagerie phénicienne*, p. 10.

selves represent otherwise, in our astronomical diagrams, the phases of the moon, or the different positions of the sun in the ecliptic?

The same meaning seems to me to be applicable to the three *swastikas* incised round a Disk on a Foot-print of Buddha (*litt.* A, No. 6). In fact, Buddha's Feet were originally the Feet of Vishnu ; Buddhism was content to attribute to the footsteps of its founder the marks already worshipped by Hindu tradition.[1] The other signs which adorn this mark seem to singularly complicate its symbolism. But it must not be forgotten that the Buddhists have accumulated, on the sacred Foot of their Master, almost all the symbols they have been able either to invent or borrow. Tradition counts as many as sixty-five! Moreover, most of these signs are also solar symbols, at least the Rosettes, the Trident, and the *trisula*, the latter representing, as I shall hereafter show, the effulgence, or the radiation of the solar fire.

Edward Thomas has fully admitted that there must be some connection between the three diurnal positions of the sun and the incised symbols on the foot-print at Amaravati. But if, in the central Disk, he discerns the noon-day sun, it is the *trisula*, on the heel, which seems to him to represent the rising sun, whilst the *swastikas* depicted on the toes might typify the last rays of sunset. As for the other *swastikas*, the two signs on the heel might symbolize the Asvins, the third, the god Pûshan.—For my part, I see nothing which can justify these latter comparisons. Mr. Thomas was more fortunate when he connected an image, taken by Sir Henry Rawlinson from an obelisk at Koyunjik, with the Hindu symbolism relating to the three positions of the sun.[2] Three solar Disks

[1] SENART. *La légende du Bouddha* in the *Journal asiatique.* Paris, 1873, vol. ii., p. 278, and 1875, vol. ii., pp. 120, 121.

[2] *Numismatic Chronicle*, vol. xx. (N. S.), pp. 31, 32.

are there represented side by side; the middle one sends forth straight rays, and a hand holding a bow (see above, fig. 11); the two others, of rather smaller dimensions, emit rays which are bent at the extremities, as if by an effect of centrifugal force.[1]

This interpretation may be further applied to the three Wheels placed on the points of the *trisula* in a Græco-Buddhist bas-relief of Yusufzaï (*litt.* A, No. 7). If, as I believe I shall prove,[2] the central Disk of the *trisulas* was an image of the sun before it became, with the Buddhists, the Wheel of the Law, as much may be said of the three Wheels which here crown the points of the ancient symbol.

In Greece, I am not aware that the mythology alludes to the " three strides " of the sun. But symbolical images sometimes take the place of figures of speech. Does not, for example, the *triscèle*, formed of three legs radiating round a disc, admit of the same interpretation as the Hindu tree with its four suns? There is, moreover, presumptive evidence that the Greeks distinguished three positions of the sun, and even that they selected distinct personages to represent those principal *moments* of its daily life. Near Lycosura, in

---

[1] Foot-prints have been used more than once as a vestige of presence, a testimonial of passage, a symbol of walking. One finds them on stones dedicated to Isis and to Venus, in the latter days of the Roman empire, where, according to Letronne's interpretation, they are equivalent to the well-known inscription, ἦλθα ἐνταῦθα, "I have been here." When the soles of both feet point each in an opposite direction, they may imply the idea of going and returning, a symbol of gratitude to the gods for a safe journey, "*Pro itu ac reditu felice.*"—On Christian tombstones of the same epoch they sometimes are accompanied by the words *In Deo*, meaning, perhaps, "Walked into God." (See RAOUL ROCHETTE, *Sur les peintures des Catacombes dans les Mémoires publiés par l'Académie des Inscriptions et Belles-Lettres*, t. xiii., p. 235.)

[2] See further, chap. vi.

Arcadia, stood the sanctuary of Zeus Lycæus, where, according to Pausanias, *bodies cast no shadow*. It was situated on a mountain between two temples, one, *to the east*, was sacred to the Pythian Apollo, the other, *towards the west*, was dedicated to Pan Nomios.[1] Apollo, the slayer of the Python, well represents the morning sun dispelling the darkness in the east. As for the Lycæan Jupiter of Arcadia, it is the sun in all its mid-day glory, at the hour when bodies cast the least shadow.[2] Lastly, Pan, the lover of Selene, has incontestably a solar character, or at least is connected with the sun when setting. M. Ch. Lenormant has brought into prominence the light-giving character of this divinity, whom Herodotus compares, without hesitation, to Chem or Min, an Egyptian personification of the nocturnal or subterranean sun.[3]

Our own popular traditions seem also to have preserved the remembrance of the three solar steps, at least in those parts of Germany and England where, till lately, the villagers climbed a hill on Easter-eve, in order to perform three bounds of joy at sun-rise. " And yet," adds Sir Thomas Browne, " the sun does not dance on that day."[4] It must be remarked that popular language still speaks of the "legs of the sun," referring to those rays which sometimes seem to move about on the ground when their focus is hidden behind a cloud.

Let us now pass to the second group (pl. ii., *litt.* B), which represents combinations of four

---

[1] PAUSANIAS, viii., 38.
[2] A. MAURY. *Religions de la Grèce antique.* Paris, 1857, vol. i., p. 59.
[3] CH. LENORMANT. *Galerie mythologique* in the *Trésor de numismatique.* Paris, 1850, p. 25.
[4] E. B. TYLOR. *Civilisation primitive*, vol. ii., p. 385.

secondary figures ranged round a central one.[1] I
will here venture—always by way of hypothesis—
an explanation similar to the preceding ones.
Equilateral crosses representing the sky, or the
horizon, have been found on Assyrian monuments.
Their extremities are sometimes ended by little
disks, ⊶.[2] It may be questioned, not only whether
these disks do not represent so many suns, as is
the case in the preceding combinations, but also
whether they do not relate to four different positions
of the luminary, which would, perhaps, suggest no
longer its daily course, but its annual revolution,
marked by the solstices and equinoxes.

However this may be, the symbol of four
Disks united by a Cross, spread, as a subject of
decoration, through Asia Minor, Greece, Italy, and
India, being sometimes simplified by the substitution of a central Disk for the Cross (pl. ii., *litt*. B,
Nos. 9 to 13), sometimes complicated by the introduction of the *gammadion* (Nos. 8, 16, and 18 to
23), without counting the variations produced by

[1] Nos. 8, 9, 12, and 19 are taken from Hissarlik pottery
(SCHLIEMANN. *Ilios*, No. 1218, 1873, 1958, and 1822); No.
10, from a cup from Nola (LUD. MÜLLER, fig. 18); No. 11,
from an archaic Athenian vase (ID., fig. 7); No. 13 from a
cylinder of Villanova (DE MORTILLET. *La croix avant le
christianisme*. Paris, 1866, fig. 39); No. 14, from a coin of
Belgian Gaul (*Revue numismatique*. Paris, 1885, pl. vi., No. 4);
Nos. 15 and 16, from ancient Indian coins (A. CUNNINGHAM.
Bhilsa Topes. London, 1854, pl. xxxi., figs. 3 and 4); No. 17,
also from an ancient Hindu coin (GREG. *Archæologia*, 1885,
pl. xix., fig. 29); No. 18, from Buddhist symbols of Tibet
(HODGSON. *Buddhist Symbols* in the *Journal of the Royal
Asiatic Society*, vol. xviii., 1st series, pl. i., fig. 20); No. 20,
from an earthenware vessel of Santorin (WARING. *Ceramic
Art in Remote Ages*, pl. xliii., fig. 2); No. 21, from a coin of
Macedon (*Numismatic Chronicle*, vol. xx., new series, pl. iv.,
No. 7); No. 22, from the bas-reliefs of Amaranati (*cf.* above,
litt. A, No. 6); lastly, No. 23, from a girdle of bronzed leaves
found in a tumulus of Alsace (DE MORTILLET. *Musée pré-
historique*, pl. c., No. 1235).

[2] VICTOR DURUY. *Symboles païens de la croix*, in the *Revue
politique et littéraire*, 14th January, 1882, p. 51, fig. 8.

the partial or general transpositions of the Disks and *gammadions*. No. 17 represents a Cross whose *gamma* character results precisely from the addition of a Disk to the right of each arm. Nos. 14 to 18 may be considered as forming a transition to the symbols 19, 20, 21, 22, and 23, where it is no longer the *gammadion* which is inscribed in or alongside the Disks, but where the Disks themselves are placed between the branches of the *gammadion*. Perhaps also the combinations reproduced at the bottom of the plate may come directly from the equilateral cross, with disks placed between the branches ⊹. The latter, after having ornamented Hissarlik pottery and the most ancient coins of Lydia, was preserved even on the coins and coats of arms of the Christian Middle Ages, its intermediate stages being the pottery of the "palafittes" in Savoy, and, later, the numerous Gallic coins on which the disks between the arms are sometimes changed into Wheels and Crescents.[1]

In these four disks or points, Mr. Greg discerns stars or small fires.[2] I wonder what *fires* would be here for. We might as well accept the four nails of Emile Burnouf. I much prefer to believe that, in conformity with the usual interpretation of the Disk, they were originally representations of the sun ; and do not these suns, perhaps, represent, to use Guignaut's expression, "always the same sun" at a different point of the celestial horizon ?

The theory that the *gammadion* symbolizes the sun's motion, has met with the objection that the ancients were not acquainted with the rotation of the sun on its own axis. But, properly speaking, there is here no question of a rotatory motion.

---

[1] L. MAXE WERLY. *Monnaies à la croix*, in the *Revue belge de Numismatique*. Brussels, 1879, pl. xii. and xiii.

[2] GREG. *Loc. cit.*, p. 296.

What they wished to denote in bending the rays of the disk, was the circular translation in space which the sun seems to undergo during the day, or the year. The proof of this is found in the symbolism of the Wheel, which likewise served to represent the progress of the sun, without, for that reason, implying a knowledge of the solar rotation.

An ancient rite, occurring in different branches of the Indo-European family, consisted in making the circuit of the object intended to be honoured, or sanctified, keeping, meanwhile, the right side turned towards it, that is to say, following the apparent direction of the sun. Known in India by the name of *pradakshina*, and still practised by the Buddhists of Tibet round their sacred stones, this custom has survived to our own times in different parts of Europe. Dr. MacLeod relates that the Highlanders of Scotland, when they came to wish his father a happy New Year, made in this manner the circuit of the house, in order to ensure its prosperity during the year. At St. Fillans, by Comrie, in Perthshire, this circumambulation, called *deasil* (deisul), was performed round a miraculous well, to which people came in search of health. A similar custom seems to have existed in the Jura Mountains.[1]

Another objection is, that a certain number of *gammadions* have their branches turned towards the left, that is to say, in the opposite direction to the apparent course of the solar revolution.[2] Prof. Max Müller has remarked that, perhaps, in this case, it was intended to represent the retrograde motion of the autumnal sun, in opposition to its progressive movement in the spring.[3] Unfortu-

---

[1] Sir JOHN LUBBOCK. *Origin of Civilisation.* London, 1870, pp. 214 and 226.

[2] F. PINCOTT, in the *Journal* of the *Roy. Asiat. Soc.*, vol. xix. (new series), p. 245.

[3] Letter to M. SCHLIEMANN. *Ilios*, p. 520.

nately, the eminent Indian scholar produces no evidence in support of this hypothesis.[1] Would it not be simpler to admit that the direction of the branches is of secondary importance in the symbolism of the *gammadion* ? When it was desired to symbolize the progress of the sun, namely, its faculty of translation through space, rather than the direction in which it turns, little attention will have been paid to the direction given to the rays. Although, in general, the form of the *swastika* predominates, the branches are turned towards the left in a great number of *gammadions* or *tétrascèles* which are undeniably connected with the personifications or the symbols of the sun.[2] The same peculiarity may, moreover, be remarked on *triscèles* whose solar character is not disputed,[3] and even on direct images of the sun, such as Disks whose rays, bent in order to render the idea of motion, are turned towards the left as well as towards the right.[4] Lastly, it sometimes happens that the same monument includes several *gammadions* whose branches are turned respec-

---

[1] However, in the last edition, recently published, of the *Report on the Old Records of the India Office* (London, 1891, pp. x-xi), Sir George Birdwood makes mention of the fact that the "right-handed" *swastika* is, with the Hindus, the emblem of the god Ganesh ; that it represents the male principle ; that it typifies the sun in its daily course from east to west, and that, lastly, it symbolizes light, life, and glory. The "left-handed" *swastika*, or *sauwastika*, on the contrary, is the emblem of the goddess Kali; it represents the female principle, typifies the course of the sun in the subterranean world from west to east, and symbolizes darkness, death, and destruction.

[2] Such, for example, are the *gammadions* inscribed between the supports of the tripod of Apollo on a coin of Damastion mentioned above, and the *gammadion* on the breast of an Apollo reproduced in our plate i.

[3] P. SIX, in the *Revue de Numismatique*. Paris, 1886, p. 147.

[4] PERCY GARDNER. *Numism. Chron.*, vol. xx., pl. iv. No. 20.

tively in the opposite direction.[1] Tradition, as we have seen, counts the two forms among the signs of good omen which adorn the feet of Buddha. The Musée Guimet possesses two statues of Buddha decorated with the *gammadion*, one, of Japanese manufacture, bears the *swastika;* the other, of Chinese origin, the *sauwastika.*

I must here call attention to an ingenious theory brought forward, in 1891, by M. E. Harroy, director of the Ecole moyenne de Verviers, at the Archæological and Historical Congress of Brussels, to account for the origin of the *gammadion*, and its connection with the equilateral cross.[2] He believes he has discovered, in the arrangement of certain cromlechs, indications which would point to their having formed a sort of astronomical dial, as exact as it was primitive. For its construction

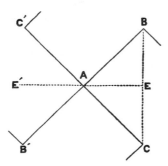

FIG. 31.

he only requires three stones. At twenty paces from a point of observation, A, let us place, he says, a stone, B, in the direction in which the sun rises on the 21st of June; then at the same dis-

[1] TH. ROLLER. *Les catacombes de Rome*, vol. i., pl. vi., 1.—*Cf.* certain disks on the Hissarlik whorls. (SCHLIEMANN. *Ilios*, No. 1951.)

[2] Proceedings of the *Congrès archéologique et historique* of Brussels, vol. i. Brussels, 1892, pp. 248-250.

tance from A place a second stone, C, in the direction in which the sun rises on the 21st of December.

The line B C will point north and south; A E east, and A E' west. A B, A E, A C, and A E, will give the directions in which the sun rises on the 21st of June, the 21st of September, the 21st of December, and the 21st of March respectively; A C', A E', A B', and A E', the directions in which it will set on the same dates. This cross, illustrating the course of the sun, will naturally become the symbol of the luminary, and four strokes might have been added to the extremities of the lines in order to give "the notion of impulsion of the rotatory movement of the regulating orb."

I will draw attention to the fact that, as the points B and C approach or go further apart, according to the latitude, this figure can only depict a cross in a fairly narrow zone of the terrestrial globe, and that, consequently, the explanation of M. Harroy is solely applicable to our latitudes. Even here, moreover, however simple the reasoning processes are which might have led to the construction of this natural observatory, there remains to be proved satisfactorily that such an idea was ever entertained and put into practice by our prehistoric ancestors.

I have admitted above that the *gammadion*, in so far as it was a symbol of the astronomical movement, may have been applied to the revolutions or even to the phases of the moon. The fact is all the more plausible since the equilateral cross seems itself to have been employed to symbolize lunar as well as solar radiation; if we may judge from a Mithraic image, where the points of the Crescent supporting the bust of the lunar goddess are each surmounted by an equilateral cross.[1] In this manner the frequent attribution

---

[1] LAJARD. *Atlas*, pl. lxxviii.

of the *gammadion* to lunar goddesses, such as the different forms of the Asiatic Artemis, might also be accounted for.

On coins of Gnossus, in Crete, the lunar Crescent

FIG. 32. CRETAN COIN.
(*Numismatic Chronicle*, vol. xx., new series, pl. ii., fig. 7.)

takes the place of the solar Disk in the centre of the *gammadion*.

A coin, which is believed to belong to Apollo-

FIG. 33. LUNAR TÉTRASCÈLE.
(BARCLAY V. HEAD. *Numismatic Chronicle*, vol. vii. (3rd series), pl. xi., fig. 48.)

nius ad Rhyndacum, shows a *gammadion* flanked by four Crescents.

On the sepulchral *stelai* of Numidia the two *gammadions* surmounting the image of the dead (see our fig. 17, where one of them is, so to speak, underlined by a Wheel) may be seen to give place, sometimes to two radiated Disks, sometimes to a Wheel and a Crescent, sometimes to an equilateral Cross and a Crescent, and, lastly, sometimes to two Crescents.[1] From which it might be concluded that the *gammadion* serves equally to replace the image of the sun and that of the moon.

M. Schliemann found at Hissarlik, in the strata

---

[1] *Stèles du Koudiat el Batoum*, in the *Comptes rendus de la Société française de numismatique et d'archéologie*, vol. ii., pl. iii , figs. 1 to 6.

lying above the " burnt city," a terra-cotta sphere
divided into parallel zones by horizontal lines.   In
the middle zone are thirteen *gammadions* drawn
up in line side by side.   The celebrated explorer
of Ilium believed he discovered therein a terrestrial sphere, on which the *gammadions*, symbols of
fire, seemed to indicate the torrid zone.   Mr.
R. P. Greg, faithful to his theory, prefers to discern therein a representation of the universe, where
the *swastikas* would seem to symbolize the supreme
power of Zeus.[1]   May I be allowed to ask, in my
turn, if there may not be seen herein a celestial
sphere, on which the thirteen *gammadions* represent
thirteen moons, that is to say, the lunar year ?

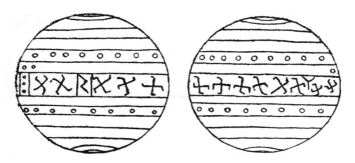

FIG. 34.   FUSAÏOLE OR WHORL FROM ILIOS.
(SCHLIEMANN.   *Ilios*, figs. 245 and 246.)

IV.   THE BIRTH-PLACE OF THE GAMMADION.

Can we determine the cradle of the *gammadion*,
or, at least, the region whence it sprang, to be
transported to the four corners of the Old World ?
To be sure, it may have been formed spontaneously here and there, in the manner of the
equilateral crosses, the circles, the triangles, the

[1] GREG.   *Archæologia*, 1885, p. 304.

flower-mark, and the other geometric ornaments so common in primitive decoration.

But the specimens which we have been examining are too identical, in their meaning as in their use, for us not to admit the original unity of the sign, or, at the very least, of its symbolical meaning.

A first observation, made long ago, is that the *gammadion* is almost the exclusive property of the Aryan race. It is found, in fact, among all the peoples of the Indo-European branch, whilst it is completely absent among the Egyptians, the Chaldæans, the Assyrians, and even the Phœnicians, although these latter were not very scrupulous in borrowing the ornaments and symbols of their neighbours. As for the Tibetans, the Chinese, and the Japanese, amongst whom it is neither less frequent nor less venerated, it is not difficult to prove that it must have come to them, with Buddhism, from India.

There was only a step from this to the conclusion that the *gammadion* is a survival of the symbolism created, or adopted, by the common ancestors of the Aryans, and this step has been easily got over. Had we not the precedents of philology, which cannot come upon the same radical in the principal dialects of the Indo-European nations without tracing its existence to the period when these people spoke the same language? We did not even stop there. Desirous of investing the *gammadion* with an importance proportioned to the high destiny imputed to it, one has endeavoured to make it the symbol of the supreme God whom the Aryans are said to have adored before their dispersion. Thus we have seen Mr. Greg exhibit the *gammadion* as the emblem of the god of the sky, or air, who, in the course of the Indo-European migrations, was converted into Indra, Zeus, Jupiter, Thor, and so forth. M. Ludwig Müller, on his side, after having by his very complete and conscientious work on the *gammadion* contributed so much to proving it to be a solar symbol, takes care to add that before receiving this signification it might well have been, with the primitive Aryans, "the emblem of the divinity who comprehended all the gods, or, again, of the omnipotent God of the universe."

To this end he draws attention to the fact that the *gammadion* is associated with divinities of different nature, and that, therefore, it might well have the value of a generic sign for divinity, in the manner of the Star which figures before the divine names in the cuneiform inscriptions of Mesopotamia : " The sign," he concludes, " expressed then figuratively the word θεός, which corresponded with *deva*, from which it is derived ; it is thus the primitive Aryans called the divinity whose symbol this sign probably was." Who knows if it did not imply and retain a still higher signification ; if, for example, the Greeks, "following the Pelasgians," did not employ it to symbolize a god elevated above the Olympians, or even the One and Supreme Being of philosophy and religious tradition, "the unknown God, to whom, according to Saint Paul, an altar was dedicated at Athens"?[1]

This is doing great honour to the *gammadion*. To reduce these theories to their real value it is only necessary to show that they are conjectures with no foundation in history. When the latter begins to raise the veil which conceals the origins of the Greeks, the Romans, the ancient Germans, the Celts, the Slavs, the Hindus, and

---

[1] LUD. MÜLLER. *Op. cit.*, p. 107.—M. Alexandre Bertrand, for whose long-promised study on the *gammadion* we are waiting with justifiable impatience, makes it, with the Gauls at least, the symbol of a nameless divinity. (*La Gaule avant les Gaulois.* Paris, 1884, p. 12.)—If, by this expression, the eminent archæologist means a divinity whose name we are ignorant of, no one will gainsay the fact. But if he alludes to a divinity who had no name, this is quite another matter.

the Persians, we find these nations adoring the vague *numina* of which they caught a glimpse behind the principal phenomena of nature, worshipping the multitude of spirits, and indulging in all the practices of inferior religions, with here and there outbursts of poetry and spirituality which were as the promise and the dawn of their future religious development.

It is probable that before historic times they had already *fetiches*, perhaps even idols, in the manner of those uncouth *xoana* which are met with in the beginnings of Greek art. But it is unlikely that at the far more distant epoch of their first separation they had already possessed symbols, that is to say, ideographic signs, figures representing the divinity without aspiring to be its image or receptacle. In any case we may here apply the adage *affirmantis onus probandi ;* upon those who wish to make the *gammadion* a legacy of the " primitive " Aryans, it is incumbent to prove that these Aryans practised symbolism ; that amongst their symbols the *gammadion* had a place, and that this *gammadion* typified the old *Diu pater*, the Heavenly Father of subsequent mythologies.

Should the same criticism be extended to the theories which make the *gammadion* a Pelasgic symbol,—whether by Pelasgians be understood the Western Aryans in general, or merely the ancestors of the Greeks, of the ancient Italians, and of the Aryan populations who, primitively, fixed their residence in the basin of the Danube ?

We can here no longer be so affirmative in our negations. It is, indeed, an undeniable fact that the *gammadion* figures amongst the geometric ornaments on certain pottery styled *Pelasgic*, because, in the bronze period, or the first iron age, it is found amongst all the Aryan peoples, from Asia Minor to the shores of the Atlantic.[1] But, to

[1] MAX COLLIGNON. *Archéologie grecque*, p. 276.

begin with, the very term Pelasgian does not seem to me a happy one, and it may be noted that there is now a tendency amongst archæologists to drop it. This term either refers to the pre-Hellenic, and the pre-Etruscan phase of civilization in the South of Europe, when it is only a word designed to hide our ignorance, or else it claims to apply to a determinate people, and then it confounds under the same denomination very different populations, of whom nothing authorizes us to make an ethnic group. Moreover, in so far as the first appearances of the *gammadion* are concerned, it is possible, and even necessary, to limit still further our geographical field of research.

Without going into the question whether geometric decoration may not have originated in an independent manner amongst different nations, it must be observed that this style of ornamentation embraces two periods, that of painted and that of incised decoration. Now, in this latter period, which is everywhere the most ancient, the *gammadion* is only found on the "whorls" of Hissarlik and the pottery of the terramares. We have here, therefore, two early homes of our symbol, one on the shores of the Hellespont, the other in the north of Italy.

Was it propagated from one country to another by the usual medium of commerce? It must be admitted that at this period the relations between the Troad and the basin of the Po were very doubtful. Etruria certainly underwent Asiatic influences; but whether the legendary migration of Tyrrhenius and of his Lydians be admitted or not, this influence was only felt at a period subsequent to the "palafittes" of Emilia, if not to the necropolis of Villanova.

There remains, therefore, the supposition that the *gammadion* might have been introduced into the two countries by the same nation.

We know that the Trojans came originally from Thrace. There is, again, a very plausible tradition to the effect that the ancestors, or predecessors, of the Etruscans, and, in general, the earliest known inhabitants of northern Italy, entered the peninsula from the north or north-east, after leaving the valley of the Danube. It is, therefore, in this latter region that we must look for the first home of the *gammadion*. It must be remarked that when, later on, the coinage reproduces the types and symbols of the local religions, the countries nearest the Danube, such as Macedon and Thrace, are amongst those whose coins frequently exhibit the *gammadion*, the *tétrascèle*, and the *triscèle*.[1] Besides, it is especially at Athens that it is found on the pottery of Greece proper, and we know that Attica is supposed to have been primitively colonized by the Thracians.

In any case, to judge from the discoveries of M. Schliemann, it was especially amongst the Trojans that the *gammadion* played an important part from a symbolical and religious point of view; which may be attributed to the belief that it was there closer to its cradle and even nearer to its original signification. "The nations who had invaded the Balkan peninsula and colonized Thrace," writes M. Maspero, "crossed, at a very early period, the two arms of the sea which separated them from Asia, and transported there most of the names which they had already introduced into their European home. There were Dardanians in Macedon, on the borders of the Axios, as in the Troad, on the borders of the Ida, Kebrenes at the foot of the Balkans, and a town, Kebrene, near Ilium."[2] Who will be astonished that these emi-

---

[1] PERCY GARDNER. *Solar Symbols on the Coins of Macedon and Thrace*, in the *Numismatic Chronicle*, vol. xx. (N. S.), p. 49 *et seq.*
[2] G. MASPERO. *Histoire ancienne des peuples de l'Orient.* Paris, 1886, p. 241.

grants had taken with them, to the opposite shore of the Hellespont, the symbols as well as the rites and traditions which formed the basis of their creed in the basin of the Danube? Doubtlessly they borrowed a great deal from the creeds of the nations amongst whom they settled. But where has the *gammadion* been discovered amongst the vestiges of the far more ancient civilization whose religious and artistic influence they were not long before feeling?

Mr. Sayce, it is true, having met with it in Lycaonia, on the bas-relief of Ibriz, maintains the impossibility of deciding if it is a symbol imported from the Trojans amongst the Hittites, or if, on the contrary, it is to be attributed to the latter.[1] Yet, whilst the oldest "whorls" of Hissarlik go back *at least* to the fourteenth or fifteenth century B.C., the bas-relief of Ibriz reveals an influence of Phrygian, and even Assyrian art, which is, perhaps, contemporaneous with King Midas, and which, in any case, cannot have risen long before the accession of the Sargonidæ; that is to say, in order to determine the age of the monument we must come down to the ninth or eighth century before our era.[2]

It is therefore not difficult, here, as everywhere else, to connect the origins of the *gammadion* with the early centres which we have assigned to it. Even when it occurs in the north and west of Europe, with objects of the bronze period, it is generally on pottery recalling the vases with geometric decorations of Greece and Etruria, and later, on coins reproducing, more or less roughly,

[1] A. H. SAYCE. *The Hittites, the Story of a forgotten Empire.* London, 1888, p. 142.

[2] PERROT et CHIPIEZ. *Histoire de l'art dans l'antiquitié,* vol. iv., pp. 728 and 794, note 1.—With the exception of the bas-relief of Ibriz, the *gammadion* has only been remarked on a single Hittite monument; it is a cylinder, probably of uncertain date. (SCHLIEMANN. *Troja,* p. 125.)

the monetary types of Greece. It seems to have been introduced into Germany, Denmark, Sweden, Norway, and Iceland, in the same manner as that in which the runic writing was brought from the Danube valley to the shores of the Baltic and the ocean. It may have penetrated into Gaul, and from there into England and Ireland, either through Savoy, from the time of the " palafittes," or with the pottery and jewelry imported by sea and by land from the East, or, lastly, with the Macedonian coins which represent the origin of Gallic coinage.

We have already seen how it was brought among the islands of the Mediterranean, and into Greece proper, then from Greece to Sicily and Southern Italy. It must be observed that even at Rome it seems to have always been connected with the traditions of the East. The only tombstone in the open air on which it has, so far, been noticed in the vicinity of the Eternal City is that of a Syrian.[1] We must not forget that the Christianity of the Catacombs was likewise a religion of Oriental origin.

In the extreme East, the origins of the *gammadion* can be traced without difficulty to the *swastika* of India. It remains to be investigated if the latter, in its turn, may be connected with the *gammadion* of the West. M. Ludwig Müller, desirous of proving that this symbol was prior to the dispersion of the Indo-Europeans, maintains that the *swastika* cannot have passed from the Hindus to the Greeks, or *vice versâ*, because the religions of these two races differed too much for an exchange of symbols to be possible. My whole book tends to prove that this is no obstacle. I will have occasion, in particular, to show how India borrowed several of its principal symbols

[1] LUD. MÜLLER. *Op. cit.*, p. 62.

from Mesopotamia, from Persia, and even from Greece. Why should the *swastika* form an exception ?

Here, however, occurs a difficulty, which we must not conceal. The *swastika* does not appear on the coins struck in Bactriana, or in India, by Alexander and his Indo-Greek successors. Even amongst the Indo-Scythians, whose coinage copies the Greek types, it is only visible on barbarous imitations of the coins of Basu Deva.[1] On the other hand, as we have shown, it adorns the coins of Krananda, and the most ancient monetary ingots of India. Moreover, Panini, who already makes mention of the *swastika*, is sometimes considered to have lived in the middle of the fourth century B.C.[2] It might therefore be possible that the Hindus had known the *swastika* before feeling in their arts, and even in their symbolism, the influence of the Greek invasion. Yet, for the best of reasons, it is neither the Chaldæans, the Assyrians, the Phœnicians, nor even the Egyptians, who can have imparted the *gammadion* to Hindustan. There only remain, then, the Persians, whose influence on the nascent arts of India was certainly felt before Alexander. But in Persia itself the *gammadion* only appears as an exception, on a few rare coins approaching our era.[3]—Perhaps we would do well to look towards the Caucasus, where the antique ornaments with *gammadions*, collected by M. Chantre, lead us

[1] PERCY GARDNER. *Coins of Greek and Scythic Kings of India and Bactria.* London, 1886, p. 160.

[2] MONIER WILLIAMS. *Indian Wisdom.* London, 1876, p. 173.

[3] M. LUDW. MÜLLER draws attention to a coin of the Achæmenidæ in the *British Museum*, which would seem to bear the *gammadion ;* but it is there a countermark which must belong to a much later period.—In the coinage prior to Alexander, the western *gammadion* does not seem to have advanced towards the east further than Asia Minor.

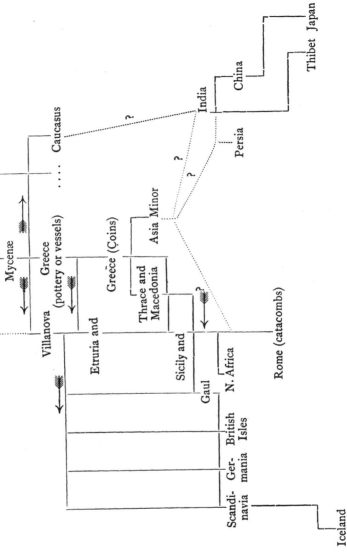

PLATE III.—TABLE ILLUSTRATING THE MIGRATIONS OF THE GAMMADION.

back to a civilization closely enough allied, by its industrial and decorative types, to that of Mycenæ.

Until new discoveries permit us to decide the question, this gap in the genealogy of the *swastika* will be equally embarrassing for those who would like to make the *gammadion* the common property of the Aryan race, for it remains to be explained why it is wanting amongst the ancient Persians.— It is right, too, to call attention to its absence on the most ancient pottery of Greece and the Archipelago, where it only appears with geometric decoration.—In reality, the problem is less a question of ethnography than of archæology, or rather of comparative art.[1]

If the *gammadion* is found amongst none of the nations composing the Egypto-Semitic group, if, amongst the Aryans of Persia, it never played but a secondary and obliterated part, might it not be because the art and symbolism of these different nations possess other figures which discharge a similar function, whether as a phylactery, or else as an astronomical, or a divine symbol ? The real talismanic cross of the countries stretching from Persia to Libya is the *crux ansata*, the Key of Life

---

[1] See the table on plate iii., where I have endeavoured to trace, in a manner, the genealogy of the *gammadion* in the Ancient World. Supposing it be necessary to change certain approximate dates, those, for example, of the centuries in which the civilizations of Mycenæ and Villanova flourished, the succession of the terms is none the less the same in each series, as is also the connection between the series themselves. It will be seen by this table that there has been, over the whole of Europe, two successive importations of the *gammadion ;* one, prehistorical, almost everywhere following the diffusion of pottery and of ornaments with geometric decorations ; and the other contemporary with the imitation of Greek coins. Perhaps we must attribute to the existence of these two successive currents the cause of the variations which M. Lud. Müller points out, amongst the Germanic nations, between the forms of the *gammadion* in the bronze period and in the iron age.

of the Egyptian monuments. As for their principal symbol of the sun in motion, is it not the Winged Circle, whose migrations I trace in another chapter? There would seem to be between these figures and the *gammadion*, I will not say a natural antipathy, but a repetition of the same idea. Where the *gammadion* predominates—that is to say, in the whole Aryan world, except Persia —the Winged Circle and the *crux ansata* have never succeeded in establishing themselves in good earnest. Even in India, granting that these two last figures really crossed the Indus with the Greek, or the Iranian symbolism, they are only met with in an altered form, and with a new meaning.[1]

In brief, the ancient world might be divided into two zones, characterized, one by the presence of the *gammadion*, the other by that of the Winged Globe as well as of the *crux ansata ;* and these two provinces barely penetrate one another at a few points of their frontier, in Cyprus, at Rhodes, in Asia Minor, and in Libya. The former belongs to Greek civilization, the latter to Egypto-Babylonian culture.

As for India, everything, so far, tends to show that the *swastika* was introduced into that country from Greece, the Caucasus, or Asia Minor, by ways which we do not yet know. However that may be, it is owing to its adoption by the Bhuddhists of India that the *gammadion* still prevails amongst a great part of the Mongolian races, whilst, with the exception of a few isolated and insignificant cases which still survive amongst the actual populations of Hindustan, and, perhaps, of Iceland, it has completely disappeared from Aryan symbolism and even folk-lore.[2]

[1] See chap. vi.
[2] Some mention might be made of the *gammadions* which have been discovered in other parts of the world. In what mysterious way did this combination of lines come to be

stranded amongst the Ashantees? There is, however, nothing against its having been conceived there, and spontaneously executed, like so many other geometric designs which are found even in the centre of the dark continent.—The same phenomena may have occurred in the two Americas. Yet, when we see it specially employed as a religious symbol amongst the Pueblo Indians, we are led to inquire if we have not here some vestige of a communication with the Old World. There can be no question of an influence subsequent to the advent of the Spaniards, for if these latter had brought the Pueblos the emblem of the Cross, it certainly would not have been under the form of the *gammadion*. There remain two ways by which the transmission of the symbol might have been effected; to the east, by the expeditions of the still pagan inhabitants of Iceland; to the west, by an influence coming from China or Japan. I would incline rather to the second theory. Mr. R. P. Greg has proved that another sign, similar to the *swastika*, the ornament known as the fret or *meander*, is frequently met with on the ancient pottery of the New World; this, too, in conditions recalling its employment amongst the nations of our extreme East. (R.-P. GREG. *The Fret or Key ornamentation in Mexico*, in *Archæologia*, vol. xlvii., pp. 157-160.)

CHAPTER III.

ON THE CAUSES OF ALTERATION IN THE MEANING AND FORM OF SYMBOLS.

Causes which may alter the primary interpretation of symbolical types.—Loss of the primitive signification.—New meanings attached to uncomprehended symbols.—Harpocrates, the god of silence.—Identical symbols applied to different traditions.—Saint George and Horus.—Daniel and the Chaldæan Hercules. — The two doves facing each other. — Chaldæan origin of the religious symbolism of the Persians.—Sources of the Christian symbolism of the Catacombs.—Causes which may alter the form of symbols. — Tendency to simplify the figures.—Tendency to beautify them.—Origins and transformations of the Thunderbolt.—The antecedents of Sagittarius. —Mistakes due to ignorance and maladroitness.—Reconstruction of a new intelligible type from degenerate elements.— Gradual transformation of linear symbols into human figures, and of human figures into linear symbols.—Substitution of one element for another in a symbolical combination.—Lily and Lotus.—Addition of new elements to a former figure.—The *perron* of Liege.

FOR two symbolical figures to have a common origin it is not always necessary that they should have the same meaning. It frequently happens that a symbol changes its meaning in passing from one country to another.

In this manner a symbol can very well become a mere ornament when, on account of its æsthetic value, or simply by reason of its originality, it is reproduced by artists who are unacquainted with its primitive acceptation. Such, for example, are those clasps in the shape of *gammadions* which are frequently offered for sale to visitors at Homburg, and which, according to M. Gaidoz, are reproductions of antique *fibulæ* found, some years ago, on the site of a Roman encampment not far from that place.[1]

A symbol, again, may retain merely a talismanic value, like those crucifixes, converted into *fetiches*, which are the only vestiges of Christianity left, among certain tribes of the Lower Congo, by the Portuguese domination of last century.

Sometimes, in similar cases, the new owners of the image will endeavour to explain it by a more or less ingenious interpretation, and in this manner they will restore to it a symbolical import, though applied to a new conception.

The rising sun has often been compared to a new-born child. Amongst the Egyptians, this comparison led to Horus being represented as an infant sucking its finger. The Greeks imagined that he placed his finger on his lips to enjoin secrecy on the initiated, and they made him the image of Harpocrates, the god of silence.[2]

This is what M. Clermont-Ganneau has very happily termed *iconological mythology ;* it is here no longer the myth which gives rise to the image, but the image which gives rise to the myth.

We may further quote, as an interpretation of the same kind, the legend related by Hygin, which made the Caduceus originate in Hermes throwing his wand between two serpents fighting. It is evident that, here also, this hypothesis, soon to be transformed into a myth by the popular imagination, was due to a desire, unconscious perhaps, to explain the Caduceus.

Most frequently it is a conception pre-existent in the local traditions which we think we find amongst the products of foreign imagery. The Egyptians of the later period sometimes repre-

---

[1] H. GAIDOZ. *Le symbolisme de la roue*, p. 113.

[2] G. LAFAYE. *Histoire des divinités d'Alexandrie hors de l'Egypte.* Paris, 1884, p. 259.

sented Horus under the form of a horseman piercing a crocodile with his spear. M. Clermont-Ganneau has shown how this symbolical image of the sun dispersing the clouds served as a model to the early representations of St. George and the Dragon.[1] The same subject had already been employed by Greek mythology to depict Bellerophon slaying the Chimæra.[2]

M. Gaidoz attributes a similar origin, not only to the image, but also to the worship of the Virgin of *the Seven Sorrows*, or rather of *the Seven Swords.* He thinks that he discovers its prototype in certain Chaldæan cylinders in which a goddess is depicted in the middle of seven arrows or swords, which radiate doubtlessly from a quiver placed behind her back. The resemblance between the two images is remarkable. This is how the author explains this transmission : " An Assyrian cylinder, or some other engraved stone, reached Italy in the Middle Ages. . . . The image of a woman could be taken for nothing else than that of the Virgin Mary. But what could be the meaning of those weapons which were seen in the figure, and seemed to transpierce her breast ? Without a doubt they were swords ; and what might they signify ? Some ingenious ecclesiastic was not wanting who assumed that they were the symbol of sorrows. . . . The swords numbered seven ; it was then only necessary to ascertain, and this was no difficult task, the seven principal sorrows in the life of the Virgin Mary."[3]

But here is a still better example : the image, so common on Chaldæan cylinders, of the mythical

---

[1] CLERMONT-GANNEAU. *Horus et saint George,* in the *Revue archéologique* of 1873, fig. 13.

[2] P. DECHARME. *Mythologie de la Grèce antique.* Paris, 1886, fig. 161.

[3] *Mélusine.* The number for November-December, 1892.

hero, Idzhubar or Gilgames,[1] seen from the front and flanked by two lions, which he holds at arm's length, was not only diffused amongst the Greeks

FIG. 35. ASSYRIAN CYLINDER.
(LAJARD. *Mithra*, pl. xliv., fig. 10.)

and Hindus to symbolize their respective solar hero in the course of his exploits, it seems also, in our Middle Ages, to have suggested certain pictorial representations of Daniel in the lion's den.

FIG. 36. ON AN OLD CHRISTIAN STAFF.
(MARTIN et CAHIER. *Mélanges d'archéologie*, vol. ii., pl. xviii.)

In these the prophet is drawn full-face, standing with arms outstretched, in the classic attitude of prayer, between two rampant lions, which he seems to keep in awe as much by his gesture as by the effect of his prayer. In this manner might be explained the peculiar fact, pointed out by the Abbé Martigny, that Daniel is often repre-

[1] According to a recent communication from Mr. Th. J. Pinches (*Babylonian and Oriental Record* of October, 1890), *Gilgames* would seem to be the definite pronunciation of this name, which has been read in such different ways in the cuneiform texts.

sented between two lions, "whilst the den contains seven."[1]

On a lintel of St. Gertrude's Church at Nivelles, in Belgium, there is a bas-relief representing Samson slaying the lion, which belongs to the oldest piece of carved stone still *in situ* in Belgium. The Biblical hero is there represented

FIG. 37. SAMSON KILLING THE LION.
(Cathedral of Nivelles.)

dressed in the Roman costume, astride of the lion, whose jaws he seizes with his hands (fig. 37). A mere glance will permit one to find in this image a reminiscence of the scene, so often reproduced

FIG. 38. MITHRA SLAYING THE BULL.
(From a bas-relief in the Louvre.)

on Mithraic bas-reliefs, where Mithras offers the bull in sacrifice (fig. 38).

The worship of Mithras was certainly practised

---

[1] MARTIGNY. *Dictionnaire des antiquités chrétiennes.* Paris, 1865, p. 201.—See also DE GAUMONT. *Mélanges d'archéologie religieuse.* Paris, 5th edition, p. 68.

in Belgium at the time of the Roman domination, for inscriptions, "*Deo Invicto Mithræ*," have been found in the Gallo-Roman cemetery at Juslenville. The Nivelles bas-relief, to be sure, is not prior to the eleventh century ; but then it must be observed that at Nivelles, and in its vicinity, traces of Roman occupation have been discovered. The sculptor of St. Gertrude may very probably have been acquainted with a local Mithraic bas-relief, in which he saw an episode of Samson's history. It may, however, be equally admitted that the model came from without.

Mediæval pictorial art, moreover, borrows frequently enough from Mithraic representations, wherein the sun and moon are depicted under the forms and with the respective attributes of the solar god and of the lunar goddess in the scene of the sacrifice.[1]

A remarkable example is seen in the bas-reliefs of the baptistery of Parma.[2]

The group of Mithras and the bull has received other adaptations again in the hands of Christian artists. M. Th. Roller has pointed out a singular instance in a Christian bas-relief of the third or fourth century. Christ is there represented in the form of Orpheus, playing on the lyre, with a Phrygian cap on the head, and the right leg reposing on the body of a lamb, which turns its head towards the musician.[3]

[1] *Cf.* especially the bas-reliefs on the baptistery at Parma. (*Revue archéologique.* Paris, 1853, vol. x., pl. 216.)

[2] In the Strasburg Cathedral there is a statue representing an individual clothed in the skin of a lion and holding in his hand a club. It was long thought to be an ancient statue to which the Christian edifice had extended its hospitality. M. Albert Dumont has shown that it was a Mediæval work, suggested probably by images of the Gallo-Roman Hercules, like those bronze ones which have been found in the neighbourhood of Strasburg. (*Revue archéologique*, 1870-71, vol. xxii., p. 246.)

[3] TH. ROLLER. *Catacombes*, vol. ii., pl. iv., No. 1.

These alterations in meaning may sometimes
be perfectly compatible with a knowledge of the
primitive signification, for one is always prone to discover in everything one's favourite image or idea.
It was in perfect good faith that the Neoplato-
nists believed they recognized the representations of their own doctrines in the symbols and in
the myths of all contemporary religions. Did not
the early Christians see the Cross in all figures
exhibiting an intersection of lines, as an anchor, a
mast and its yard, a standard, a plough, a man
swimming, a bird flying, a person praying with
outstretched arms, the Paschal Lamb on the spit,
and even the human face, in which the line of the
nose crosses that of the eyes? When the Serapeum at Alexandria was destroyed, the Christian
writers of the time relate that a certain number of
cruces ansatæ were found in it. They themselves
observe that in these figures was recognized the
old Egyptian symbol of life; which avowal,
however, does not prevent them from seeing in
this emblem a prophetic allusion to the sign of
the Redemption. Sozomen adds that this fact
brought about many conversions amongst the
pagans.[1]

A legend, widely diffused throughout the ancient
world, related that Zeus, wishing to know the
centre of the earth, let fly at the same moment
from the ends of the world, in the east and west,
two eagles (other versions say two crows), which
came and settled at the same time on the *omphalos*
of Apollo in the temple at Delphi.[2] It may be
questioned if this tradition was not perhaps suggested by the desire to account for a representation of the *omphalos*, similar to the image of a
temple found amongst the jewels collected by
Dr. Schliemann at Mycenæ. It is a sort of shrine,

[1] Sozomen. *Hist. ecclés.*, vii., 15, p. 725 B.
[2] Strabo. *Liv.* ix., ch. iii.

which stands between two doves facing one
another.

The origins of this representation must, in their

FIG. 39. JEWEL FROM MYCENÆ.
(SCHLIEMANN. *Mycènes.* Paris, 1879, fig. 423.)

turn, be sought for in the symbolism of the worship paid, in Asia Minor, to the Great Goddess of
Nature, venerated by the Phœnician populations
under the name of Astarte. The doves played a
part in this worship, either as personifications of
the goddess, or as sacred birds reared in the
temples.[1] Two doves appear on some *stelai* in

FIG. 40. PUNIC STELA.
(*Corpus inscript. semit.*, i., part iii., No. 183.)

Libya, and, later, on imperial coins of Cyprus ; in
the former they are facing one another on the
opposite sides of one of those conical *bethels*

[1] FRANÇOIS LENORMANT, in the *Gazette archéologique* of
1878, p. 75 *et seq.*

which represented the goddess (fig. 40); in the latter they are back to back on the roof of a temple containing a Sacred Stone (fig. 41).

FIG. 41. COIN OF PAPHOS.
(GUIGNAUT, vol. iv., pl. liv., fig. 206.)

This combination of figures might all the more easily relate to the *omphalos*, since the latter was a white stone, a real *bethel*, round at the top. I am not aware that it has ever been found represented between two crows or eagles, but Strabo informs us that near the Sacred Stone (ἐπ' αὐτῷ), in the sanctuary at Delphi, there was an image of the two birds mentioned in the fable.[1]

Let us now pass over a dozen centuries, and, from the shores of the Ægean Sea, direct our steps towards the valley of the Sambre. Coins of

[1] Since the publication of the French edition of this work Sir George Birdwood has pointed out to me two representations of the *omphalos* where the Sacred Stone is found with two

FIG. 42.

doves on its sides; one (fig. 42*a*) is taken from a coin of Cyzicus (*Numismatic Review*, vol. vii. (3rd series), pl. i., No. 23), the other from a marble bas-relief found at Sparta (*Mittheilungen des Deutschen Archäologischen Instituts in Athen*, 1887, vol. xii., pl. 12).

the Principality of Liege, struck at Thuin under Bishop Otbert (1092-1119), offer to our view the well-known type of the Temple,—which Charlemagne borrowed from ancient Italy,—with this

FIG. 43. COIN OF THUIN.

(DE CHESTRET. *Numismatique de la province de Liege*, pl. iii., No. 52.)

difference, that here the gable stands between two doves *affrontée*.

M. le baron de Chestret has drawn a parallel between this image and a legend relating to the siege of the monastery of Lobbes, in 955, by the Huns, who had invaded the territory of Thuin. The Lobbes chronicle relates that two pigeons, having escaped from the church, had flown three times round the barbarians' encampment, and that forthwith a violent shower of rain, by swelling their bows, had put the besiegers to rout.[1] As Folcuin, the writer of the chronicle, became abbot of Lobbes in 965, it cannot be maintained that this narrative was prompted by Otbert's coin ; but the legend will probably have contributed towards establishing in the coinage of Thuin a type whose antecedents, perhaps, date back, across classic antiquity, to the sacred dove-cots of Phœnicia.[2]

It may also happen that the signification of a

[1] DE CHESTRET. *Numismatique de la province de Liege.* Brussels, 1888, p. 54.

[2] The same subject seems to have passed into India, if we are to judge from the doves and other birds found facing one another on the roofs of the palaces represented in the Buddhist bas-reliefs of Boro-Budur. (LEEMANS. *Boro Boedoer op het eiland Java.* Leyden, 1873. Atlas, pl. lxvi., fig. 102; cxliv., fig. 22, etc.)

foreign symbol is intentionally modified in order to adapt it to an idea or a belief, till then devoid of all material expression, or confined to a few rudimentary figurations.   When the Persians had taken possession of Mesopotamia, they converted to their own use almost the whole imagery of the conquered people, in order to give a concrete form to their own religious conceptions, which the absence of a national art left without well-defined plastic representations.   The Assyrian *genii*, with a double pair of wings, provided a body for the seven superior spirits of Mazdeism, the Amshaspands.   The Chaldæan demons, with their hideous and bestial forms, were employed to represent the *devas*, those Iranian personifications of all that is false, dark, and impure.   Lastly, as we shall see in another chapter, Ahura Mazda appropriated the symbol of Ashur, the great god of the Assyrian pantheon, and the Iranian Holy Tree, whose sap averts death, borrowed its shape from the conventional Trees of Mesopotamian pictorial art.

In the same manner, when the Christians began to reproduce on the walls of the Catacombs the scenes of the Old Testament and the parables of the New, it was from classic, and even mythological art that they they took their first models. Hermes' Criophoros furnished the type of the Good Shepherd.[1]   Orpheus taming the wild beasts became a symbol of Christ and of his preaching. The Christian clinging to the Cross, in order to overcome temptations, was represented by Ulysses bound to the mast of his ship, so as to resist the song of the Sirens.   By an ingenious application of a myth, which paganism had already spiritualized,

---

[1] The origin of this type is found, perhaps, among the Phœnician people, where it was merely meant to represent the believer, or the sacrificer, bringing the sheep or the ram destined for the sacrifice.   (*Cf.* PERROT et CHIPIEZ, vol. iii., figs. 307, 308, and 402.)

Psyche offered the image of the human soul united to Love, replaced by an angel.[1] The religions of Gaul and of India have offered instances of similar assimilations from the day they came into contact with the symbolism of more advanced nations.

In general, there must be an analogy between the old and the new interpretation sufficient to justify the transition from the one to the other. On the monuments of Egypt and of Mesopotamia divinities or *genii* are frequently met with possessing a double pair of wings, one raised, the other lowered; the Phœnicians easily made therefrom a symbolical image of perpetual motion.[2] Amongst the Egyptians, the Phœnix rising from its ashes represented the sun resuscitating every morning in the glow of dawn. Depicted on a pyre, and encircled by a halo of glory, this solar Bird became, amongst the Romans, the emblem of the imperial apotheoses, and then passed to the *sarcophagi* of the Christians, as a symbol of the Resurrection.

The connection, however, is not always so easy to trace, whether in the form or in the idea, especially when it is a question of metaphysical conceptions embodied, at a later date, in a symbol of naturalistic origin. So long as symbols remain the image of some object or perceptible phenomenon, the mental operation which produced them can always be reconstituted. But in the domain of abstract ideas the field of analogy is as vast as that of individual fancy, and the same image may be used to render the most dissimilar ideas. How could we ascertain the origin of so abstract a symbol as the representation of the world under the form of a serpent biting its tail, if the texts did not inform us that in the cosmogony of Egypt, of Chaldæa, of Greece, and of India, the

---

[1] TH. ROLLER. *Les catacombes de Rome.* Paris, vol. ii., pp. 370-372.

[2] *Sanchoniathonis Fragmenta,* ed. Orelli, p. 38.

earth was believed to be circumscribed by an ocean or celestial river, whose circular course is compared to a serpent ?

We must observe that even in naturalistic religions one image may be applied to very different objects. The serpent, for instance, has also served to symbolize the lightning, solar rays, clouds, rivers, and even the course of the stars in the sky.

Symbols may even differ in appearance and yet be genealogically connected with one another. This leads us to examine the causes which may alter the form of symbolical representations.

There is a tendency, in the first place, to reduce or abbreviate the figure in order either to enclose it in a smaller space, or else to lessen the work of the artist, especially when it is a complicated image in frequent use. In all systems of writing where the characters first appeared under the form of hieroglyphs, the letter need only be glanced over in order to find the symbol. It is known that our vowel A was originally a bull's head, a bucrane, and that the latter, in its turn, represented the whole animal, in conformity with the popular rule that the part is equal to the whole in the matter of symbols, as well as of sacrifices. It is thus, again, that in the signs of the Zodiac the Lion is merely represented by its tail.

At other times, on the contrary, we have additions and embellishments suggested by æsthetic considerations. Such, in particular, was the fate of nearly all the symbols adopted by Greece, whose art, so powerfully original, never accepted foreign types without stamping them with profound and happy modifications. We will see an important example of this in the transformations of the Caduceus.

The Thunderbolt is another symbol which lent itself to all the refinements of classic art; here, however, the germs of those improvements, like the origins of the symbol itself, must be sought for further towards the East. On bas-reliefs at Nimrud the Thunderbolt is represented in the left hand of a god holding an axe in his right; at Malthaï it is brandished in each hand by the god Merodach struggling with the monster Tiamat, the mythical assailant of the moon. We may add that in these Mesopotamian sculptures its antecedents are recognized without difficulty; it appears there, indeed, as a double trident, or rather as a trident doubled in the manner of the blade in the two-

FIG. 44. ASSYRIAN THUNDERBOLT.
(LAYARD. *Monuments of Nineveh*, 2nd series, pl. v.)

edged axe, or of the hammer in the Two-headed Mallet.

Almost all nations have represented the lightning by a weapon. Among the Chaldæans it was depicted by a trident as well as by a pitch-fork and an axe. The Trident, with branches which zigzag like lightning, is frequently exhibited in the hands of the Assyro-Chaldæan gods. On a cylinder dating back to the oldest times of Chaldæan art the handle of a Trident held by the god of the storm lets fall a jet of water into the mouth of a deer.

The Assyrian artist who—with the intention, perhaps, of accentuating the power of the god—first doubled the Trident, or rather produced from it the trifid sheaf, of which Greek art was to make such good use, secured thereby for the old Mesopotamian symbol an advantage over all the

FIG. 45.

(RAWLINSON. *The Five Great Monarchies*, vol. ii., p. 251.)

other representations of lightning with which it was to compete.

The Greeks, like all the Indo-European nations, seem to have figured to themselves the light of the storm under the form of a bird of prey. When they had received the image of the Thunderbolt from Asia Minor, they placed it in the talons of the eagle, and made it the sceptre, and even the symbol, of Zeus; explaining, in return, according to their custom, this symbolical combination by a myth: it was, said they, the eagle that brought the Thunderbolt to Zeus, when the latter was preparing to fight the Titans.[1]

Roman Italy transmitted the Thunderbolt to Gaul, where, in the latter centuries of paganism, it alternated with the Two-headed Hammer on Gallo-Roman monuments; it is even found on amulets of ancient Germany, Scandinavia, and Brittany.

In the East it penetrated into India in the track of Alexander. It had there to compete with other symbols having the same signification: "the sparrow-hawk with golden wings," and "the stone with four points," of which the Vedas speak,—the

[1] GUBERNATIS. *Zoological Mythology*. London, 1872, vol. ii., p. 196.

St. Andrew's Cross (itself perhaps a double fork) which forms the *vajra*, the redoubtable weapon of Indra, god of the stormy sky ;[1] the Drum and the Axe which figure in the hands of Siva ; lastly, its own antecedent, the Trident, which the Hindus had already borrowed from the West, or else imagined themselves spontaneously.

Siva, who succeeded Zeus on the coins of the Indo-Scythic kings when the last glimmering of Greek civilization in north-west India had died out, holds in his hand sometimes the Thunderbolt, sometimes the Trident,[2] and if the latter remains the essential weapon of the god in the later imagery of the Hindu sects, the Thunderbolt made none the less its way amongst the Buddhists, who transported it with their symbolism as far as China and Japan. Even at the present time it can

FIG. 46. DORDJ.
(From a specimen belonging to the author.)

be recognized there under the form of the *dordj*, a small bronze instrument shaped like a double sheaf, with six or eight branches, which, held between the thumb and forefinger, is used by the lamas and bonzes to bless the faithful, and to exorcise demons.[3]

A legend which M. Gustave Le Bon found in Nepaul claims to justify the presence of the

[1] In the Vedas Indra's weapon is defined as " the stone with four points which brings the rain " (Rig. Veda, 4, 22, 1-2). Now the *vajra* of Indra had so exactly the form of a St. Andrew's cross that the term *vajrarupa*, " vajra-shaped," is the equivalent of our expression "in the form of the letter X." (Cf. *Dictionnaire de Saint-Pétersbourg*, 6, 630.)

[2] BARCLAY V. HEAD. *Catalogue of Indian Coins in the British Museum*. London, 1886, p. 147 *et seq.*

[3] The *dordj* appears already on the bas-reliefs of Sanchi.

Thunderbolt in the temples of the country by stating that Buddha had wrested it from the god Indra.[1] The assertion is true in this sense, that Buddhism, after having precipitated from his supreme rank the Master of the Brahminical Olympus, made of his terrible and capricious instrument an ally of man in the struggle against the powers of evil. It is interesting to note the fact that with us, too, the antique and redoubtable attribute of the Master of the Thunder has become the emblem of lightning removed from the blind direction of natural forces and placed by science at the service of human industry. Are there many other symbols which can boast of such a long and fruitful career?

This happy disposition of Greek genius reacted even on symbols of strange religions wherever their form was not invariably regulated by the canons of a perennial tradition. M. Menant has pointed out the hand of Greece in the transformation of the winged bulls which kept watch of old at the entrances to the Assyrian palaces. Their function as gate-keepers or guardians, in condemning them to remain immovable, imposed upon them, in spite of their wings, rigid contours and massive forms, calculated to give at once an impression of repose and force. With the advent of the Persian religion, in which the bull was a mythical character invested with a wholly active function, as representing Gayomert, the first-born of creation, it was no longer deemed necessary to fasten his images to the ground; the bull moved its wings, started at a gallop into space, brandished a bow, and ended, under the Greek rule of the Seleucidæ, by assuming, on cylinders, the well-known physiognomy of Sagittarius.[2]

[1] GUSTAVE LE BON. *Voyage au Népaul* in the *Tour du Monde*, 1886, li., p. 266.
[2] J. MENANT. *Pierres gravées de la Haute-Asie*, vol. ii., p. 191.

Beside the improvements due to the artistic
taste of their authors we must place the disfigura-
tions brought about by the maladroitness or ignorance of the copyist, as may be remarked on so
many Gallic coins, where Greek symbols have
assumed the most singular forms.

Sometimes those corruptions tend to produce
a new type, which, in passing through a whole
series of intermediate forms, takes the place of the
old. It is like those dissolving views where the
outlines of the two succeeding pictures are blended
in an image which is no longer the one, and is not
as yet the other, but exhibits features borrowed
from both.

Nothing is more curious than to follow the
gradual stages of the degeneration which, on Gallic
coins, has finally transformed into the letter E
the bust of Apollo,[1] and into the letter H, on coins
of Valenciennes, the type of the Carlovingian
temple formed of four columns placed on a base-
ment and surmounted by a pediment.[2]

FIG. 47. DEGENERATION OF THE *Temple* TYPE.

A metamorphosis of the same kind may be
noticed in the carved work on paddles from New
Ireland, which were exhibited in 1872 by General
Pitt Rivers at the annual session of the British
Association for the Advancement of Science. We
see here a whole series of deformations, which at last

---

[1] C. A. SERRURE. *La numismatique et l'archéologie gauloise,*
in the *Annales de la Société d'archéologie de Bruxelles,* vol. iv.,
p. 58.

[2] CH. ROBERT. *Lettre à M. R. Chalon,* in the *Revue
belge de numismatique* of 1859, p. 133 *et seq.* It must be
observed that the letter H is the first in Hannonia (Hainault).

change a human form into a crescent placed on the point of an arrow.   Had the intermediate figures not been found, the connection between the two extremes would never have been admitted, nor even suspected.

FIG. 48. POLYNESIAN CARVINGS.
(FLAMMARION. *Etoiles et curiosités du ciel*, p. 445.)

As a counterpart of the metamorphoses which thus convert a face into a sign or instrument we will see further on examples of symbols which, purely linear in the beginning, have gradually assumed a human physiognomy.[1]   These transformations may, in certain cases, be systematic and premeditated; but generally they originate in a desire to give an intelligible character to a shapeless symbol by approximating it to the image which it seems most to resemble.

When a foreign or antiquated symbol is formed of several images combined, it sometimes happens that one or more of its constituent parts are modified in order to better agree with the religious traditions, the æsthetic preferences, the national predilections, or even with the geographical peculiarities of its new environment.   It is thus that, in the symbolism of Europe, the Lily has generally taken the place which the Orient assigned to the Lotus.

There are also symbolical combinations in which several superposed elements, dating back to different periods, can in some measure be distinguished. The most curious monuments to be studied in this

----

[1] See chaps. v. and vi.

connection are the *perrons* or *pérons* which, in the Middle Ages, constituted the symbol of communal liberties in several cities of eastern Belgium. The

FIG. 49. THE PERRON OF LIEGE.
(*Revue de Liège*, vol. vi. (1846), p. 86.)

most celebrated of those *perrons* is still standing, above a fountain, on the market-place at Liege;

FIG. 50. HERALDIC PERRON.
(LOYENS. *Recueil héraldique*, passim.)

it consists of a white marble column placed on a square base with five steps, guarded by four lions. The capital is surmounted by the three Graces, who support a Crown encircling a Fir-cone with a small Cross on its point.

In other towns of the same country, at Namur, for instance, the *perron* only comprised a column on a pedestal with three steps.[1]

The *perron* of Liege has had a very chequered existence, which makes it all the dearer to its fellow-townsmen. Transported to Bruges by Charles the Bold in 1467, after the defeat of the citizens of Liege, and solemnly restored to the old episcopal city ten years later, twice blown down in a storm, in 1448 and in 1693, it figured as early as 1303 on the banner of the trades leagued together in defence of their privileges, as also on the gemel blazon of the two annual burgomasters, or temporary masters, of the city.[2]

In still earlier times it is seen on coins of the bishop-princes from the end of the twelfth century. On one of them, dating back to Rodolphe de Zæringen (1167-1191), it only appears in the form of a column surmounted by a ball, above which is

FIG. 51. COIN OF ROD. DE   FIG. 52. COIN OF JEAN
ZÆRINGEN.   D'APS.

(DE CHESTRET. *Numismatique de la principauté de Liège*, pl. vi., No. 119, and x., No. 192.)

a cross, and the inscription PERU VOC(OR) (fig. 51). On a coin of Jean d'Aps (1229-1238), however, the Fir-cone is plainly visible at the top of the column (fig. 52).

The meaning and origin of the *perrons* have been much discussed.[3]   M. Ch. Piot, general

---

[1] JULES BORGNET. *L'Hôtel de ville et le Perron de Namur*, in the *Messager des sciences historiques*. Ghent, 1846, p. 235.

[2] LOYENS. *Recueil héraldique des bourgmestres de la noble cité de Liège*. Liège, 1720.

[3] The name itself means simply "stone" (from *petronem*). It

archivist of Belgium, has proved in a conclusive manner that they were, in the Middle Ages, " stones of justice," marking the place where the holders of municipal jurisdiction sat in the open air; and thus it is easily explained how they everywhere became the symbol of municipal life, as also of popular privileges.[1] But this explanation leaves the question of their origin untouched. Moreover, why were these stones surmounted by a column, and why did this column itself support a Fir-cone and a Cross?

According to some, the *perron* might simply be a sort of Calvary, or even an elevated Cross, like that which figures on the farthings of Charlemagne, and on some coins of the bishop-princes;[2] according to others, it might date from the Eburons, and represent an ancient druidical stone;[3] there are those, again, who attribute it, together with the Fir-cone, to one or other of the Germanic races who successively occupied the basin of the Meuse;[4] whilst some, lastly, would wish to make it a legacy of the Roman domination in Belgium.[5]

For my own part I consider that the *perron* of Liege may be resolved into five elements belonging

is generally used in the sense of a stone with steps, a stone staircase. Yet, in the vicinity of Verdes, in France, there are several artificial mounds, composed of heaps of stones, which are named *perrons* or *perroux*, and which have given rise to many legends. (*Une visite à Verdes*, by M. Ludovic Guignard (from the *Bulletin de la Société Dunoise*. Chateaudun, 1891.)

[1] CH. PIOT. *Observations sur le perron de Liège*, in the *Revue belge de numismatique*, vol. iii., p. 369 *et seq.*

[2] BARON DE CHESTRET. *Le perron liégeois*, in the Reports of the *Institut archéologique liégeois*, vol. xviii. (1885), p. 175 *et seq.*

[3] HÉNAUX. *Le Péron de Liège*, in the *Revue de Liège*, vol. vi. (1846), p. 86 *et seq.*

[4] CH. RAHLENBEEK. *Le Perron de Liège*, in the *Revue de Belgique*, vol. lxv. (1890), p. 31 *et seq.*

[5] EUG. DOGNÉE. *Liège*, in the *Collection nationale*, Brussels, 1 vol. ill., pp. 24-27.

to as many different periods. Putting aside the lions and the Crown, which date from the Middle Ages, and the group of the Graces, which, in 1693, replaced three copper figures representing, it would appear, scoundrels embracing rods, there remain :

1. The *column*, which represents the common element of monuments of this kind, and which may date back, as M. Rahlenbeek thinks, to the Germanic tribes settled in western Belgium.—Tacitus bears witness to the presence of sacred columns amongst the Frisians who occupied the valley of the Lower Rhine, nor far, consequently, from the Meuse ; he even calls them Pillars of Hercules ; however, he hastens to recall to mind that many things are fathered upon Hercules which do not belong to him.[1] The Saxons, that is to say the inhabitants of the right bank of the Rhine, venerated, on their side, wooden or stone pillars dedi-

Fig. 53. Column of Hildesheim.
(Kratz. *Der Dom zu Hildesheim*, 2nd part, pl. vii., fig. 2.)

cated to the god Irmin; such was the famous Irminsul demolished by the order of Charlemagne. A stone column dug up at Eresburg or Stadt-

[1] *De mor. German.*, xxiv.

bergen in Westphalia, under Louis the Débonnaire,
and placed in the cathedral of Hildesheim, where
it still serves as a candelabrum, exhibits a striking
resemblance to the ancient representations of the
perron of Liege.

M. Piot, again, has proved that people were
sworn on the *perron*. Now we learn from the
Saga of Gudrun that amongst the Scandinavians
they swore "by the holy white stone."[1] Moreover, there have been preserved until our own
times, on the *tumuli* or *haugs* of the Scandinavian
Peninsula, pillars of white stone to which the
lower classes accord a certain veneration. One of
these stones, now in the Bergen Museum, presents
the similitude of a small pillar with an enlarged top
three feet high and sixteen inches in diameter.[2]

Were the pillars of the Germanic nations dedicated to the divinities of the sky, or of war ? Did
they exhibit a *simulacrum* of Thor, of Odin, or of
a god Irmin ? Had they a phallic acceptation, as
M. Holmboe thinks with respect to the Scandinavian *cippi*, or did they provide a cosmogonical
symbol, as might be inferred from a passage in
Adam of Bremen to the effect that, the Saxons
venerated in their Irminsul the image of "the
universal pillar which supports all things"?[3] All
that can be said for the moment is that these
pillars had a religious character, and that they had
to play a part in the social life, so intimately connected, amongst all barbarians, with the religious
life of the people.

2. *The Fir-cone.*—This is, according to M.
Henaux, "the symbol of an existence united but
distinct," and represents the union of the tribes

---

[1] "At enom hvita helga Steini" (*Godrunar-Harmr*, str. 47).
(In *Edda Saemundar Hinns Fróda*, Stockholm, 1818, p. 237.)

[2] HOLMBOE. *Traces de Bouddhisme en Norvège*, fig. 10.

[3] *Gesta Hammenburgensis Ecclesiæ pontificum*, Hamburg,
1706, lib. i., ch. vi.

leagued together against the dominion of Rome.[1]
We do not find, however, that the Fir-cone admitted
of this interpretation in the symbolism of the
ancient Germans, or even of the Gauls. To tell
the truth, we possess very little information on
the particulars of Germanic symbols and even
forms of worship. To make up for this, however,
we know that, in the Græco-Roman paganism, the
fruit of the pine discharged prophylactic, sepulchral,
and phallic functions.—Amongst the Etruscans
the Fir-cone occurs frequently in tombs and on
urns, sometimes alone, sometimes on the top of a
pillar.[2] Does it there figure a representation of the
flames on an altar, and does it consequently symbolize the persistency of life in death? The pillar,
whole or broken, and often adorned with bas-
reliefs, was a fairly common monument on Belgo-
Roman tombs.[3] But we nowhere find that it
supported a Fir-cone, and nothing permits us to
suppose that the *perrons* ever ·had a sepulchral
acceptation.—Moreover, the Thyrsus of Bacchus,
composed of a stalk crowned by the fruit of the
pine, was a familiar emblem in classic paganism.[4]
An emblem of the same kind was borne by Syl-
vanus Dendrophorus, that old god of the Latin
forests, assimilated at a later date, on so many
Gallic monuments, to one of the principal divinities

[1] HENAUX. *Loc. cit.*, p. 91.

[2] G. DENNIS. *The Cities and Cemeteries of Etruria.* London, 1848, vol. ii., pp. 157, 193, and 492.—*Cf.* JOS. MICALI.
Monuments antiques. Paris, 1824, tab. xxxvi.

[3] L. VAN DER KINDERE. *Introduction à l'histoire des insti-
tutions de la Belgique au moyen âge.* Brussels, 1890, p. 86.

[4] It must be also taken into consideration that the burning
altar often represented, as is seen at Mycenæ (see below,
fig. 74), by a cylindrical pyre surmounted by a triangular-
shaped flame, was accounted the centre and palladium
of the city in the most ancient republics of antiquity. (*Cf.*
FUSTEL DE ·COULANGES. *La cité antique.*)—But this tradition does not seem to have spread beyond Greece and
Italy.

of the Celtic pantheon, if not its supreme god—the god with the Mallet :

Et teneram ab radice ferens, Sylvane, cupressum.[1]

It may therefore be asked if the addition of the fir-cone to the *perron* of Liege is not due to the syncretic influence of Gallo-Roman art, which would thus have brought the Germanic column within the limits of classic paganism, as, at a later period, the Church introduced it into Christian society by surmounting it with a Cross. Perhaps also it was thus desired to keep alive in the monument a phallic signification, whilst correcting whatever too great coarseness this symbol might have had in its primitive form.

It is probable that the *pyr* of Augsburg, that gigantic Fir-cone, depicted, from time immemorial,

FIG. 54. THE PYR OF AUGSBURG.

on the arms, the coins, and the seals of that town, dates from the time of the Roman occupation. It has been found, indeed, at Augsburg itself, on a Roman monument, now in the museum of that town, and known as the altar of the *duumviri*. The pine-fruit is there sculptured at the top of a pillar ornamented with flower-work, which separates the statues of the two municipal magistrates, exactly as, at Liege, the *perron* figures between the coats of arms of the two annual burgomasters.[2]

[1] *Georg.*, i., 20.
[2] VON RAISER. *Die romischen Alterthümer zu Augsburg.* Augsburg, 1820, pl. xxi.

It must be observed that the *pyr* rests on a capital; now, every capital supposes a column, that is to say, that we have here the remains of a veritable *perron*, which was never baptized by the apposition of a Cross, but was merely shortened by the suppression of the shaft, in order to be more easily introduced into armorial bearings and coins.

I have been assured, but have not been able to verify the fact, that in Rome itself, in front of the church of SS. Nereo et Achilleo, built on the ruins of a temple of Isis, there was still to be seen, some years ago, an antique column surmounted by a Fir-cone with a Cross on the top.

We have likewise the proof that the Fir-cone,

FIG. 55. BUCKLE FROM ENVERMEU.
(COCHET. *La Normandie souterraine*, pl. xii., No. 4.)

FIG. 56. BUCKLE FROM EPRAVE.
(A. BEQUET. *Soc. arch. de Namur*, vol. xv., p. 315.)

placed at the end of a stalk or pillar, figured amongst the objects held in veneration by the Franks, who occupied, in the fifth century, the East of Belgium and the North-east of France.

The Abbe Cochet and M. Alfred Bequet have separately found, the former in the Merovingian cemetery of Envermeu, near Dieppe, the latter in the cemetery of Eprave, not far from Namur, silver belt-buckles adorned with an identical figure, in which I have no hesitation in recognizing a prototype of the *perrons*. We have there, in the middle of a support or pedestal, which is placed between two peacocks facing one another, a long stalk, capped by a conical object, whose resemblance to the Fir-cone at once struck the Abbe Cochet, though at that moment he was little thinking of the *perrons* of Belgium (figs. 55, 56).[1]

It is to be remarked that the two birds facing one another are also met with on the sides of the

FIG. 57. SEAL OF LIEGE *ad legata*.
(LOYENS. *Recueil héraldique des bourgmestres*, p. 2.)

perron on the earliest coin of Liege, on which an attempt is made to represent this monument with the Fir-cone (fig. 52), and also on a seal which Loyens attributes to the year 1348 (fig. 57).

If the fact be insisted upon, that the stalk engraved in the Frankish image seems to be of wood, I will remark that the symbolical pillars of

[1] Abbé COCHET. *La Normandie souterraine.* Paris, 1855, p. 344.—A. BEQUET. *Nos fouilles en 1880*, in the *Annales de la Société archéologique de Namur*, vol. xv., p. 315.

the ancient Germans were made of wood as well as of stone. This was particularly the case with the Irminsul, which the oldest chronicles define as the trunk of a tree erected in the open air.[1] The Hessians of the eighth century, who lived on the Lower Rhine, still venerated, at the time when they were evangelized by St. Boniface, the trunk of a tree, which was to them the *simulacrum* of the god Thor.[2]

Do not our May-Poles, often a mere stalk surrounded with ribbons, take us back to the time when Lucan sang of our forefathers :

> *simulacraque mœsta deorum*
> *Arte carent, cæsisque extant informia truncis* [3] *?*

Lastly, old chroniclers relate that in the thirteenth century the destruction of the Irminsul by Charlemagne was still commemorated at Hildesheim on the Saturday following the Sunday of the *Lætare*, by planting in the ground, on the cathedral square, two poles six feet high, each surmounted by a wooden object one foot in height, and shaped *like a pyramid or cone*. The young people then endeavoured with sticks and stones to overthrow this object. Does not this tradition directly connect the Irminsul, or rather the Irminsuls, with the stake which, surmounted by a Cone, is presented to our view in the Frankish buckle, just as the stone column of the Hildesheim cathedral links them with the *perrons* of Belgium ? The same custom, or rather the same popular sport, existed elsewhere too in Germany, at Halberstadt in particular ; here, however, it was the canons

---

[1] "Truncum quoque ligni non parvæ magnitudinis in altum erectum sub divo colebant patria eum linguâ Irminsul appelantes, quod Latine dicitur universalis columna quasi sustinens omnia." (*Op. cit.*, liv. i., ch. vi.)

[2] "Robur Jovis sive Thori deastri." (ECKART. *Commentarii de rebus Franciæ orientalis.* Wurzburg, 1729, p. 344.)

[3] *Pharsalia*, iii, 412.

who indulged in it on the Sunday of the *Lætare* itself.[1]

We have, moreover, a more direct proof that the representation of the stalk, surmounted by a Fir-cone, and placed between animals facing one another, figured in Christian imagery from the eighth century of our era. The sculptures in question are taken, one from the parapet of the cathedral of Torcello, near Venice (fig. 58), and

FIG. 58. FROM THE CATHE- FIG. 59. FROM THE ATHENS
DRAL OF TORCELLO. CATHEDRAL.

the other from a bas-relief on the Athens cathedral (fig. 59). Both of them are reproduced in the remarkable work of M. R. Cattaneo, *L'architecture en Italie.*[2]

3. *The Cross.*—Tradition relates that the Christian missionaries everywhere overthrew, amongst the Belgians, the altars of Thor and of Wodan. But the fate of the column of Hildesheim shows us how monuments of this kind managed to escape destruction by placing themselves, so to speak, under the protection of the new faith. At Hildesheim, they placed a Virgin on the column, transformed into a candelabrum. At Liege, a Cross

---

[1] ECKART. *Op. cit.*, p. 221.—MEIBOM. *De Irminsula Saxonica*, p. 20.

[2] Translated into French by M. Lemonnier. Venice, 1891, figs. 19 and 165.

was placed on the *perron*, and the oaths which were
taken on the " sacred whitestone" continued to
be taken on the Cross which sanctified the ancient
simulacrum.   In Sweden also *cippi* are found,
similar to the one I have mentioned above, on the
top of which the Cross has been incised.[1]

The Abbe Cochet thinks that the figures engraved on the Envermeu plate denote a Christian
symbol, because we find in the Catacombs, and
even in Roman architecture, the symbol of a
bunch of grapes between two peacocks facing one
another, depicting the soul quenching its thirst at
the eternal fountain of life.   Nothing, however,
entitles us to distinguish a bunch of grapes in the
object placed at the end of the stalk ; moreover,
its resemblance to the ordinary representation of
the *thyrsus* is incontestable.   Lastly, we have
already seen in the present chapter that the custom
of figuring sacred objects between two winged
animals facing one another was spread throughout
the whole Mediterranean basin long before the
birth of Christian art.   It is especially on the side
of sacred stones and trees that they are met with,
as I shall have an opportunity of pointing out in
the following chapter.   Now, in so far as it was a
cosmogonical column, related to the Scandinavian
Yggdrasill, the Irminsul is just as much connected
with the tradition of the Universal Pillar as with
that of the Tree of the World, both of which seem
to have received their first plastic expression
amongst the Assyro-Chaldæans.

Curiously enough, the Tree of Life between two
peacocks facing one another is even found in the
symbolism of modern India (fig. 60).

---

[1] LILIEGREN.   *Nord Fomlemningar*, ii., No. xci.—*Cf.* CAR-
TAILHAC.   *La France préhistorique.*   Paris, 1889, p. 317 :
" Many unhewn pillars in the departments of the Yonne, Côtes
du Nord, Finisterre, Morbihan, Indre, Creuse, Puy-de-Dôme,
Saône-et-Loire. etc.. bear Crosses and even Madonnas."

It will be observed that here each of the two peacocks holds a serpent in its beak. Now the peacock was held amongst the ancients to kill serpents, and this also may be one of the reasons

FIG. 60. CLOTH FROM MASULIPATAM.
(Sir G. BIRDWOOD. *The Industrial Arts of India.* 1880.

which brought about its introduction into Christian symbolism.[1]

It is evident that, at least in its outlines, all this iconography takes us backwards, far beyond Christianity, into the very midst of antique symbolism.

Lastly, it is proper to remark that traces of Christianity are entirely wanting in the cemeteries

---

[1] MACCARIUS. *Hagioglypta.* Paris, 1856, p. 205.

of Envermeu and Eprave, as well as in nearly all the Frankish cemeteries of that period.

Thus, to sum up, the *perron* of Liege includes in harmonious order the legacies and, so to speak, the *witnesses*, of all the civilizations which have succeeded one another in this part of Belgium. In this respect it is more than a symbol of municipal liberty; it is the embodiment of the very history of the nation.[1]

[1] My dissertation upon the origins of the *perron* has had the privilege of reviving, in Belgium, the controversies which this subject seems never to exhaust. We must instance, in particular, the recent works of MM. Léon Van der Kindere, Léon Naveau, and Eugène Monseur.

M. Naveau has no hesitation in adopting the theory of M. the Abbé Louis, that the *perron* of Liege was, from the beginning, a real Calvary, with a purely religious signification. Liege, which, as he points out, was at one time a mere village, only became an important city from the time of St. Lambert, its first bishop and veritable founder. Now, he asks, is it credible that a bishop would have chosen a pagan symbol as an emblem of his city? (*Le Perron Liègeois*, from the *Bulletin de l'Institut archéologique Liègeois*. Liege, 1892.)

M. L. Van der Kindere admits, on his side, that the *perron* was in all times an elevated Cross, but he adds that this Cross had essentially a secular and administrative import. It was the symbol of the *Weichbildrecht*, that is to say, of the right granted to the towns to establish a market under the protection of the imperial authority, and it was thus it came to symbolize the whole of the municipal liberties. In reference to this, he recalls to mind the Rolandsäulen, those columns serving as a support to the image of a warrior, bearing the name of Roland, which, from the thirteenth century onwards, are noticed in many towns in northern Germany. He considers that these statues might have replaced the Cross as a symbolical representation of the imperial power. (*Notes sur les Perrons*, in *le Bulletin de l'Académie royale de Belgique*. Brussels, 1892, vol. xxi. (3rd series), p. 497.)

According to M. Monseur, whose opinion I am rather inclined to accept, *perrons*, Rolandsäulen and Irminsäulen, would be forms, differing according to time and place, of the post, sometimes adorned with a shield, which the ancient Germans used to erect in their public meetings, and which were consecrated to the patron god of those assemblies, probably Tiews, whose name, the Germanic equivalent of Zeus, is met with in the word Tuesday. This god bears the epithet of "god of the assembly" (*thingsaz, i.e., Zeus agoraios*), a surname which has been pointed out in an inscription in England. This post was probably erected on a stone; whence the expression, met with in old Alsatian texts, to have ",post and stone in a village," meaning, to have jurisdiction there. At a later date these posts had the Cross placed on them in Belgium, as in Germany they were surmounted by the statue of the hero whom the "chansons de geste" represented as the paladin above all others, and whose name, besides, probably offered a certain consonance with Hrodo, like Irmin, one of the names of the god Tiews. (*Supplément littéraire de l'Indépendance belge* of the 3rd of May, 1891.)

CHAPTER IV.

SYMBOLISM AND MYTHOLOGY OF THE TREE.

I. The Sacred Tree and its acolytes.—The Tree in the art and symbolism of Mesopotamia.—The Tree between two animals, or two monsters; adoption of this theme by the Persians, Phœnicians, Greeks, Hindus, Arabs, and Christians. —The Tree between two human personages; its migrations into Persia, India, and the extreme East.—Characteristic features of the images derived from these two themes.—The variety of certain details does not preclude relationship between symbolical combinations.—Substitution of sacred objects for the Tree between its acolytes.

II. Interpretation of the Sacred Tree amongst the Semites.— The Sacred Tree does not merely represent a plant venerated for its uses.—*Simulacra* of the Goddess of Nature ; the *asherîm.* —The representation of the artificial fertilization of the palm-tree became, in Assyria, the symbol of fecundation in general.— Myths and symbols relating to the Tree of Life.—The Cosmo-gonical Tree in the cuneiform texts.—The Tree of Knowledge. —The Calendar Plant or Lunar Tree.

III. The Paradisaical Trees of the Aryans.—Mythical Trees of the Hindus.—The Tree of Knowledge amongst the Buddhists, and its connection with the Cosmic Tree.—Contests for the fruit of the Tree.—Analogous myths amongst the Persians, Greeks, and Scandinavians.—How far this similarity of traditions denotes a common source.—Logical coincidences in the applications of vegetable symbolism.—Enrichment and approximation of mythologies by the mutual exchange of myths and symbols.

I. The Sacred Tree and its Acolytes.

THE Tree is one of the oldest and most widely diffused subjects in Semitic pictorial art, especially in Mesopotamia.[1]   It first appears, on Chaldæan

[1] JOACHIN MENANT. *Les pierres gravées de la Haute-Asie.* Paris, 1883-86, vol. i., figs. 41, 43, 71, 86, 104, 115, 120, 121,

cylinders, as a stem divided at the base, surmounted by a fork, or a crescent, and cut, mid-way,

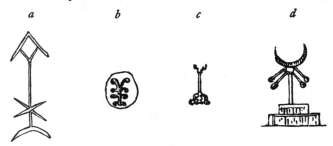

a   *b*   *c*   *d*

FIG. 61. RUDIMENTARY FORMS OF THE SACRED TREE.[1]

by one or more cross-bars, which sometimes bear
a fruit at each extremity.

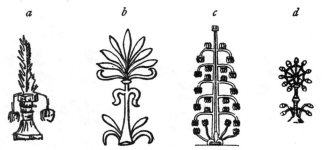

a   *b*   *c*   *d*

FIG. 62. VARIETIES OF SACRED TREES.[2]

This rudimentary image frequently changes into

and 142; vol. ii., figs. 11, 13, 17, 18, 19, 36, 41, 54 to 61, 85,
110, 208, 213, etc.

[1] *a* is taken from a Chaldæan cylinder (J. MENANT, *Pierres
gravées*, vol. i., fig. 71); *b*, from a cylinder of Nineveh (LAYARD,
Monuments of Nineveh, 2nd series, pl. ix., No. 9); *c*, from a
Chaldean cylinder (J. MENANT, *Pierres gravées*, vol. i., fig. 115);
d, from an Assyrian cylinder (PERROT et CHIPIEZ, *Histoire de
l'art dans l'antiquité*, vol. ii., fig. 342).

[2] *a* (MENANT, *Pierres gravées*, vol. i., fig. 86); *b* (LAJARD,
Mithra, pl. xxxix., fig. 8); *c* (PERROT et CHIPIEZ, *Histoire de
l'art*, vol. ii., fig. 235); *d* (Seal of Sennacherib, MENANT,
Pierres gravées, vol. ii., fig. 85).

the palm, the pomegranate, the cypress, the vine, etc. (fig. 62).

On the monuments of Nimrud and Khorsabad, beginning with the tenth century before our era, the

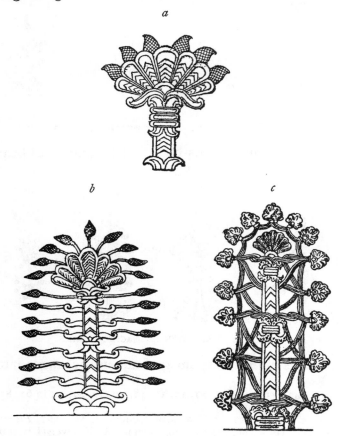

FIG. 63. CONVENTIONAL TREES OF ASSYRIAN BAS-RELIEFS.

Tree becomes still more complex; it would sometimes seem to be composed of fragments belonging to different kinds of plants. The stem, which suggests a richly ornamented Ionic column, is crowned by a palmette; the base is concealed

behind a bunch of slender leaves, which, in some
cases, recall our *fleur-de-lis* (fig. 62*c*), or else it
rests upon a pair of fluted horns, which recur again
at the top and even in the middle of the stem
(fig. 63). On both sides branches spread out
symmetrically, bearing conical fruits (fig. 63*b*), or
fan-shaped leaves (fig. 63*c*), at their extremities.
Sometimes the ends of these branches are connected by straps which form a net-work of the
most pleasing effect.[1]

Whatever the ornamental value of this figure
may be, it is certain that it has, above all, a reli-

FIG. 64. THE ACOLYTES OF THE SACRED TREE.
(LAJARD. *Mithra*, pl. xlix., fig. 9.)

gious signification. It is invariably associated
with religious subjects, among the intaglios of the
cylinders, the sculptures of the bas-reliefs, and the
embroidery of the royal and sacerdotal garments.
Above it is frequently suspended the Winged
Circle, personifying the supreme divinity, Assur at
Nineveh, Bel or Ilu at Babylon. Lastly, it nearly

---

[1] LAYARD. *Monuments of Nineveh*, 1st series, pl. 6, 7, 8, 9,
25, 39, 44.—G. RAWLINSON. *The Five Great Monarchies of
the Ancient Eastern World*. London, 1862-67, vol. ii., pp. 236,
237.—See also *passim* in the Atlas, appended by Félix Lajard
to his *Introduction à l'étude du culte de Mithra*.

always stands between two personages facing each other, who are sometimes priests or kings in an attitude of adoration, sometimes monstrous creatures, such as are so often met with in Assyro-Chaldæan imagery, lions, sphinx, griffins, unicorns, winged bulls, men, or *genii*, with the head of an eagle, and so forth.

Hence we have two types, or symbolical combinations, whose migrations we can easily follow.

A. The Tree between two animals facing each other makes it first appearance on the oldest

a   b

Fig. 65.

(From the *Catalogue* of the de Clercq collection, vol. i., pl. ii., 15, and pl. vii., 61.)

cylinders of Chaldæa. In the de Clercq collection it is seen on engraved stones which are attributed, one to the archaic art of Chaldæa, the other to the school that flourished, according to M. J. Menant, in the city of Agadi at the time of Sargon I., some four thousand years before our era.[1]

---

[1] The object engraved between the two monsters in fig. 65*a* is, according to the *Catalogue* of the de Clercq collection, a candelabrum. I think that we must rather see in this a tree of the kind reproduced above (fig. 62*c*), from a bas-relief in the Louvre. Moreover, the Tree, the Candelabrum, and the Column, are images which merge into one another with the greatest ease (*cf.* below, fig. 76). The two objects have not only a resemblance of form, but also of idea, on which matter I cannot do better than refer the reader to the chapter entitled *The*

EXPLANATION OF PLATE IV.

Figure *a* is a bas-relief of Nineveh, reproduced from LAYARD (*Monuments of Nineveh*, 2nd series, pl. xlv., fig. 3).

Figure *b* is taken from a Phœnician bowl discovered at Cærium by M. de Cesnola, and reproduced by M. CLERMONT-GANNEAU (*L'Imagerie phénicienne.* Paris, 1880, pl. iv.).

Figure *c* comes from a Persian cylinder inscribed with Aramean characters, the property of M. Schlumberger, and reproduced by M. PH. BERGER (*Gazette archéologique* for 1888, p. 143).

Figure *d* belongs to a bowl which was found, together with products of Sassanian art, near the White Sea (J. R. ASPELIN. *Antiquités du Nord Finno-Ougrien.* Helsingfors, fig. 610).

Figure *e* is copied from a capital of the temple of Athene at Priene (O. RAYET et A. THOMAS. *Milet et le golfe Latinique.* Paris, 1887, pl. xlix., No. 5).

Figure *f* reproduces the ornamentation of an archaic vase of Athens belonging to the British Museum (RAYET et COLLIGNON. *Histoire de la céramique grecque*, fig. 25).

Figure *g* comes from the sculptures on the baptistery at Cividale (LE MONNIER. *L'Architecture in Italie.* Venice, 1891, fig. 36).

Figure *h* comes from the bas-reliefs of Bharhut, probably anterior to our era (A. CUNNINGHAM. *The Stupa of Bharhut*, pl. vi.).

Figure *i* is copied from a Tanjore carpet at the India Museum in London (SIR GEORGE BIRDWOOD. *The Industrial Arts of India.* London, 1880, p. 53).

Figure *j* is taken from a tympanum of the church at Marigny, in the Calvados department (DE CAUMONT. *Rudiments d'archéologie. Architecture religieuse.* Paris, 5th edition, p. 269).

PLATE IV.

FIG. *a*. Bas-relief of Nineveh.

FIG. *b*. From a Phœnician Bowl.

FIG. *c*. From a Persian Cylinder.

FIG. *d*. From a Sassanian Bowl.

FIG. *e*. Capital of the Temple of Athene at Priene.

FIG. *f*. Archaic Vase of Athens.

FIG. *g*. Bas-relief of the Baptistery of Cividale.

FIG. *h*. Bas-relief of Bharhut.

FIG. *i*. Tanjore Carpet.

FIG. *j*. From a Tympanum of the Church at Marigny.

However this may be, it was only at the time of the Assyrian domination that it received its definite and so highly artistic shape. While the Tree becomes larger and more conspicuous, the two animals, no longer embracing or crossing one another, assume a more natural and strictly symmetrical attitude (see pl. iv., fig. *a*).

From Mesopotamia this subject passed on the one hand among the Phœnicians and into the whole of Western Asia, on the other among the Persians after the fall of Babylon.

The latter confined themselves to copying the Assyrian type on their seals, their jewels, their cloths, and their bas-reliefs, until the end of the empire of the Sassanidæ, in the seventh century of our era (pl. iv., figs. *c* and *d*).

From Persia it passed into India, doubtlessly during the period immediately preceding the invasion of Alexander. The presence of the Tree between two lions facing one another among the Buddhist sculptures of Bharhut is even one of the indications that help to prove the influence of Iranian art on the most ancient monuments of Hindu architecture (pl. iv., fig. *h*).[1]

In the bas-reliefs of Kanheri, where the symbols of Buddhism are mingled with the reminiscences of an earlier form of worship, the Sacred Tree is sculptured as an object of veneration between two elephants facing one another, whilst in other bas-reliefs it is transformed, flanked by the same two elephants, into the Lotus-flower which forms the Throne of Buddha.[2] Lastly, after the extinction of Buddhism in India, it was resumed by the

Jewel Bearing Tree in Mr. W. R. Lethaby's recent work, *Architecture, Mysticism, and Myth.*

[1] A. CUNNINGHAM. *The Stupa of Bharhut.* London, 1879, pl. vi. and vii.

[2] FERGUSSON and BURGESS. *Cave Temples of India.* London, 1880, p. 350.

Brahmanical sects, which confined themselves to replacing Buddha on his Lotus Throne (still between the two elephants), by Parbati, the spouse of Vishnu.[1]   Moreover, we again meet with the Tree—in which Sir George Birdwood does not hesitate to recognize the Tree of Life—between two animals facing one another on the cloths, the carpets, the vases, and the jewels of contemporary India.[2]   In this last case, however, it is not always easy to discriminate whether we are in the presence of a survival of pre-Islamitic symbolism, or of a reaction of Sassanian art introduced into India by the Islamic invasions (*cf.* fig. 60 and pl. iv., fig. *i*).

The Phœnicians borrowed it from Mesopo-

FIG. 66.   STELE FROM CYPRUS.
(PERROT et CHIPIEZ, vol. iii., fig. 152.)

tamia more than a thousand years anterior to our era, developing its artificial appearance until all semblance of its arboreal origin has well-nigh vanished, to be replaced by an interlacing of spirals and strap-like curves (pl. iv.,

[1] MOOR. *Hindu Pantheon*, pl. 30.
[2] Sir GEORGE BIRDWOOD. *Industrial Arts of India.* London, 1880, p. 350.

fig. *b*). Some of those combinations, in which winged sphinxes cling to the spirals, betray a singular medley of Egyptian influences, whilst at the same time already suggesting the elegant modifications of Greek art.[1]

This type, as conventional as it is æsthetic, occurs wherever Phœnician influence was felt, more especially among the archaic pottery of Corinth and of Athens (pl. iv., fig. *f*). Perhaps it had already penetrated directly into Greece through Asia Minor, for it is seen on an *amphora*, discovered by General de Cesnola at Curium, which MM. Rayet and Collignon place among the vases with geometric decorations belonging to an

FIG. 67. VASE FROM CURIUM.
(CESNOLA. *Cyprus*, chap. i., p. 55.)

earlier time than the period of Phœnician influence. The Tree preserves here a more natural appearance; it is placed between two quadrupeds standing on their hind legs and overlooking the stem. This brings us back to the Chaldæan prototype of our fig. 65.

If it did not furnish the Greeks with the first idea of the palmette and the honeysuckle ornament, it certainly suggested the decoration of certain capitals, such as those of the temple of Apollo at Didyme, and of Athene Polias at Priene (pl. iv., fig. *e*).[2]

[1] SARA YORKE STEVENSON. *On certain Symbols of some Potsherds from Daphnæ and Naucratis.* Philadelphia, 1892, p. 13 *et seq.*
[2] O. RAYET and A. THOMAS. *Milet et le golfe Latinique.* Paris, 1877, pl. xvii., No. 9, and pl. xlix., No. 5.

Greece, however, seems only to have made use of it by way of exception.   If it penetrated into Italy, and even into Gaul, along with the other products of Oriental imagery, it did not become an ordinary motive of classic art.   We may draw attention to ˙ts presence, by the way, in a decorative painting ᴀt Corneto,[1] and on a Gallic coin found near Amiens, and attributed to the commencement of our era.

Following in the footsteps of M. Hucher, I had at first taken the object engraved on this coin be-

FIG. 68. GALLIC COIN.
(HUCHER.   *L'art gaulois*, vol. ii., p. 36.)

tween two quadrupeds to be a cup or drinking vessel.   But my attention has been directed to some intaglios of Cyprus, and even of Chaldæa, where the tree assumes the form of a staff supporting a semicircle, as in the figure 61*d* given above.   M. Hucher, with his usual perspicacity, thinks that the subject engraved on this coin belongs "to the same train of thought as that which in antiquity brought face to face the lions of Mycenæ on the gates of that town, and the lions of the Arab or Sassanian fabric of Mans on the shroud of St. Bertin, or even, in the thirteenth century, the doves with serpents' tails on the capitals of the cathedral at Mans."   It is strange to note the presence of the same theme, dealt with in an identical manner, on a *fibula* discovered

---

[1] J. MARTHA.   *Archéologie Etrusque et Romaine*.   Paris, fig. 8.

near Geneva, which M. Blavignac considers to be of Christian origin.[1]

However, it is by another way that it was introduced into Christian symbolism. It was, in fact, taken directly from the Persians by the Byzantines about the seventh century of our era. The influence of Sassanian art had made itself felt in the Byzantine Empire from the time of the death of Theodosus, if not earlier. " The Byzantines," says M. Charles Bayet, " did not invent all the ornamental combinations from which they got such pleasing effects; in this instance again they borrowed them from the East, and on the monuments of Persia models are found from which they drew their inspirations." [2] The same writer proves that in the sixth and seventh centuries the apartments of the rich, and even the treasures of the churches, were filled with stuffs which came from Persia, or which reproduced the subjects of Persian art.[3] It is related that even Justinian had employed a Persian architect to decorate several buildings in Constantinople.[4] Under these circumstances, how could the Byzantines help adopting one of the most pleasing and widely diffused Sassanian themes of decoration, which lent itself both to the refinements of ornamentation and to the fancies of the symbolical imagination ? This is, moreover, the way by which the whole fantastic fauna of the East entered Europe, to form the Christian symbolic menagery of the Middle Ages.[5]

[1] J. D. BLAVIGNAC. *Histoire de l'architecture sacrée à Genève.* Paris, Atlas, pl. ii., fig. 2.
[2] *L'Art Byzantin.* Paris, p. 60.
[3] *Id.*, chap. iii.
[4] BATISSIER, quoted by E. SOLDI. *Les Arts méconnus.* Paris, 1881, p. 252.
[5] The Tree between two lions facing one another appears already on an ivory casket which Millin attributes to an early period of the Byzantine Empire, and which is now in the

From the Grecian provinces it was introduced
into Italy, where it is often found in religious
architecture between the seventh and the eleventh
centuries in Sicily, at Ravenna, and especially at
Venice (see pl. iv., fig. *g*, and also fig. 58). Here
it was even taken up and reproduced by the
Renaissance, as may be seen at Santa Maria del
Miracoli, at the Scuola of San Marco, etc.[1]

Finally, it crossed the Alps with Roman art.
M. de Caumont was one of the first to draw attention to its presence amongst the sculptures of the
Roman period, in particular on a tympanum of
the church at Marigny, in the Calvados department. It is here sculptured between two lions,
which hold the stem with their fore-paws, and
bite at the extremities of the middle branches
(pl. iv., fig. *j*).[2]

What a strange fate for this antique symbol,
which, after being used for several thousand years
in the long since vanished worships of Higher Asia,
came thus to be stranded, in the western extremity
of Europe, on the sanctuary of a religion possessing
also amongst its oldest traditions the reminiscence
of the Paradisaical Trees of Mesopotamia![3]

cathedral of Sens. (*Voyage dans les Départements du Midi.*
Paris, 1807, pl. x. of Atlas.)

[1] BACHELIN DEFLORENNE. *L'Art, la Décoration et l'Orne-
ment des Tissus.* Paris, pl. iv. and xiii.

[2] It is generally the griffin which is chosen in preference,
perhaps because it symbolizes vigilance.

[3] The Arabs adopted it in their turn, when they had overthrown the Sassanian dynasty, but divesting it of all religious signification. Through their agency it reached Europe
towards the beginning of the Middle Ages, together with the
stuffs which are still extant in private and public collections, in
treasures of churches, and so forth. (See *Anciennes étoffes* in
the *Mélanges d'archéologie* of MM. Ch. Cahier and A. Martin,
vol. i., pl. 43; vol. ii., pl. 12 and 16; vol. iii., pl. 20 and 23;
vol. iv., pl. 24 and 25.) It is also to be seen on a golden vase,
adorned with enamelled partition work, which belongs to the
church of Saint-Martin-en-Valais, and which is said to have
been sent to Charlemagne by the Caliph Haroun Al Rashid.

EXPLANATION OF PLATE V.

Figure *a* is taken from an Assyrian cylinder (LAJARD. *Mithra*, pl. lxi., fig. 6).

Figure *b*, from the ornamentation of a Phœnician bowl (CLERMONT GANNEAU. *L'Imagerie phénicienne*, pl. vi.).

Figure *c*, from an imperial coin of Myra in Lycia (COLLIGNON. *Mythologie figurée de la Grèce*. Paris, Bibliothèque des Beaux-Arts, p. 10).

Figure *d*, from a Persian seal (LAJARD. *Mithra*, pl. xliv., xlvi., No. 3).

Figure *e*, from the sculptures in the caves of Kanerki (FERGUSON and BURGESS. *Cave Temples of India*, pl. x., fig. 35).

Figure *f*, from the bas-reliefs in the cave of Karli (MOOR. *Hindu Pantheon*, pl. lxxii.).

Figure *g*, from a wooden group in the Musée Guimet.

Figure *h*, from a Chaldean cylinder (LAJARD. *Mithra*, pl. xvi., fig. 4).

Figures *i* and *j*, from coins of the Javanese temples (MILLIES. *Monnaies de l'Archipel Indien*, pl. vi., fig. 50, and pl. ix., fig. 67).

Figure *k*, from a Maya manuscript known by the name of the *Fejervary Codex* (Publications of the *Bureau of Ethnography*. Washington, 1882, vol. iii., p. 32).

Figure *l*, from the ornamentation of a modern Syrian copper dish inscribed with cufic characters, presented by the Count Goblet d'Alviella to Sir George Birdwood.

Figure *m*, from the bas-reliefs of the cathedral at Monreale (D. B. GRAVINAT. *Il duomo di Monreale*. Palermo, 1859, pl. xv., *H*).

PLATE V.

FIG. *a*. From an Assyrian Cylinder.

FIG. *b*. From a Phœnician Bowl.

FIG. *c*. Imperial Coin of Myra in Lycia.

FIG. *d*. Persian Seal

FIG. *e*. Indian Sculpture.

FIG. *f*. Indian Sculpture.

FIG. *g*. Japanese Group.

FIG. *h*. From a Chaldean Cylinder.

FIG. *i*. Javanese Coin.

FIG. *j*. Javanese Coin.

FIG. *k*. Mexican Manuscript.

FIG. *l*. Syrian Ornamentation.

FIG. *m*. Sicilian Bas-relief.

B. The image of the Tree between two human (or semi-human) personages invariably facing one another followed at first almost the same route as the type whose migrations I have just described. The two themes are sometimes combined, as we see, in Assyria itself, on the cylinder reproduced above (fig. 64). Modified considerably by Greek art, like all symbols which made use of the human figure (pl. v., fig. *c*, and below, figs. 69 and 83), it remained more faithful to its earliest type in Phœnicia (pl. v., fig. *b*), in Persia (pl. v., fig. *d*), and even in India, where the two Assyrian eagle-headed *genii* (pl. v., fig. *a*), which advance towards the Tree holding the symbolical Cone, became the two *naga-rajahs*, or "snake-kings,"—their heads entwined with *cobras*—who support the stem of the Buddhist Lotus (pl. v., fig. *e*). In the grottoes of Karli this stem, which serves as a support to the Throne of the Master, stands erect both between two of those *naga-rajahs* and two deer facing one another (pl. v., fig. *f*).

These sculptures date back to a period which cannot be prior to the reign of Asoka, *i.e.*, the middle of the third century B.C., nor much later than the beginning of our era. It is interesting to again come across them, at an interval, perhaps, of two thousand years, in Japanese wooden groups of the seventeenth century belonging to the Guimet Museum. In one of them the *naga-rajahs* bear a genuine dragon on their shoulders; this substitution, together with some differences in the costume and the figure of these personages, is almost the only liberty which the native art took with the old Buddhist subject, long since forgotten in its original home (pl. v., fig. *g*).

From India it reached, in company with Buddhism, the island of Java, where we meet with it upon those curious medals of temples which the natives, although converted centuries ago to

Islamism, continue to wear by way of talismans. It occurs there, amongst other Buddhist symbols, between two figures with human bodies and beasts' or birds' heads,—which is surely the Mesopotamian conception in all its integrity (pl. v., figs. *i* and *j*).

It is also found in China on Taoist medals, recalling the coins of the Javanese temples.[1] Here, however, the disposition of the Tree, as also the costume of the personages, refer to quite a different type, whether it be that we are here in the presence of a corruption of Javanese coins, or that these, in imitating the Taoist coins, cast, so to speak, the subject of the latter in a mould provided by the Buddhist symbols of India.

From the Indian Archipelago—or from Eastern Asia—it may have even reached the New World, if we are to judge from the resemblance of the scene depicted on the Javanese medals to certain images found in manuscripts connected with the ancient civilization of Central America.

We have seen that the Cross was used, in the symbolism of the ancient inhabitants of America, to represent the winds which bring the rain. These crosses sometimes assume a tree-like form, and are then composed of a stem bearing two horizontal branches, with a bird perched on the fork, as in the famous *stele* of Palenque.[2] Moreover, this tree is sometimes placed between two personages facing one another, with a sort of wreath of feathers on their heads, who cannot but recall the monstrous aspect of the beings depicted on both sides of the Tree upon the medals of Javanese temples.   The reproduction which I

[1] Specimens of these medals are to be found in the department of medals in the Bibliothèque Nationale at Paris.

[2] A bird perched on the fork of the Sacred Tree is likewise seen on certain Persian cylinders. (LAJARD. *Mithra*, pl. LIVe fig. 6.)

here give (pl. v., fig. *k*) from the Fejervary Codex [1] shows up this parallel all the more, since it is placed close to medals of Java and underneath a Chaldæan cylinder which might be almost made the prototype of all these images (pl. v., fig. *h*).— We have here certainly fresh evidence in favour of the theory which already relies upon so many symbolical and ornamental similarities in order to discover, in the pre-Columbian civilization of America, the traces of intercourse with Japan, China, or the Indian Archipelago.

Finally, by a singular case of atavism, this subject, which already adorned the Chaldæan cylinders of five or six thousand years ago, re-appears in our own times in the decoration of the copper vases or plates, known as *mosouli*, which are still manufactured in Syria, on the banks of the Euphrates and the Tigris (pl. v., fig. *l*). There is still the palm-tree between its two acolytes,— henceforth dressed as *fellahin*,—who are engaged in plucking the two large fruits, or rather conventional *clusters*, suspended side by side beneath the crown.

On the other hand, it was quite adapted to furnish the first Christian artists with a model of the scene of the Temptation ; all that was needed was to give a different sex to the two acolytes (pl. v., fig. *m*). Already in the art of the Catacombs it frequently occurs with this application.[2]

The cabinet of antiquities at the Bibliothèque Nationale of Paris possesses a cameo which has likewise been held to represent the scene of the Temptation, although it depicts the quarrel between Poseidon and Athene under the sacred olive-

[1] CYRUS THOMAS. *Notes on certain Maya and Mexican Manuscripts*, in the publications of the *Bureau of Ethnology*. Washington, 1881-82, vol. iii., p. 32.

[2] GARUCCI. *Storia del'Arte christiana*. tab. xxiii., 1.

tree, in the presence of the serpent Erichthonios.[1]
What makes the case very interesting is, not only
that we have here engraved upon the stone the
Hebrew text of Genesis III. 6, but that we
also find at work those touching-up processes
which were sometimes made use of in order to

FIG. 69. ANTIQUE CAMEO.
(BABELON.   *Cabinet des Médailles*, pl. xxvi.)

adapt a pre-existent image to the expression of a
new tradition.

The olive-tree has been changed into an apple-
tree. Neptune's Trident and Minerva's Spear have
been scraped out. The attempt has even been

[1] BABELON. *Le Cabinet des Médailles à la Bibliothèque
nationale.* Paris, 1888, p. 79.

made to transform into some sort of a head-dress
the helmet, inappropriate enough, to be sure, on
the head of our first mother, and in her companion's hand has been placed a round object,
which may pass for an apple.

To be sure, the occurrence of the representation
of a tree between two animals or personages, even
when facing one another, is not in itself sufficient
for one to infer that it is connected with the types
described above. Yet, in the examples I have
given, the original identity of the inspiration may
be verified, not only by a general resemblance
spread throughout the whole image,—we might
call it a family likeness,—but also by the presence
of certain features, its ineffacable characteristics,
so to speak, by which it may everywhere be
recognized.

In the first place, there is the symmetry in the
expression and attitude of the two acolytes, often
also in the form of the Tree and the arrangement
of the branches. Then we have the presence,
often unaccountable, of a pair of volutes between
which the stem rises. These two spirals sometimes represent branches, or petals, of flowers
(pl. iv., figs. *a, b, c, e, g, i, j*, ; pl. v., figs. *a, d, h,
i, l*), sometimes curved horns (figs. 63, 64 ; pl. iv.,
figs. *a, b, e, f, g, i, j* ; pl. v., figs. *a, b, f, i, k*).
We may, perhaps, attribute their origin either
to the conventional representation of the *clusters*
which adorn the image of the Chaldæan Palm-
tree, or to the introduction of the horns which
were amongst the Assyrians a distinguishing sign
of the divinity.

Finally, a detail which seems to be equally
characteristic of the Sacred Tree in the most different countries is the appearance of serpents,
which sometimes twine themselves round the
stem (figs. 60, 69, 83 ; pl. iv., fig. *d* ; pl. v., figs. *c,
e, f, g, m*), and sometimes figure merely in the

background of the image (fig. 59, and pl. v., fig. *h*).

It must be observed that it is not the identity of the species of plants which constitutes the essential feature of the symbol through all its local modifications, but rather the constant reappearance of its hieratic accessories.

Each nation seems, indeed, to have introduced into this symbolical combination the tree which it deemed the most valuable. Thus we see depicted in turn the date-palm in Chaldæa, the vine or a cone-bearing plant in Assyria, the lotus in Phœnicia, and the fig-tree in India.[1]

Moreover, following in the footsteps of the Assyrians, who had inserted into this Tree features which were quite extraneous to the vegetable kingdom, some creeds replaced the plant itself by other sacred objects.

The Phrygians placed the representation of a pillar, a *phallus*, or an urn, between winged sphinxes,

FIG. 70. TOMB AT KUMBET.

(PERROT et CHIPIEZ. *Histoire de l'Art*, vol. v., fig. 84.)

lions, or bulls, facing each other, as is still to be seen on the pediments of the tombs hewn in the rocks of Phrygia. As M. Perrot observes : "Though one element is substituted for another,

[1] M. Didron observes, in his *Manuel d'iconographie chrétienne* (Paris, 1845, p. 80), that each Christian nation chose the plant which it preferred to represent the Tree of Temptation ; the fig and orange-trees in Greece, the vine in Burgundy and Champagne, the cherry-tree in the Isle of France, and the apple-tree in Picardy.

the group preserves none the less the same character." [1]

On a cylinder, which M. Menant considers of

FIG. 71. HITTITE CYLINDER.
(*De Clercq collection*, vol. i. of *Catalogue*, pl. xxviii., No. 289.)

Hittite origin, the arborescent stalk becomes a Winged Globe.

The Pelopides of Mycenæ, and, later, the Persians, put in its stead a pyre or fire-altar. [2]

FIG. 72. PERSIAN CYLINDER.
(CH. LENORMANT, in the *Mélanges d'archéologie*, vol. iii., pp. 130 and 131.)

The group which formerly surmounted the celebrated gate of Mycenæ certainly represented an object of this nature between lions facing one another (fig. 73).

The Buddhists introduced their principal "jewels" into the image, as may be seen in the following reproduction of a small portable altar, where the object, portrayed between two animals in a crouching attitude, represents perhaps the

<hr />

[1] PERROT et CHIPIEZ. *Op. cit.*, vol. v., p. 220.

[2] See a painted vase in the Blacas collection. (*Mém. de l'Acad. des inscr. et bel.-lett.*, vol. xvii., pl. viii.)

astronomical emblem of the nine planets, the

Fig. 73. Gate of Mycenæ.
(Schliemann. *Mycènes.*)

nava-ratna, borrowed by Buddhist symbolism from the Hindus (fig. 74).

Fig. 74. Tibetan Symbol.
(Hodgson. *Journ. of the Roy. Asiatic Soc.,* vol. xviii., 1st series, pl. i., No. 18.)

In Chinese and, perhaps, Japanese art, the "great jewel" becomes a pearl, frequently depicted between two dragons facing one another, with partly-open jaws. We may, perhaps, find a curious application of this symbol in the customs of the Chinese. M. de Groodt relates that in the festival of lanterns they lead about a dragon made of cloth and bamboo, before whose mouth they wave a round lantern like a ball or pearl of fire,—whether this scene represents the conflict of the celestial bodies with the devouring dragon, in keeping with the Chinese conception of eclipses, or the vain efforts of falsehood to swallow up truth.[1]

We have seen above that the Greeks, in imitation of the Phœnicians, represented between

FIG. 75*a*. BAS-RELIEF ON A SARCOPHAGUS.
(MILLIN. *Voyage dans le Midi*, pl. lxv.)

FIG. 75*b*. CHRISTIAN SCULPTURE OF THE THIRD CENTURY.
(ROLLER. *Catacombes*, vol. i., p. 53.)

two birds the *bethel* of the Cyprian Aphrodite and the *omphalos* of the Delphic Apollo, thus creating a new theme less extravagant and fantastic. The Christians, in their turn, from the time of the Catacombs, placed two figures on the sides of their principal emblems,—not only of the Cross, which is

[1] *Les fêtes annuelles à Emoui*, in vol. xi. of the *Annales du Musée Guimet*. Paris, 1886, p. 369.

also called "a Tree of Life," but also of the Chrism, the *labarum*, the *rouelle*, the Crown, the bunch of Grapes, the eucharistic Cup, and so forth.[1] Sometimes these figures are lambs, and sometimes peacocks, or doves (fig. 75, *a* and *b*).

Among the wooden ornaments of Romoaldus' episcopal throne in San Sabino at Canossa, we even find the mystic candelabrum thus sculptured between two griffins:

FIG. 76.   WOODEN SCULPTURE AT CANOSSA.
(H. W. SCHULTZ. *Kunst des Mittelalters in Italien*, pl. vi., fig. 1.)

Then chivalry placed its coats of arms between the two creatures facing one another,—lions, leopards, unicorns, griffins, giants, etc.   Charles Lenormant was not mistaken in saying, with respect to the filiation of these types: "When the use of armorial bearings began to develop in the West, Europe was deluged with the manufactured articles of Asia, and the first lions drawn on escutcheons were certainly copied from Persian and Arabian tissues.   These tissues themselves dated back, from one imitation to another, to the models from which, perhaps, over a thousand years before Christ, the author of the bas-reliefs of Mycenæ, drew his inspiration." [2]

The same tendency is still at work.   When, more than half-a-century ago, the *Royal Institute of British Architects* wished to have *armes parlantes*,

[1] ROLLER.   *Catacombes*, vol. i., pl. xi., figs. 3, 4, 19 to 34, etc.
[2] *Mélanges d'archéologie*, by MM. Martin and Cahier, vol. iii., p. 138.

it chose a Corinthian column, on the sides of which it placed two British lions facing each other.

Fig. 77. Seal of the *R. Inst. of British Architects.*

Some time ago, while on a visit to the fine estate, well-known in the country round Liege under the name of the Rond-Chêne, I observed, sculptured on a mantelpiece of recent construction, an oak of pyramidal form with a heraldic griffin on either side. On inquiring whether these were not the old armorial bearings of the domain, I was told that it was merely an artistic conceit, suggested by the name of the locality. I could not give a better instance of how the sculptor, or engraver, even whilst yielding to quite a different inspiration, upholds, nevertheless, a tradition unbroken for thirty centuries, and obeys, more or less consciously, a law which may be formulated thus: *When an artist wants to bring into prominence, as a symbol, the isolated image of an object which lends itself to a symmetrical representation*, particularly a tree or pillar, *he places on either side two creatures facing one another,*—giving rise sometimes, in return, to a myth or legend in order to account for the combination.

II. Signification of the Sacred Tree amongst the Semites.

We have just seen that the adoption of a complex symbol, such as the Assyrian image of the Sacred Tree, does 'not necessarily imply the acceptance of the myths with which it is connected in its original home. But if distrust is wise when it is a question of interpreting the earliest meaning of these images by means of the beliefs which they represent amongst nations unconnected with the Assyrians, such as the Hindus, the Greeks, the Christians, and the ancient inhabitants of America, this is no longer the case when we have to deal with nations belonging to the same race, or possessing at least a common fund of mythological traditions, as, for instance, almost all the inhabitants of Anterior Asia, from the Tigris to the Mediterranean; though, even then, we have to ascertain whether the interpretation which certain branches of the Semitic race give to their Sacred Trees meets with any confirmation in the texts of Mesopotamia properly so called.—We might afterwards, perhaps, go a step further, and find out, amongst some at least of the nations belonging to other races, whether, in their own traditions, there are not points of contact which justify or explain the assimilation of the Assyrian symbol.

The first question to be inquired into is as to whether we are not in the presence of a mere case of tree-worship. Nearly all nations, and the Semites in particular, venerated the trees which impressed them by the singularity of their forms, the vastness of their proportions, their great age, and especially by the usefulness of their fruits. The first beings, according to the Phœnician traditions, "'" consecrated the plants which grew on the earth; they made gods of them, and wor-

shipped the very things on which they lived,
offering up to them libations and sacrifices." [1]

M. Bonavia, a botanist who has subjected to a
minute examination the flora of the Mesopotamian
monuments, maintains that the sacred tree of Assyria
is merely an amalgamation of the plants formerly
venerated in that country by reason of their uses ;
the palm for its dates, the vine for its juice, the
pine-tree and the cedar for their timber and fire-
wood, the pomegranate for its services in the production of tannin and in the preparation of
sherberts. As for the horns grafted on the stem,
they would represent the horns of animals,—oxen,
wild-goats, ibex, and so forth,—which doubtless
were suspended from the branches to ward off the
evil eye. [2]

I would be the first to admit that purely utili-
tarian considerations of this kind had originally
suggested to the Mesopotamians the worship of
certain trees which were afterwards used to represent the Sacred Tree. Yet the boldly conventional
form of the latter,—the nature of its hieratic accessories, starting with the symbolical horns of the
divinity,—its frequent association with the figure
of the supreme God,—the prominence everywhere
accorded, in public worship, to its representations,
—already imply that it not only exhibits the image
of a plant venerated for its natural qualities, but
that it must be something more ; either the vegetable symbol of a divine power, like the *ashêrah*
mentioned in the Bible, or the *simulacrum* of a
mythical plant like the Winged Oak, on which—
according to a Phœnician tradition quoted by
Pherecydes of Syros—the supreme God had woven
the earth, the starry firmament, and the ocean.

Let us therefore carefully consider what share

---

[1] EUSEBIUS. *Præparatio Evangelica*, i. 9.
[2] E. BONAVIA. *The Sacred Trees of the Assyrian Monuments*,
in the *Babylonian and Oriental Record*, vol. iii., pp. 1-6.

conceptions of this kind may have had in the mythology of the Semitic nations.

In the first place, these peoples frequently represented by a tree the female personification of Nature, who, under various names, and even with different attributes, seems above all to have embodied in their opinion the conceptions of life, of fecundity, and of universal renovation : Istar, Mylitta, Anat, Astarte, Tanit, and others.—At Heliopolis, where the worship of the Great Goddess prevailed, coins present to our view a cypress of pyramidical form, planted beneath the peristyle of a temple, in the very place where other medals have either a Conical Stone, the well-known representation of Astarte, or else the image, or bust, of the Goddess herself.[1]

Movers informs us that the Venus of Lebanon bore the local name of the Cypress.[2] At Rome there is an altar of the Palmyrene which exhibits on one of its sides the image of a solar god, and on the other a cypress of pyramidical form, whose foliage admits a child carrying a ram upon its shoulders.[3] M. Lajard quotes in this instance the story related of Apuleius, who, wishing to paint the son of Venus in his mother's lap, depicted him in the foliage of a cypress.[4] To the same class of images belongs the pine in which Cybele imprisons the body of Atys till the spring-time. This tree has been thought to be the *simulacrum* of the solar god ; it seems to me more logical to seek therein the symbol of the Matrix in which Atys awaits his annual resuscitation.

We are all acquainted with the legend of Myrrha,

---

[1] F. LAJARD, in the *Mémoires de l'Académie des inscriptions et belles-lettres*. Paris, 1854, vol. xx., 2nd part, pl. vi.

[2] MOVERS. *Die Phönicier*, vol. i., ch. xv.

[3] *Mémoires de l'Académie des inscriptions et belles-lettres*, vol. xx., pl. i., fig. 2.

[4] *Ibid.*, vol. xx., p. 221.

another Asiatic variety of Artemis-Aphrodite. Myrrha, bearing Adonis, was transformed into a tree, and, according to a version recorded by Hyginus, was set free by the stroke of an axe. Now, on an imperial coin of Myra, in Lycia, a tree is seen whose fork supports the image of a goddess (pl. v., fig. c). On either side is a wood-cutter with a raised axe. Whatever the meaning of this scene may have been in the local mythology of the period, it is difficult not to refer it to the Oriental representations of the Sacred Tree, in so far as it was a *simulacrum* of the Goddess.

In Palestine, the Bible tells us, they venerated, beside the *stelai* or *hâmmânim* symbolizing Baal, *simulacra* of Ashtaroth, representing this goddess of the fruitful and nourishing earth under the form of a tree, or rather stake, begirt with drapery and bandelets. These are the *ashêrîm* which the Hebrews, in spite of the upbraidings of the prophets of *Yahveh*, did not cease to " construct " and " plant," in imitation of the former inhabitants of the country, from the time when the twelve tribes settled in the land of Canaan [1] till the day on which the King Josiah burnt, near the Kedron, the *ashêrah* set up by Manasseh in the temple of Jerusalem itself.[2]

The *ashêrah* must then have been a *simulacrum*, which, like our May-Poles laden with conventional attributes, was at once artificially constructed and planted in the ground. The Sacred Tree of the Mesopotamian monuments exhibits this feature more than once. From the earliest times of Chaldæan engraving, it occurs, as I have above mentioned, under the form of a staff placed on a support and crowned by two branches. On a cylinder found by M. de Sarzec at Telloh, two long strings, plaited like whip-cord, are even seen

---

[1] *Judges* iii., 7.
[2] *2 Kings* xxi., 3, and xiii., 6 and 7.

descending from the fork of the tree. According
to M. J. Menant, all that it has been possible to
find out from the archaic inscription on this cylinder
is that it relates to a goddess invoked by a prince
who proclaims himself her servant.[1]

FIG. 78. CHALDÆAN CYLINDER.
(HEUZEY. *La Masse d'armes*. Paris, 1887, p. 15.)

On other cylinders, reproducing scenes of
adoration, or of sacrifice, the rudimentary tree
sometimes accompanies and sometimes replaces
the image of a naked woman with her heels
touching and hands turned towards her breasts.
Now, this hieratic type is incontestably the representation of Istar, not the chaste and warlike Istar
who was worshipped at Nineveh, but the voluptuous and procreative Istar venerated in particular
at Babylon, and more or less related to the goddess
of the *ashêrim*.[2]

This might justify the hypothesis of M. François
Lenormant, who not only sought an equivalent of
the *ashêrah* in the Sacred Tree of Mesopotamia, but
who also descried,—in the combination so often reproduced in Assyria of the Winged Circle suspended over the Sacred Tree,—the old cosmo-

---

[1] J. MENANT. *Les pierres gravées de la Haut-Asie*, vol. i.,
p. 220.
[2] ID., *ibid.*, vol. i., pp. 170 *et seq.*

gonical pair of Assur and his companion, the creative heaven and the productive earth.[1]

It ought to be noticed that the representations of the Sacred Tree in art become particularly frequent under the Sargonidæ. According to Mr. Boscawen, the symbolical image of the Tree between the two *genii* is not found prior to the ninth century before our era;[2] and, with rare exceptions, is met with on Assyrian, not on Babylonian monuments. Now it was especially at the time of the Sargonidæ or at least during the second Assyrian empire, that Istar was placed beside Assur as a divinity of the first rank.

There remains to be seen what could have given the Semites the idea of representing by a tree their Great Goddess of Nature. I will here call attention to the interesting essay which Mr. Edw. B. Tylor published in the *Proceedings of the Society of Biblical Archæology* of June, 1890, under the title of *Winged Figures of the Assyrian and other ancient Monuments.* The learned Oxford professor points out that in by far the greater number of cases the Sacred Tree of the Assyrian monuments exhibits the form of the palm, and also that the two *genii* seem to hold towards the tree the point of a conical object, with a reticulated surface, exactly similar to the inflorescence of the male palm. On a bas-relief in the Louvre one of the *genii* is even seen putting this object into one of the palmettes at the end of the branches.

We have therefore here a representation of the fertilization of the palm by the artificial transference of the pollen to the clusters of the female or date-bearing tree, a process which was known to

---

[1] F. Lenormant. *Les origines de l'histoire.* Paris, 1880, vol. i., p. 88.

[2] *Babylonian and Oriental Record*, vol. iv., No. 4, p. 95.— Yet in the Louvre there is a specimen found in the palace of Ashur-bani-pal (tenth century B.C.).

the Mesopotamians, as passages from Herodotus and Theophrastus formally prove.[1]

Others have maintained that this object was the cone of a pine or cedar, a fruit well known for

FIG. 79. ASSYRIAN BAS-RELIEF.
(PERROT et CHIPIEZ. *Histoire de l'Art antique*, vol. ii., f. 8.)

its prophylactic reputation amongst the Assyrians. In adopting this theory, M. Bonavia adds that the fir-cone doubtlessly performed the function of an *aspergillum*. The *genii* would have it to be-sprinkle the Tree with the lustral water taken from the receptacle which they carried in the other hand, a receptacle which M. Bonavia takes to be

[1] "Palm-trees," says Herodotus in his description of Chaldæa, "grow in great numbers in the whole of the flat country; most of them bear a fruit which supplies the inhabitants with bread, wine, and honey. They are cultivated like the fig-tree, particularly in the following respect: The natives tie the fruit of the male palm, as the Greeks call it, to the branches of the date-bearing palm, in order to let the gall-fly enter the dates and ripen them and prevent the fruit from falling off. (*Hist.*, liv. i., 193.—See also THEOPHRASTUS. *Hist. plant.*, ii., c. 2, 6, and 7, 4.)

a metal bucket, and Mr. Tylor a wicker basket. We would thus be in the presence of a true scene of exorcism such as are described in the magic texts of the period. Water, consecrated by certain *formulæ*, figures indeed with many nations among the procedures employed to put demons to flight.[1]

M. Bonavia, besides, adduces the testimony of an Oriental, alleging that certain sects use to this day a fir-cone for their sacred sprinklings.[2]

Nevertheless, the monuments seem to decide in favour of Mr. Tylor, who places side by side the Cone represented in the hand of the *genii* and

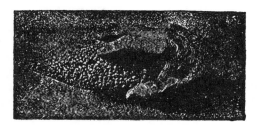

FIG. 80. INFLORESCENCE OF THE MALE DATE-PALM.

the inflorescence of the male date-palm copied from nature (fig. 80).

As a complete representation of the scene already become mythical, Mr. Tylor reproduces a bas-relief on which—in front of the two *genii* who advance towards the Tree with the inflorescence in one hand—we find two personages kneeling in an attitude of invocation, and holding the end of

---

[1] M. F. LENORMANT quotes the following passage from the *Cuneiform Inscriptions of Western Asia*, vol. iv., pl. 16, 2 : "Take a vase, put water into it, place therein white cedar-wood, introduce the charm which comes from Eridu, and perfect thus potently the virtue of the enchanted waters." (*Origines de l'Histoire*, vol. i., p. 84, note.)

[2] *Babylonian and Oriental Record*, vol. iv., No. 4, p. 96.

an undulating ribbon which falls from the Winged
Disc depicted above the tree.

These personages have generally been taken to
be praying, and the two ribbons to be the symbol
of the tie which unites the god to his worshippers.

FIG. 81. ASSYRIAN BAS-RELIEF.
(LAYARD. *Monuments of Nineveh*, pl. 59A.)

Mr. Tylor sees therein two cords by which the
deities guide or maintain the solar Globe above
the palm-tree in order to hasten the ripening of
the dates, whilst the two customary genii prepare
to accomplish their fertilizing mission.

The representation of the Sacred Tree, in which
the traces of a deep and mysterious symbolism
have so often been sought, would therefore only
have the practical import of a scene drawn from
everyday life. As for the intervention of superhuman personages in an operation generally
accomplished by the hand of man, this would be
merely a proof of the importance which the
Mesopotamians attached to the cultivation of
their palms and the fertilization of their fruits—at
most an historical myth, attributing to gods the
invention of one of the processes which have most
contributed towards securing these results.—Is
this not what seems to be designated by the
presence of the inflorescence in the hand of a
personage dressed in the skin of a fish, Dagon or
Oannes, the amphibious god who is held to have

instructed the Chaldæans in agriculture, as also in literature, the arts, and the other elements of civilization?

I consider that Mr. Tylor has thoroughly grasped the primitive and somewhat material meaning of the subject handled in his essay. I have, however, already had occasion to show that, amongst the Assyrians, this subject had above all a symbolical acceptation. It must be remembered that they could not attach to the cultivation of the date-palm the same importance as the inhabitants of Lower Chaldæa. In fact, though the palm grows in Assyria, the date does not ripen there. They must therefore have seen in this figured representation something else and something more than the artificial fertilization of the palm.

Mr. Tylor himself suggests, by way of hypothesis, that the *genii* facing one another might either represent the fertilizing winds, or the divinities whose fertilizing influence was typified by the artificial fecundation of the palm. This operation would therefore have become the symbol of *natural* fertilization, or rather of fertilization brought about by what we call natural agents, and which the Mesopotamians looked upon as personifications of the divine forces of Nature.

May we not go further, and inquire if this process might not have supplied a symbol of fertilization *in general*, a symbolical representation of the mysterious operation everywhere performed, under the most different forms, by the fertilizing forces of Nature?

The Tree thus represented is—as we have seen —far from being always a palm; sometimes it is a vegetable species which does not admit of this method of fertilization. Moreover, there are monuments on which the *genii* are seen holding the Cone, not towards a tree, but towards the face of a king or some other personage. The object in question must here have a vivifying, or at least a prophylactic import, like the cedar or fir-cone. " Take the fruit of the cedar "—we read in one of the passages on which François Lenormant hinged his assumption that the *genii* held a fruit of this tree in one hand—" and hold it to the face of the sick person ; the cedar is the tree that produces the pure charm and drives away the unfriendly demons, spreaders of snares." [1]

On an archivolt of Khorsabad two winged *genii* are seen holding the inflorescence in the direction of a Rosette. According to Mr. Tylor,

FIG. 82. BAS-RELIEF OF KHORSABAD.
(V. PLACE. *Nimroud et l'Assyrie*, vol. iii. pl. 15.)

this Rosette would be nothing else than the crown of a palm-tree seen from below or above. But, in general, the Rosette—whether derived from the rose, the lotus, or any other flower—forms an essentially solar symbol, and the *genii* who here advance towards it can have no other function—if this scene has a symbolical import—than to revive the power of the sun, to fertilize the calyx from which he issues forth at each succeeding dawn, or perhaps to gather his vivifying emanations for the replenishment of their sacred instrument. It is noteworthy that they hold the latter exactly as the gods of Egypt sometimes handle the Key of Life.

[1] *Origines de l'histoire.* Paris, 1880, vol. i., pp. 83-84.)

In short, the Assyrians seem to have drawn from the sexual relations of plants, or, properly speaking, of the palm, the same symbolism, relating to the renewal and communication of life, as did other nations from human sexuality. It is, moreover, quite conceivable that the inflorescence of the date-palm may have performed the symbolical function which elsewhere devolved upon the *phallus*, as the pre-eminent emblem of the fertilizing force. As for the palm, it naturally became, in this order of images, the symbol of generative nature, or, to be more exact, of the Universal Matrix so plainly personified amongst the Mesopotamians, and even the Semites generally, by the great astral, or terrestrial goddess, represented in the *ashêrah*.

Yet the two *genii* with the inflorescence are not the only acolytes who appear, in Assyria, round the Tree. We have seen (pl. v.) that the latter are often two monsters—griffins, unicorns, or sphinxes—represented for quite a different purpose. On a cylinder reproduced above (fig. 64) both *genii* stand erect on a sphinx which places a foot on one of the lower branches of the Tree, and puts forward its head as if to bite at one of the pomegranates at the end of the branches. This change of attitude would seem to correspond with a variation of the myth; the monsters approach the Tree as if they intended to pluck a fruit or a flower, and this idea becomes still more accentuated if we pass to the neighbouring nations, such as the Phœnicians and Persians, who took from the Assyrians the type of their Sacred Tree, but without either the two winged *genii*, or the inflorescence of the male palm. Now, we know that the Persians possessed the tradition of a Tree of Life, the *haoma*, whose sap conferred immortality. We find also, amongst the Western Semites, the belief in a Sacred Tree whose fruit had the same power. It will be remembered that the Book of Genesis places in the Garden of Eden two Paradisaical Trees, " the Tree of Life in the midst of the garden, and the Tree of Knowledge of good and evil."[1] When the first human pair, following the treacherous advice of the serpent, had tasted of the fruit of the Tree of Knowledge in spite of the explicit command of the Creator, the latter drove out the guilty ones from the Garden of Eden, saying : " Behold ; the man is become as one of us to know good and evil : and now, lest he put forth his hand and take also of the Tree of Life, and eat, and live for ever ; "[2] therefore He drove them out, and placed at the east of the Garden of Eden *kerubim* with the flaming sword which turned every way, to keep the way of the Tree of Life.

It is now no longer possible to interpret the traditions of the Hebrew people without connecting them with the beliefs of the other Semitic nations. Have we not learnt from the version of the Deluge, discovered some years ago in the cuneiform writings, how the Israelitish nation preserved certain Chaldæan myths, whilst transfiguring them by doing away with their polytheistic elements and by introducing a moral factor ? The Bible itself dates its oldest traditions from Chaldæa, particularly the narratives referring to the Garden of Eden and its Paradisaical Trees. We will not here enter into the question as to whether the traditional Eden should be located in Mesopotamia or further towards the north-east. But the *kerubim* who guard its entrance certainly seem to be a creation of the mind revealed in the art and the creeds of Mesopotamia. They have nothing in common with the chubby *cherubs* of the Christian imagery ; they bear a far stronger resemblance to the monstrous *genii* who guard the approaches to the Assyrian palaces ; their name

---

[1] *Gen.* ii., 9.   [2] *Gen.* iii., 22-24.

in the Bible itself alternates with *shôr*, "a bull," and numerous indications lead us to assume that they were either winged bulls with the face of a man,[1] or winged *genii* with the head of an eagle.[2] In the description of the Temple which Ezekiel has left us, he says that the ceiling was "made with *kerubim* and palm-trees, so that a palm-tree was between a *kerub* and a *kerub*."[3] This is exactly the position of the Sacred Tree between its acolytes on the monuments of Mesopotamia.

Moreover, certain cuneiform texts seem to prove that the Assyro-Chaldæans were acquainted with a "Tree of Life." Whether it was thus styled because it served as a *simulacrum* of the Goddess of Life, or whether it represented this divinity by reason of its own mythical function, the fact is none the less certain, according to Mr. Sayce, that the "divine Lady of Eden," or Edin, was termed in Northern Babylonia "the goddess of the Tree of Life,"[4] and Babylon, before receiving from the Semites the name of *Bab Ilu*, "Gate of God," was called, in the old language of the country, Tin-tir-ki, or Dintir-ra, which most Assyriologists translate as "the place of the Tree (or Grove) of Life."[5]

As for the fruits depicted on the Sacred Tree, whether they be clusters of dates, or bunches of grapes, they are naturally adapted to a Tree of Life, since they yield some of those fermented liquors which in ordinary language still bear the name of *eau de vie*.[6]

---

[1] PERROT et CHIPIEZ. *Histoire de l'art dans l'antiquité*, vol. iv., p. 305.—Regarding the word *kerub* = bull, *cf.* LENORMANT. *Orig. de l'hist.*, vol. i., p. 112.

[2] Ezekiel defines the kerubim as beings with a double pair of wings, having beneath their wings a man's hand.

[3] *Ezekiel* xli., 8.

[4] A. H. SAYCE. *The Religions of the Ancient Babylonians.* London, 1887, p. 240.

[5] F. LENORMANT. *Origines de l'histoire*, vol. i., p. 76.

[6] In the Assyrian language the vine was called *karânu*,

Sometimes they unquestionably represent pomegranates. Now the pomegranate, which contains hundreds of seeds, has at all times been considered an emblem of fertility, of abundance, and of life. All Semitic nations have used it, as a symbol, on the most different kinds of religious monuments, from the pillars of Solomon's temple [1] to the *stelai* dedicated to the divinities of Libya.[2] The Tree of Life depicted amongst the bas-reliefs of the Parma baptistery bears pomegranates for its fruit,[3] and it is also a pomegranate which, according to a tradition related by M. de Gubernatis, was the fruit that Eve offered Adam.[4]

It must be remarked that, on some Assyrian bas-reliefs, the climbing plant interlacing the sacred tree bears a strong likeness to the *Asclepias acida*.[5] Now, as we shall see further on, this is the very shrub which supplied the Hindus and the Persians with their elixir of life.

Finally it is the Lotus-flower, which, contrary to all the rules of botany, sometimes blossoms upon the Sacred Tree and is plucked or smelt by the two acolytes.

We have seen how this flower, which discloses itself every morning to the sun's rays, evoked ideas of resurrection and immortality amongst all the ancient nations of the East. When, therefore,

which means, according to M. Terrien de la Couperie, *the Tree of the Drink of Life*. (*Babylonian and Oriental Record*. October, 1890, p. 247.)

[1] *Kings* vii., 18-20.

[2] PH. BERGER. *Représentations figurées des stèles puniques*, in the *Gazette archéologique* for 1877, p. 27.

[3] M. LOPEZ, in the *Revue archéologique* for 1853, vol. xx., p. 289.—Here again the Tree, embraced by a dragon, stands between two animals facing one another.

[4] *Mythologie des plantes*, vol. ii. p. 167.

[5] Sir George Birdwood, who understands the subject in his two-fold capacity of naturalist and archæologist, bears witness to this resemblance in the most explicit terms (*Industrial Arts of India*, part ii. p. 430).

we find it on the Sacred Tree of the Phœnicians or the Assyrians, we have every reason to believe that it there represents a " flower of life." This divine flower, like the fruit of the Tree of Life, will doubtlessly have figured in myths whose text has not come down to us, but whose existence is sufficiently revealed by the monuments. In any case, the meaning of this symbolical efflorescence seems to be plainly enough indicated in a scene engraved upon a bowl of Phœnician origin, which M. de Cesnola discovered at Amathus in the island of Cyprus. The Sacred Tree here stands, in its most artificial form, between two personages clad in the Assyrian manner, who with the one hand pluck a Lotus-blossom from its branches, and in the other hold a *crux ansata* (see above, pl. v., fig. *b*). The Phœnicians, whose symbols were almost all derived from Egypt on the one side and Mesopotamia on the other, must have known what they were about in thus connecting the Sacred Tree with the Lotus-flower and the Key of Life. It would have been difficult to better express the equivalence of these two symbols.[1]

It is evident that, in the absence of texts serving as a direct commentary on the representations of the Sacred Tree amongst the Semites, other hypotheses again may be formulated upon its original or derived meaning.

Thus the Chaldæans must be included amongst the nations who saw in the universe a tree whose summit was the sky, and whose foot or trunk was the earth.[2]

[1] In Egypt itself, on a monument of the sixth dynasty, the Atlas of Lepsius shows us a queen with the Key of Life in one hand, and in the other a lotus whose calyx she holds to her nose.

[2] M. W. MANSELL points out that the term *gis*, a tree, occurs in a lexicographical tablet amongst the figurative expressions which serve to designate heaven (*Gazette archéologique*, 1878, p. 134.)

To be sure, this somewhat puerile conception of the universe seems to have been early thrown into the shade, in Mesopotamia, by the more subtle cosmogonical system which, according to Diodorus, made of the earth a boat floating upside down on the watery abyss.[1] The boat in question was one of those, shaped like a bowl or cauldron, which are portrayed in the bas-reliefs of Mesopotamia, and are still used at the present day in the basin. of the Euphrates. The hollow interior formed the region of darkness, the domain of the dead and of the terrestrial spirits ; at the top stood an immense mountain whose summit served as a pivot to the firmament, and from whose sides flowed the principal rivers.

This "Mountain of the World," or axis of the universe, became the object of quite an especial veneration. The Assyrians located it in the high chains of mountains north-east of Mesopotamia. The Chaldæans named after it some of the great staged temples which they built in the plains of their country.[2] It must be observed, however, that some hymns address it in terms which are perfectly applicable to a huge tree : " O thou who givest shade, Lord who casteth thy shadow over the land, great mount, father of the god Mul ! "[3] Another hymn terms it a " mighty mountain whose head rivals the heavens and whose foundations rest on the pure deep." [4]

Texts, moreover, prove in a decisive manner that the notion of the Cosmogonical Tree had endured into the traditions, at least, of certain local mythologies. A bilingual hymn of Eridu, that ancient centre of civilization which, at the dawn of

---

[1] Diod. Sicul. *Hist.*, vol. ii., 31.

[2] Sayce. *Op. cit.*, p. 405 *et seq.*

[3] Quoted by De Gubernatis. *Mythologie des plantes*, vol. i., p. 45.

[4] Sayce. *Op. cit.*, p. 362.

history, flourished on the borders of the Persian Gulf, mentions a dense tree that grew on a holy spot. " Its root (or fruit) of white crystal stretched towards the deep. . . . . Its seat was the (central) place of the earth; its foliage was the couch of Zikum the (primæval) mother. Into the heart of its holy house which spreads its shade like a forest hath no man entered; there (is the home of) the mighty mother who passes across the sky; (in) the midst of it was Tammuz." [1]

This passage seems to connect the Cosmogonical Tree with the Great Goddess of Nature. Whether the latter be regarded as a celestial, telluric, or lunar divinity, Tammuz, the sun, is at once her spouse and child. A cylinder, which M. Menant attributes to the ancient art of Chaldæa, shows us the goddess beside the Sacred Tree, with an infant seated in her lap.[2] Perhaps we ought to see in this the prototype of similar representations wherein Isis, Tanit, and other mother goddesses appear, each with her son, the young solar god.

Another reference to the Cosmogonical Tree occurs in a passage concerning the exploits of Izdhubar or Gilgames, the Chaldæan Hercules. This mythical personage having reached the "gates of the Ocean" encounters a forest of trees "resembling the trees of the gods" which bore "fruits of emerald and crystal." Marvellous birds live amongst the branches; they build "nests of precious stones." The hero strikes one of these birds in order to pluck " a large crystal fruit," and then he wishes to withdraw; but he finds the door

---

[1] SAYCE. *Op. cit.*, p. 238.—M. F. Lenormant has published a slightly different translation of this passage (*Origines de l'histoire*, vol. ii., p. 104). But the variations do not bear upon the cosmogonical character of the Tree. M. Terrien de la Couperie considers that the plant in question is not so much a tree as a stem similar to the stakes which support the tents (*Babylonian and Oriental Record*, vol. iv. No. 10, p. 221).

[2] J. MENANT. *Pierres gravées*, vol. i., fig. 104.

of the garden closed by one of the female guardians who live "in the direction of the Ocean." The rest of the passage is missing. These details, however, suffice for us to infer that here again the subject in question is a celestial tree, bearing, for fruits, the planets, the stars, and all the "jewels" of the firmament.[1] One cannot but be struck by the strange similarities which this story offers to the legend of Herakles carrying off the golden apples from the garden of the Hesperides, "in the direction of the night, beyond the ocean stream."[2]

Might not the Sacred Tree have likewise served to portray, amongst the Chaldæans, an equivalent of the tree designated, in the Bible, as giving the knowledge of good and evil? M. Sayce does not seem unwilling to admit this comparison. He gives prominence to the fact that the name of the god Ea was written upon the heart of the cedar. Now not only was Ea the god of wisdom, but the possession of his sacred names communicated his own knowledge to him who pronounced them.[3] A passage explicitly associates with the cedar "the revelation of the oracles of heaven and earth."[4]

Moreover, the scene of the Temptation is believed to have been discovered on a cylinder in the British Museum. Two personages, in whom Mr. G. Smith thought he recognized a man and a woman, stretch forth a hand towards a tree from which hang two large fruits; behind the woman a serpent erects itself on its tail (see above, pl. v., fig. h).[5] M. J. Menant, however, maintains that both personages belong to the stronger sex; in any case, he adds, nothing authorizes us, in face of

[1] G. W. Mansell. *Un épisode de l'épopée chaldéennes,* in the *Gazette archéologique* for 1879.
[2] Hesiod. *Theogony,* v. 274-275.
[3] A. H. Sayce. *Op. cit.,* p. 133 *et seq.*
[4] *Id.,* p. 242.
[5] G. Smith. *Chaldæan account of Genesis.* London, p. 91.

the silence of the texts, to discern in this scene the Scriptural account of the "original sin."[1] At the same time—whilst pointing out that subjects of this kind may lend themselves to innumerable interpretations—he calls attention to another cylinder which might still better be compared with the Biblical narrative. It is the representation of a garden where trees and birds are visible; in the middle stands a palm, whose fruits two personages are engaged in plucking, whilst a third, himself holding a separate fruit, seems to address them.[2]

The comparison attempted by M. Baudissin between the Tree of Knowledge and the Prophetic Trees whose office was to reveal the future seems to be less exposed to criticism.[3] The Chaldæo-Assyrians, in the manner of all the Semitic nations, practised *phyllomancy, i.e.,* the art of divination by the rustling of leaves, which was held to be the voice of the divinity.[4] Now, endeavours to gain a foreknowledge of the decrees of the divine will are often considered an encroachment upon the celestial power, a rash act, or even a sacrilege, which calls for punishment.

Cuneiform tablets, commented upon by Mr. Sayce, tell the story of a god Zu who, covetous of the supreme rank, abstracted the "tablets of fate" as well as the attributes of Bel, and having made good his escape in a storm, began to divulge the knowledge of the future. After consulting the principal gods, Bel, to punish him, contented himself with changing him into a bird of prey and exiling him, like another Prometheus, upon a distant mountain. According to Mr. Sayce, Zu is

---

[1] J. MENANT. *Pierres gravées*, vol. i., pp. 189-191.

[2] J. MENANT. *Pierres gravées*, vol. i., fig. 121.

[3] W. BAUDISSIN. *Studien zur semitischen Religiongeschichte*, vol. iii., p. 227.

[4] F. LENORMANT. *La divination chez les Chaldéens*. Paris, 1875, p. 85.

none other than " the bird of the storm," common to so many mythologies, which, in the rolling of the thunder, discloses to mankind the secrets of the future, the knowledge of good and evil.[1] It might almost be said that this legend lies mid-way between the Scriptural account of " the original sin " and the Aryan traditions, which we are about to investigate, regarding the theft of fire and ambrosia from the branches of the Cosmogonical Tree.

Finally, Professor Terrien de la Couperie, having noticed that the Sacred Tree of Mesopotamia frequently exhibits the same number of branches (7, 14, 15 or 30), thinks he finds therein an accordance with the days of the lunar month. He instances, in this connection, a Chinese tradition, prior to our era, which tells of a wonderful plant that appeared on both sides of the staircase of the imperial palace, during the reign of Yao.[2] On this plant a pod grew every day of the month till the fifteenth ; then one fell every day till the thirtieth ; if the month had only twenty-nine days, a pod withered without falling off. It is not difficult to descry in this plant a lunar tree ; the Chinese themselves termed it the Calendar Plant, *lik-kiep.*

We must wait for more decisive proofs before admitting that the Sacred Tree of the Assyrians permitted of a similar interpretation on account of the number of the branches, which does not always agree—indeed quite the contrary—with the subdivisions of the lunar month. We have, however, evidence that the Calendar Plant was not unknown to the Semites, and that it occurred amongst them in connection with the Tree of Life. The Apocalypse (xxii., 2), places in the midst of the celestial Jerusalem "the Tree of Life, which bare twelve manner of fruits, and yielded her fruit every month:

---

[1] SAYCE. *Op. cit.,* pp. 294-300.
[2] *The Calendar Plant of China,* in the *Babylonian and Oriental Record* for September, 1890, p. 218.

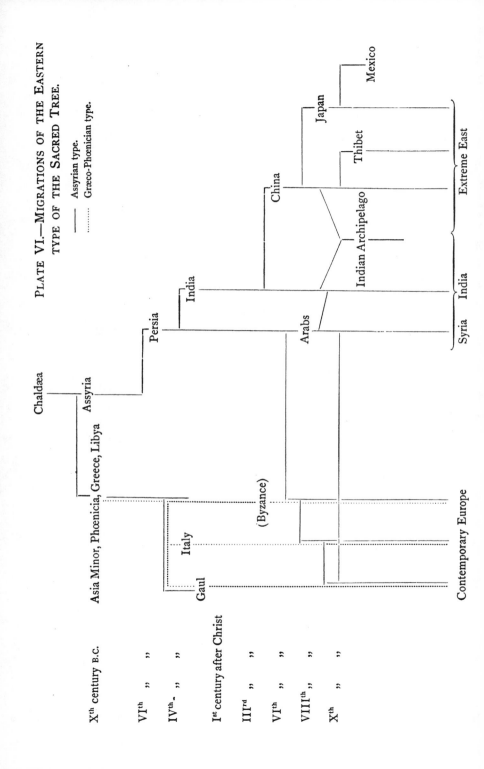

PLATE VI.—MIGRATIONS OF THE EASTERN TYPE OF THE SACRED TREE.

——— Assyrian type.
.... Græco-Phœnician type.

and whose leaves were for the healing of the nations."

Moreover, M. Terrien de la Couperie has shown that the belief in a Tree of Life existed amongst the Chinese. Traditions mention seven wonderful trees which grew on the slopes of the Kuen-Lün mountains. One of them, which was of jade, conferred immortality by its fruit.[1] The question—which I do not pretend to decide—is as to whether this tradition crossed directly from Mesopotamia into China, some forty centuries before our era, or whether it reached that country either by way of Persia or of India at a less distant period.

III. The Paradisaic Trees of the Aryans.

Not only do the different species of mythical trees which we have just met with amongst the Semites occur amongst the Indo-Europeans, and the Hindus in particular, but nowhere can the ties which link the Tree of the Universe to the Tree of Life and the Tree of Knowledge be more clearly perceived than amongst the traditions of the latter nation.

The Vedas make mention of the tree whose foot is the earth, and whose summit is heaven.[2]

Sometimes it is the tree of the starry firmament whose fruits are precious stones, at other times it is the tree of the cloudy sky whose roots or branches shoot out over the canopy of heaven, like those sheaves of long and fine-spun clouds which, in the popular meteorology of our country, have been named *Trees of Abraham*. Amongst its branches it holds imprisoned the fire of the light-

---

[1] *Babyl. and Oriental Record* for June, 1888, pp. 149-159.

[2] "Which is the forest," asks the Vedic poet, "which is the tree wherein they have hewn heaven and earth?" (*Rig-Veda*, x., 81, 4.)

ning. Through its leaves it distills the elixir of life, the celestial *soma* or *amrita, i.e.,* the vivifying waters "which Mitra and Varuna, the two kings with the beautiful hands, watch amidst the clouds."[1] It also forms the way to the other side of the atmospheric ocean, beyond the river which possesses or procures everlasting youth.[2] Under its dense branches, Yama, the king of the dead, "drinking with the gods, entices our elders by playing on the flute."[3]

It is finally the Tree of Knowledge. Its sap begets poetic and religious inspiration.[4] In approaching its foliage, man remembers his previous existences.[5] From its top resounds in sonorous rolling the celestial voice, *vac,* which reveals the will of the gods, the divine messenger, engendered in the waters of the clouds.[6]

This latter aspect of the Sacred Tree is developed especially amongst the Buddhists. M. Senart has shown, in his learned and able *Essai sur la légende du Bouddha,* how the sacred fig-tree (*Urostigma religiosum*) under which Buddha attained perfect illumination, in spite of the exertions of Mâra and his demons, is directly connected with the Cosmic Tree of Indo - European mythologies, which produces ambrosia, and dispenses salvation.[7] But to the disciples of the new faith who loathed life and longed for extinction, the old Celestial Tree which led to immortality became

---

[1] *Rig-Veda,* i., 71, 9. In the Vishnu Purâna (i., 9), the *amrita* and the Tree of Paradise (the *pârijata*) are generated in succession by the churning of the sea of milk, *i.e.,* of the primordial or atmospheric ocean.

[2] A. DE GUBERNATIS. *Mythologie des plantes,* vol. i., p. 178.

[3] *Rig-Veda,* x., 135.

[4] E. SENART. *Journal Asiatique* for 1874, vol. iii., p. 289.

[5] *Id., ibid.,* p. 305.

[6] J. DARMESTETER. *Essais orientaux.* Paris, 1883, p. 179.

[7] E. SENART. *Essai sur la légende du Bouddha,* in the *Journal Asiatique* for 1875, vol. iv., p. 102.

merely the *buddhidruma*, the Tree of Wisdom, a symbol both of the truths which lead to *nirvâna* and of the Master who discovered and taught them.[1] The *Royal Asiatic Society* continued in the same vein when, in its turn, it chose as emblem, with the well-devised motto, *tot arbores quot rami*, one of the Sacred Trees of the Buddhists, the banyan-tree (*Urostigma indicum*), whose branches take root on touching the ground, and become so many fresh stems.

Thus, eternal life, productive power, perfect happiness, supreme knowledge, all these divine attributes are in India the gifts of the Tree which represents the Universe. Vedic and post-Vedic traditions tell us the story of the rivalries which occur between the *devas* and *asuras* for the possession of this Tree or its produce. The Vedas relate that the Tree of the *soma* was guarded by *gandharvas*, kinds of centaurs in whom is generally seen the personification of the winds or clouds. A swift sparrow-hawk with golden wings, Agni, took flight one day from the summit, carrying with it the broken end of a branch. Hit by the arrow of a *gandharva* it let fall a feather and a claw. These produced the plants which recall the bird of prey by their pennated leaves or sharp thorns, as well as those whose sap supplies the terrestrial *soma*, the intoxicating liquor of Vedic India.

---

[1] See the description of the Tree of Brahma, as the Tree of Knowledge, in the Anugita (*Sacred Books of the East*, vol. viii., pp. 370-371). A Buddhist legend, recorded by Mr. Hardy, tells of an immense Tree, adorned with four boughs, from which great rivers flow unceasingly; it bears golden pips which are carried down to the sea. "This description," M. Sénart adds (*loc. cit.*), "may convince the most sceptical that the tree *bô* must not be separated from the Cosmic Tree of Indo-European mythologies." It may be added that these details especially remind one of the Tree of Life with its wonderful fruits, planted in the middle of that Garden of Eden from which flowed four great rivers.

It is unnecessary, after Kuhn's *Herabkunft des Feuers und des Gœttertranks*, to dwell upon the purport of those traditions which go towards explaining at once the shape of the universe, the phenomena of the storm, the production of fire, the fertilization of the ground by rain, and, lastly, the virtues of certain plants.

In a different reading, the *amrita* was in the possession of the *asuras* who alone at that time were immortal.   Indra, the god of the stormy sky, succeeded in abstracting it, and thus it is that the *devas* obtained in their turn the privilege of immortality.[1]

According to the *Mahabharata* it is a genius half eagle and half man, which, after subduing several monstrous animals on the borders of a lake, takes advantage of the negligence of the dwarfs who guard the Sacred Tree to break off and carry away the branch of the *soma*.[2]

The Persians placed on the borders of a lake two trees, each of which was guarded by a *gandhrawa*.   One of these trees is the white *haoma* or *homa*, which, according to the *Yasna*, wards off death and confers " spiritual knowledge ; "[3] the other, according to the *Bundehesh*, is the Tree of All Seeds, which is also called the Eagle-tree. According to the version of the myth recorded by Kuhn, when one of these birds flies away, a thousand branches grow on the tree, and as soon as it returns to the nest it breaks a thousand branches, and causes a thousand seeds to fall.[4] The sap of the *haoma*, however, is not only the fertilizing rain ; like the *soma* of India, it is also

---

[1] A fragment quoted by Weber in his *Indische Studien*, vol. iii., p. 466.

[2] *Mahâbhârata*, i., 1345.

[3] *Yasna*, ch. ix. and x. (*Trans.* by M. de Harlez.   Paris, 1876, vol. ii.)

[4] *Revue germanique*, 1861, vol. xiv., p. 375.

the fermented liquor which was obtained by pound-
ing the twigs of an asclepiad, or some allied plant,
and which, considered as the drink of the gods,
played an important part in the sacrificial rites of
the two nations.

The Greeks seem likewise to have been acquainted with a Tree of Heaven. This was the oak
whose hollow trunk sheltered the Dioscuri from
their enemies, and from which hung the golden
fleece "on the shores of the Ocean, there where
the sun's beams are imprisoned in a chamber of
gold."[1] Perhaps we ought to include in the same
category of mythical trees the Oak of Dodona, in
whose foliage was heard the prophetic voice of
the master of the thunder.

The juice of the grape, personified in Bacchus,
that Greek equivalent of the god Soma, grants also
a knowledge of the future : " This god is a prophet,"
says Euripides ; "for, when he forces his way into
the body, he makes those whom he maddens fore-
tell the future."[2]

The name ἀμβροσία, which the Greeks gave to
the food of the Olympians, corresponds phoneti-
cally with the amrita. But the Aryans of Greece,
faithful to their custom of referring everything to
man, and inspired, perhaps, by a Phrygian myth,
in preserving the old Indo-European tradition
changed the theft of the liquor into the abduc-
tion of the cup-bearer ; and it was Ganymede
whom they made Zeus, transformed into an eagle,
carry off "in the midst of a divine whirlwind."
We may add that it is doves which, in the
Odyssey, bring ambrosia to Zeus.[3]

The Greeks, again, more than any other branch
of the Aryan race, developed the myth of the hero

---

[1] *Minnerme* (fragm. 11), quoted by M. P. DECHARME,
Mythologie de la Grèce antique. Paris, 1886, p. 607.

[2] *Bacchæ*, iii., 265.

[3] *Odyss.*, xii., 62.

overtaken by the divine wrath for having communicated to mankind the use of fire and the possession of knowledge.   Prometheus was considered
not only to have stolen the fire from Zeus by
lighting his torch either at the wheel of the sun or
at Vulcan's forge, but also to have modelled the
first man from clay and then infused into him the
spark of life.   Without adding comments which
no text would justify, we may yet draw attention
here to a small monument reproduced by M.
Decharme in his *Mythologie de la Grèce antique.*[1]
Prometheus is there represented as engaged in
moulding the first man, with the help of Minerva,
behind whom stands a tree encircled by a
serpent.

Lastly, we find again in Greece a third cycle of
mythical tales which refer us still more directly
to the Hindu tradition of the Sacred Tree; this is
the expedition of Hercules to the garden of the
Hesperides, whence he carries off the Golden
Apples guarded by dragons.   Whether these
Apples represent the luminous rays or the healing
waters, another reading of the myth records that
Hercules handed them over to Minerva, who put
them back in the place where they must always
remain, "for they are immortal." [2]   It is noteworthy
that, on a Greek vase reproduced by Guigniaut, the
Tree round which the dragon is coiled is depicted
between two Hesperides, one of whom gathers the
fruit for Hercules whilst the other diverts the
attention of the dragon by offering it a jar—which
scene may be more or less connected with oriental
representations of the Tree of Life, adapted to the
requirements of Hellenic taste and Hellenic
mythology (fig. 83).

The Edda of Scandinavian mythology exhibits
a perfect type of a cosmogonical tree : this is the

[1] *Mythologie de la Grèce antique*, fig. 82.
[2] *Ibid.*, p. 533.

ash Yggdrasill, the most beautiful of trees, which has three roots. One spreads out towards the upper spring, *Urdur*, where the Ases hold council and where the Nornes, whilst settling the duration

FIG. 83. THE DRAGON AND THE HESPERIDES.
(GUIGNIAUT. *Religions de l'antiquité*, vol. iv., pl. 181.)

of the lives of men, pour water from the spring over the Tree in order to secure for it an endless sap and verdure. The second root stretches towards the land of the giants of the Frost; under this root springs the well of Mimir the first man and king of the dead; in this well all knowledge and all wisdom dwell; Odin himself, in order to quench his thirst with its waters, had to leave one of his eyes in pledge. As for the third, it descends to Nifleim, the Scandinavian Hades, where it is ever gnawed at by a dragon. On the highest bough of the stem an eagle perches whilst other animals occupy the lower branches. Finally, Odin spent nine nights under its shade before discovering the runes,[1] an act which recalls the great meditation of Buddha under the sacred fig-tree.

Other passages in the Edda show us the contests for the possession of the hydromel, the liquor

[1] R. B. ANDERSON. *Mythologie scandinave*, trans. by Jules Leclercq. Paris, 1886, p. 34 *et seq.*

which is at once the drink of the gods and the source of poetry. It was carried off by Odin, who, in the form of a serpent, surreptitiously entered the den of the giant who was its guardian. Another myth which alludes more directly to life-imparting fruits is the legend of the goddess Idhunn who kept in a box the Apples of Immortality. This was the fruit which, on approaching old age, the gods partook of in order to renew their youth. Enticed into a neighbouring forest by the faithless Loki, Idhunn was abducted, together with her treasure, by a giant disguised as an eagle. But the gods, feeling themselves growing old, obliged Loki to transform himself into a hawk and go and bring back Idhunn and her Apples during the absence of their abductor.[1]

As regards the Slavonic peoples, MM. Mannhardt and de Gubernatis have recorded more than one legend bearing witness to their belief in a cosmogonical tree. Such is, amongst the Russians, the Oak-tree of the island Bujan, on which the sun retires to rest every evening and from which it rises every morning; watched by a dragon, it is inhabited by the Virgin of the Dawn, just as is the oak of Eridu by Tammuz and his mother.[2]

---

[1] ANDERSON, p. 124.

[2] A legend, given by M. de Gubernatis, relates that the Tree of Adam reaches to hell by its roots and to heaven by its branches; in its top lives the infant Jesus (*Mythologie des plantes*, vol. i., p. 18).—For traces of the belief in a Tree of Knowledge in Celtic folk lore, see JOHN RHYS *Celtic Heathendom* (London, 1888, p. 557). The Finns and Esths possess on their side, several legends relating to a cosmogonical tree. The Lapps are acquainted with an Oak or Tree of God which covers the heavens with its golden branches; it is uprooted by a dwarf, who afterwards transforms himself into a giant. The Esthonian legend develops this myth still further. The divine tree is here a Tree of Plenty; from its trunk come houses, cradles, and tables. The chief of these dwellings has the moon for a window; the sun and stars dance on the roof (DE GUBERNATIS. *Mythologie des plantes*, vol. ii., p. 76).—As regards the tree with fruits of precious stones, consult the interesting little

In brief, both Semites and Aryans were acquainted with the Tree of Heaven, the Tree of Life, and the Tree of Knowledge. The first has for fruit the igneous or luminous bodies of space; the second produces a liquor which secures eternal youth; the third confers foreknowledge and even omniscience. This valuable produce is the object of mythical rivalries between superhuman beings, the gods, *genii*, and fabulous animals, on the one hand, who have the treasure in their possession or in their keeping, and the divinity, the demon, or the hero, on the other, who strive to get possession of it. Curious similarities crop up in the different accounts of this conflict, which sometimes ends in the victory of the assailant, and sometimes in his defeat or exemplary chastisement.

Do such coincidences suffice to justify the assumption that all these traditions have one and the same origin or even that they represent an old stock of folk-lore bequeathed to the Aryans and Semites by their common ancestors?

More than thirty years ago, Frederic Baudry recapitulating, in the *Revue germanique*, Kuhn's work upon the myths relating to the origin of fire and nectar, drew attention, incidentally, to the tradition of the Paradisaic Trees as evidence " of a pre-historic communication between the Semites and Aryans, taking us back to the remotest times, before the fixation of languages and grammars. " [1] François Lenormant, going further still, saw therein an indication of the community of origin between the two races.[2]

volume in which M. Lethaby recently endeavoured to prove that the religious architecture, and even all the symbolism of the early civilizations, have a cosmogonical bearing, *i.e.*, tend to reproduce the image of the universe according to the conceptions of the period (*Architecture, Mysticism and Myth*, London, 1892, chap. v.).

[1] *Revue germanique* for 1861, vol. xiv., p. 385.

[2] *Origines de l'histoire*, vol. i., chap. ix.

First of all I will point out the fact that the
original unity of a tradition by no means implies
the relationship of the nations amongst which
it is found.   The researches conducted in our own
times, regarding the migration of fables, have
shown with what ease a tale brought into being on
the banks of the Ganges or the Nile may have
made its way to the islands of Japan, the shores of
the Atlantic, or the plains of southern Africa
among nations differing widely in race and language.   Of course, if the resemblance of the
traditions is strengthened by the identity of the
names they contain, especially when the people who
hold them in common belong to the same linguistic
group, we may admit that the formation of these
beliefs preceded the separation of the different
branches.   Such, in particular, is the conclusion to
be drawn from the connections noticed, amongst
certain Aryan nations, between the names *soma* and
haoma, *amrita* and *ambrosia*, *gandharva*, *gandhrawa*, and *kentauros*.

Nothing similar, however, exists between the
Semites and Indo-Europeans amongst the words
used by the two races to respectively designate
either the Tree of Life and its produce or the personages concerned in its legend.   Baudry, it is
true, gets out of the difficulty by supposing that
the communication might have taken place before
the fixation of languages and grammars.   This is a
desperate effort to justify one assumption by
another.   The etymological independence which
we find here, suggests, on the contrary, that the
tradition of the Paradisaic Trees either crossed, at
some period, from one race to another, or else that
it sprang up separately in each of the two centres.

At first sight it may seem unlikely that myths
which correspond so well in detail were produced
simultaneously in several places.   Yet there is not,
in all these tales, a single peculiarity whose pre-

sence cannot be connected with the most ordinary processes of mythical reasoning, and that cannot be found, at least in a fragmentary state, amongst a number of nations related neither to the Aryans nor to the Semites.

The idea of referring to the form of a tree the apparent conformation of the universe is one of the most natural methods of reasoning which can occur to the savage mind.

The Mbocobis of Paraguay still say that when they die they will climb up the Tree which unites heaven and earth.[1] To the Maoris heaven and earth formerly clave together; it was a Divine Tree, the Father of the Forests, which rent them asunder by placing itself between them.[2] The Khasias of India take the stars to be men who scaled heaven by climbing up a Tree, and were obliged to remain in the branches, their companions, who had stopped on earth, having cut down the trunk.[3]

We will leave out the Khasias, who may have come into contact with the mythology of the Hindus. But will anyone maintain that the traditions of Paraguay, or of New Zealand, are connected with those of the Semites or Aryans? As well might we pretend that old La Fontaine and Virgil before him were inspired by the cuneiform texts or the Vedic poems when they described the mighty oak :

> *De qui la tête au ciel était voisine*
> *Et dont les pieds touchaient à l'empire des morts.*

The Tree of Life is no more difficult to account for than the Cosmogonical Tree. Is not a plant one

---

[1] E. B. TYLOR. *Early History of Mankind.* London, 1878, p. 358.
[2] A. REVILLE. *Religions des peuples non civilisés.* Paris, 1883, vol. ii., p. 28.
[3] E. B. TYLOR. *Primitive Civilization*, vol. i. of French translation, p. 333.

of ‚the symbols most capable of expressing the abstract idea of life ? Whilst an animal evokes, above all, complex ideas of motion, strength and passion, the functions of the plant are concentrated, so to speak, in life, not alone in life subject to the conditions of birth and death, but also in life liable ʇo periodical successions of inactivity in winter, and of re-animation in spring.

What more natural and obvious symbol could there be than the " Gardens of Adonis," those pots of ‚early flowers which were made to blossom, and then left to wither under the rays of the sun, in order to recall the death of the young god ?[1] The Tahitans symbolize death by the *Casuarina*, a leafless tree, allied to our horse-tails, which they plant upon graves.[2] Is it not from the vegetable kingdom that we ourselves borrow our metaphors when we speak of a life " blooming," or cut down in its flower ?

> *Rose, elle a vécu ce que vivent les roses,*
> *L'espace d'un matin.*

We know what lofty precepts the mysteries of Greece drew from the constantly recurring phenomena of vegetation.[3] Egyptian monuments reproduce a sarcophagus from which an acacia emerges with the motto : " Osiris springs forth," as if to call the god to witness that life comes from death.[4] It was especially trees with evergreen foliage, such as the pine, the cedar, and the cypress, which were employed to represent the hope in an eternal life beyond the tomb. M. Lajard has brought together some singular examples in his researches *Sur le Culte du Cyprès,*

---

[1] C. P. TIELE. *Histoire des Religions de l'Égypte et des peuples sémitiques,* p. 291 in French translation. Paris, 1882.

[2] LETOURNEAU. *Sociologie.* Paris, 1880, p. 217.

[3] See preface, page 2.

[4] TIELE. *Religions de l'Égypte et des peuples sémitiques,* p. 83.

a worship which occurs, with this symbolical meaning, amongst the Greeks, the Etruscans, the Romans, the Phœnicians, the Arabs, the Persians, the Hindus, and the Chinese, without taking into consideration the nations of the New World.[1]

The plant, however, has not only the faculty of typifying life. The power of communicating and of renewing life can also be attributed to it. By means of its grains or fruits it provides mankind with fresh strength ; by its fermented juice it increases our vitality tenfold; finally, it furnishes remedies, or *simples*, to which is ascribed the faculty of restoring the sick to health, and of recalling the dying to life.

Now these qualities are met with precisely in most of the vegetable species from which the Aryans and Semites derived the outlines of their Sacred Trees. There is the oak, whose acorns the western Aryans gathered for food in the primeval forests. There is the asclepiad, from which the eastern Aryans got their elixir of life. Then there are the cone-bearing plants, whose prophylactic reputation amongst the Semites of Babylonia is proved by numerous texts. Above all there is the palm-tree, whose fruits still form a considerable part of the food of the people inhabiting the Lower Euphrates, and whose fermented juice produces an intoxicating liquor well known to the Arabs. There is even the vine, which, according to M. Lenormant, was termed, in the ancient language of Chaldæa, *ges-tin*, literally " wood of life,"[2] whilst the goddess of the Tree of Life, named " the Lady of Eden " in the North of Mesopotamia, is called in the South " the Lady of the Vine." [3]

Lastly rain, which revives Nature periodically,

---

[1] F. LAJARD, in the *Mémoires de l'Académie des inscriptions et belles-lettres*, vol. xx., second part.

[2] F. LENORMANT. *Orig.*, vol. ii., p. 254.

[3] SAYCE. *Op. cit.*, p. 240, note.

appears among nearly all nations as a seed of life. When therefore the configuration of the universe is referred to the type of the tree, it is natural enough to look upon rain as the sap which flows from its trunk or branches. In the island of Ferro, in the Canaries, a tradition of the Guanches told of a wonderful Tree whose top is surrounded by clouds, and whose branches let fall every morning, before sunrise, the water necessary for quenching the thirst of the natives.[1]

Here we see the Tree of Life become connected with an allied class of myths which we find fully developed amongst the Aryans: the belief, namely, in the existence of a spring, river, or lake which prolongs or renews life. This tradition was not wanting in Chaldæa either; the poem of the descent of Istar into Hades places in the gloomy realm of Allat, queen of the dead, a fountain of life which could revive the dead, were its approaches not jealously watched by the *anounas* or spirits of the earth. Istar herself must immerse herself therein before returning to the light of day and taking her place again amongst the gods.[2]

This fresh analogy between the Aryan and Semitic traditions, however, seems to me to be rather an assumption in favour of their original independence. On both sides, to be sure, there is the notion of natural waters which renew life upon earth; but whilst in India, and even among the nations of Europe, the annual re-awakening of Nature is chiefly brought about by the rains which fall from the Celestial Tree, in Chaldæa—as all travellers in that country bear witness—the fertility of the soil, and even the existence of the civilization, are dependent not upon the celestial

---

[1] RAMUSCO. *Historia delle Indie occidentali*, quoted by de Gubernatis, *Mythologie des plantes*, i., 36.
[2] SAYCE. *Op. cit.*, p. 221 *et seq.*

waters but upon rivers, wells, and canals, which
some sixty centuries ago made of this land, now a
desolate and pestiferous waste, a vast and luxu-
riant garden.[1]

There is therefore nothing to preclude the supposition that the Aryans and Semites might have
separately imagined their Tree of the Universe,
and even their Tree of Life, under the more or less
rudimentary forms belonging to the traditions still
to be observed amongst a number of uncivilized
or savage peoples. The borrowal, or rather
mutual infiltration of the two mythologies, had
only to deal with the details and episodes which
everywhere spontaneously clustered round this
common nucleus, and which, spreading in the
neighbourhood, without disappearing from their
respective cradles, ended not in obliterating but
in enriching and assimilating the original tradition
of each race.[2]

Let it be granted, for instance, that both races
vaguely pictured to themselves heaven under the
form of a tree. If one race likened the heavenly
bodies to the tree's fruits, can we wonder at the
other doing the same, as soon as they became
acquainted with this development of the myth

---

[1] In other countries this fountain of perpetual youth might
again be accounted for in another way. We find, indeed, a
similar tradition existing amongst the Malays, certain Poly-
nesians, and the inhabitants of the Antilles ; *i.e.*, amongst
insular peoples who see, every evening, the dying sun vanish
in the sea to arise from it in the morning, endowed with fresh
life. The Maoris, according to Tylor (*Civilisation primitive*,
ii., 383), imagine that the sun descends every evening to the
bottom of a cave, where he bathes in the Wai Ora Tane (water
of life), returning, at dawn, to the upper world.

[2] This seems, on the whole, to be what M. Tiele means
when he suggests that the myth of the elixir of life originated
doubtlessly in a non-Aryan race, although he discovers points
of contact in similar myths belonging incontestably to the
Aryans (*Manuel de l'histoire des Religions*, translation of M.
Maurice Vernes, 2nd. ed., pp. 153, 154).

amongst their neighbours ? Let us assume that
the Chaldæans learnt from the Indo-Iranians, or
vice versâ, or yet again both from a third people,
the art of making intoxicating liquors with the
juice of certain plants: does it not appear likely
that the myths suggested by this invention in its
original home were transmitted along with the art
itself ? Thus it is that Christian infiltrations, by
blending with the old stock of local traditions,
unquestionably contributed in such a degree
towards forming the legends recorded in the
Edda of the Scandinavians and the Kalevala of
the Finns, that it is now no longer possible for us
to ascertain the proper share which either of those
elements had in the formation of these legends.

Comparative archæology shows clearly how
these exchanges are brought about, when it
enables us to see how the Mesopotamian type of
the Sacred Tree was adopted by the Persians
to represent their Tree of Immortality, by the
Buddhists to typify their Tree of Wisdom ; and by
the Christians to symbolize their Tree of Temptation.

Each race, each religion has its independent
type, which it preserves and develops in accordance with the spirit of its own traditions, approximating it, however, by the addition of extraneous
details and accessories, to the equivalent image
adopted in the plastic art of its neighbours. Thus
the current which makes the Lotus of Egypt
blossom on the Paradisaic Tree of India has its
counter-current which causes the *Asclepias acida*
of the Hindu Kush to climb upon the Sacred Tree
of Assyria. Art and mythology comply, in this
respect, with the usual processes of civilization,
which is not the fruit of a single tree, but has
always been developed by grafts and cuttings between the most favoured branches of the human
race.

CHAPTER V.

ON THE TRANSMUTATION OF SYMBOLS.

Theory of the blending of symbolic forms.—Fusion of equivalent symbols.—Production of intermediate types.—Axe and Drum.—Wheel and Rosette.—Chrism, Wheel, and *crux ansata* —Transformations of the *triscèle*—Symbols which have had an influence upon the representation of the conical *bethels* among the Semites.—Permutations between the triangle, Winged Globe, *crux ansata*, human profile, table of offerings, cuneiform Star, and Sacred Tree.

WHILST inquiring into the cause of the changes occurring in the forms of symbols, sufficient importance is not always attached to the attraction which certain figures exercise upon one another. We might almost state it as a law that, when two symbols express the same or approximate ideas, they display a tendency to amalgamate, and even to combine in such a manner as to produce an intermediate type.

Through not taking into consideration that a symbol may thus unite with several figures differing greatly in origin and even in appearance, many archæologists have wasted their time in debating upon the origins of a sign or image which both sides were right in connecting with different antecedents—like those knights in the legend who broke a lance over the colour of a shield of two hues, one of the adversaries having only seen the front and the other the back.

When the necessity of seeking known or extremely simple antecedents in complex figures is not lost sight of, the study of symbols often re-

sults in the most singular verifications, especially
in countries like India, where all the manifestations of art have a symbolical import. One should
note in Moor's *Hindu Pantheon* how the Disk, the
Conch, the Lotus, the Flame, the Axe, and so forth,
frequently assume each other's forms—each of
these symbols going part of the way to meet the
others. Take, for example, two of the attributes
which oftenest figure in the hands of Siva, the
Axe and the Drum, and see them merge into one
another :

FIG. 84.   HINDU SYMBOLS.
(MOOR.   *Hindu Pantheon*, pl. vii., xiv., xvi., xlvii.)

Sir George Birdwood, one of the authors most
conversant with the industrial arts of India, records how the principal decorative and symbolical
types of India combine and interchange, regardless
even of the distinction between the animal and
vegetable kingdom. An identical phenomenon
may be noticed in Phœnician art. There is a
symbol inscribed on Cyprian pottery and Syrian
coins which recalls at the same time the Winged
Disk of Asia Minor, the Sacred Tree of Assyria,
the *trisula* of the Buddhists, the Bee of Ephesus,
and certain patterns of the Greek Thunderbolt (see
below, fig. 114).

Are these mere coincidences ? To answer this
question we must seek, in each particular case, not

only the antecedents of the figures which impress us by their complexity, but also the communications which may have taken place between their prototypes, and, if need be, we must reconstitute the successive stages of these symbolic transmutations.

Let us take, for instance, the image of the Wheel. This figure, which offers the twofold advantage of possessing a circular form, and suggesting the idea of motion, is one of the commonest symbolical representations of the sun.

Now different nations, amongst whom the sun is likewise symbolised by an expanded flower, have attempted to blend the two images. Thus it is that in Buddhist bas-reliefs we find Wheels whose spokes are replaced by petals of the Lotus-flower, while in the island of Cyprus some coins bear Roses whose leaves are hemmed in by bent spokes, or are even arranged in the form of a wheel.

In the same way the solar *rouelle*—that amulet *par excellence* of the Gauls—readily became the monogram of Christ, either in the form of the combined initials I and X (Ιησοῦς Χριστός)

a   b

FIG. 85. ROUELLE AND CHRISM.
(ROLLER. *Catacombes*, vol. ii., pl. xliii. and lxxxvii.)

(fig. 85a), or X and P (XPιστός) (fig. 85 b). In the latter case it is only necessary to add a loop to the top of one spoke to get the commonest type of the Chrism, which M. Gaidoz has accurately defined as "a six-rayed wheel without the rim, and with a loop at the top of the middle spoke."[1]

Thus, again, in Egypt the Chrism was combined with the Key of Life through a whole series of modifications which have been found in inscriptions on the island of Philæ dating from the first Christians of Nubia, who were anxious to make the sacred sign of their new faith correspond with the principal emblem of their former religion.

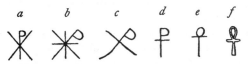

a   b   c   d   e   f

FIG. 86.   EGYPTIAN CHRISMS OF PHILÆ.[2]

We have seen how, amongst the Gauls, the steeds of the solar *quadriga* had combined with the arms of the *gammadion* in such a manner as to produce the complex figure of four horses' busts radiating round a disk.[3]   The transformations of the *triscèle* exhibit no less singular instances of similar combinations, whilst permitting us to ascertain, so to speak, the different stages of the operation.

The sun, which, as I have had occasion to point out, was often typified in Asia Minor by a disk from which radiated three legs united at the thighs, was likewise symbolised there by different animals, such as the lion, the wild boar, the dragon, the eagle, and the cock.   Now some Asiatic coins exhibit the cock beside the *triscèle* (fig. 87); on

---

[1] *Le dieu gaulois du soleil et le symbolisme de la roue.* Paris, 1886, p. 77.

[2] *a*, Greek chrism; *b*, *c*, *d*, monograms of Christ at Philæ (LETRONNE.   *La croix ansée a-t-elle été employée pour exprimer le monogramme du Christ?* in the *Mémoires de l'Académie des inscriptions et belles-lettres*, vol. xvi., pl. i., fig. 47, 48, 49); *e.* key of life.

[3] See above, fig. 28, p. 57.

others, the *triscèle* is superposed upon, or rather
stuck to the body of, a bird, or a lion, without the
aspect of the latter being changed on that account

FIG. 87. COIN OF ASPENDUS.
(HUNTER, pl. vii., No. 15.)

(fig. 88) ; elsewhere, finally, the two parallel symbols, first placed near and then upon each other,

FIG. 88. COIN OF ASPENDUS.
(HUNTER, pl. vii., No. 16.)

literally blend together, the three legs of the
triscèle being transformed into cocks' heads, or

FIG. 89. LYCIAN COIN.
(BARCLAY V. HEAD, pl. iii., No. 35.)

monsters' busts, which revolve in the same direction round a central point (fig. 89).

One's thoughts turn involuntarily to those
figures drawn, in different positions, or with diffe-

rent faces, on cardboard disks, which are spun quickly in the hand to produce the illusion of a single image animated by a motion of its own.

On some coins of Magna Græcia and of Sicily the *triscèle* is composed of three Crescents ranged round a Disk. Certain archæologists have concluded from this that the *triscèle* had a lunar significance. It is quite admissible that the *triscèle*, as a symbol of astronomical movement, was sometimes used—like the *tétrascèle* and *gammadion*—to typify the circular course, or even the phases of the moon. The Gobineau collection possesses a Persian cylinder exhibiting a *triscèle* formed of three monsters, which seem about to swallow as many Crescents.

FIG. 90.   LUNAR TRISKELION.
(*Revue archéologique*, vol. xvii., 1874, pl. iv., No. 56.)

Are we, however, to infer from this, as Mr. Robert Brown does, that the *triscèle* originated in the intentional grouping together of three Crescents ?[1]   At first sight, this hypothesis would seem to find its confirmation in the comparison of certain coins which establish an actual transition from the *triscèle* to symbols that are undeniably lunar.

But these coins belong unquestionably to a later period than the oldest Lycian coins, on which, as I have above shown, the *triscèle* has a solar import.   Instead of exhibiting the ante-

[1] R. Brown, junior. *The Unicorn, a mythological investigation*, London, 1881, p. 66.

cedents of the *triscèle*, the witnesses, and the
stages of its independent development, is it not
more likely that they represent lunar symbols
gradually modified by the plastic attraction of the
triscèle; or, to put it plainer, that little by little

a   b   c

FIG. 91.   TRISCÈLE AND CRESCENTS.[1]

they so arranged their component parts as to
assume the form of the *triscèle* whilst preserving
their original meaning ?

This adaptation of the *triscèle* to the lunar
movements is the more easily explained since the
ancients seem especially to have distinguished in
the queen of the night her three phases of crescent,
half-moon, and full-moon, whence the *Hecate trifor-
mis*, depicted with three faces.[2]

If it be desired to find the antecedents of the
triscèle they must rather be sought for, like those
of the *tétrascèle*, in the figure of the Disk which
projects three curved rays indicating motion.[3]
Under this form it is already met with amongst
the " whorls " of Hissarlik.   At Mycenæ it may
be referred to the following type :

---

[1] *a*, R. BROWN, fig. 73 (coin of Metapontum) ; *b*, HUNTER,
pl. 22, fig. 13 (coin of Croton) ; *c*, ID., pl. 36, fig. 22 (coin of
Megarsus).

[2] "She was depicted with three faces," says Cleomedes,
"because the ancients observed the moon under her three
aspects of bicornous, half, and full " (*cf.* MONTFAUCON, i., pl.
i., p. 252).

[3] See above, chap. ii., § 3.

FIG. 92. TRISCÈLE FROM MYCENÆ.

It is easy to understand how a figure of this kind may have sometimes assumed the form of three crescents, and sometimes that of three legs, according to the vagaries of art, or the dictates of symbolism.

Another symbol, whose history gives perhaps a still better explanation of how an image may undergo in its development the influence of several distinct symbols, and react in its turn on the form of these latter through a real phenomenon of transmutation, is to be found in those conical stones whose figurative representation plays such an important part in the graphic arts of the western Semites. We know that they were *simulacra* of the Great Goddess, at once telluric and lunar, who was worshipped under different names by all the Semitic nations. Tacitus informs us that Aphrodite was represented at Paphos by a stone of this kind, shaped like a pyramid.[1] His description, corroborated by other ancient writers, is illustrated, so to speak, on coins of Paphos, Byblos, Sidon, and other places, which exhibit several kinds of conical stones erected in the midst of the sanctuary.

---

[1] Tacitus, speaking of the simulacrum placed in the sanctuary of Paphos, says : *Simulacrum deæ. . . . . continuus orbis latiore initio tenuem in ambitu metæ modo exsurgens (Hist.,* ii., 3).—Similar cones of stone have been discovered in the ruins of the Gigantea, in the island of Malta, as also about the site of the temple of Tanit at Carthage (*cf.* FR. LENORMANT, in the *Gazette archéologique* for 1876, p. 130).

On other monuments—coins, slabs, and amulets—the same symbol is found by itself with

FIG. 93. SACRED STONE OF BYBLOS.
(*Corpus inscript. semitic,* vol. i., fasc. i., pl. vi.)

changes of form in which is revealed the influence, the *attraction,* of figures belonging to another class of images.

M. Renan reproduces, in his *Mission de Phénicie,* the following symbol taken from a stone which was found near Damascus :

FIG. 94. STONE OF DAMASCUS.
(RENAN. *Mission de Phénicie,* p. 351.)

"This sign," M. Renan adds, "is common on Phœnician monuments; it seems to come from the image of a person praying, a figure no less frequent on the top of Phœnician *stelai.*"

We shall see that the supposed "persons praying" are merely a slightly altered form of the Sacred Cone. The relation of the sign on the Damascus stone to the *simulacrum* of Paphos is not to be questioned; it is even visible in the two small circles on either side of the triangle.[1] On the other hand we at once recognize the general similarity of this figure to certain ornithomorphic Globes of Asia Minor, with their triangu-

[1] See above, the stone of Paphos (fig. 41, p. 92).

lar tails, outstretched wings, and rectilinear horns
(see next chapter).

The secret of this twofold resemblance is discovered in the engraving of a Moabite cylinder

FIG. 95. MOABITE CYLINDER.
(DE VOGUÉ. *Mél. d'archéol. orient.*, p. 89.)

published by M. de Vogué, and attributed by
M. J. Menant to the beginnings of Phœnician
art.

We have here unquestionably in their separate
state the two symbols which are combined on the
stone of Damascus, *i.e.*, the Cone and the Winged
Globe, one suspended over the other, with the same
pair of small circles which flank the sides of the
Cone.

Another combination which occurs fairly often
on monuments of Phœnician origin exhibits on
the point of the *bethel*, or rather of its triangular
representation, a horizontal cross-bar, on the middle
of which rests a Disk, or a handle.

FIG. 96. ANSATED CONES.[1]

It seems to me difficult to call in question the
resemblance of the Cone thus modified to the

[1] *a*, On a coin of Paphos. *Corpus inscript. semitic*, vol. i.,
fasciculus i., p. 6; *b*, on a coin of Carthage (BARCLAY V.
HEAD. *Coins in the British Museum*, pl. xxxv., No. 38); *c*,
on intaglios of Sardinia (J. MENANT. *Pierres gravées de la
Haute-Asia*, vol. ii., Paris, 1886, pp. 256 and 258); *d*, on a
Phœnician seal (*Idem.*, p. 234).

Egyptian symbol of the *crux ansata* or Key of
Life. Widen the foot of the latter somewhat, or
contract the base of the former, and the resulting
images will be identical.

To such a degree, indeed, do these figures resemble one another, that it is impossible to determine to which of the two symbols belong

FIG. 97. KEY OF LIFE.
(LEPSIUS. *Denkmäler*, Abth., ii., Bl. 86.)

certain intermediate figures, such as, for instance,
the representation of the object erected behind the
principal person on the famous seal of Abibal,
father of Hiram (fig. 96 *d*). The narrowness of
its base recalls the Key of Life, but the Disk, encircled by the Crescent, which takes the place of
the handle, as well as the position of the object
on the ground, suggest rather a modification of
the Sacred Cone.

How is this resemblance of forms to be accounted for if not by the attraction which one of
the two symbols will have exercised upon the
other? Now the Key of Life was certainly not
formed under the influence of the Sacred Cone, if
we may judge from their relative ages. There
were *cruces ansatæ* upon the monuments of Egypt
long before the Phœnicians had learnt to manipu-
late the chisel, perhaps even before the Semites
had reached the shores of the Mediterranean.

The *crux ansata* has alternately been taken for
a Nilometer (Plucke), a key for regulating the inun-
dations of the Nile (Zoëga), a vase placed on an
altar (Ungarelli), a perversion of the Winged Globe
(Lajard), a *phallus* (Jablonski), and the sort of apron

which the Egyptians wound round themselves by
way of a waist-band (Sayce). Regarding its meaning, however, there is no diversity of opinion.

In the hieroglyphic writings it forms an ideogram, which renders the sound *anχ*, and means *to
live, living*.[1] On inscribed monuments it seems to
be used by the gods as an instrument for awaken-
ing the dead to a new life. A bas-relief of the
twelfth dynasty, which shows the goddess Anuke-t
holding the Key of Life to the nostrils of King
Usertesen III., is accompanied by this inscription :
"I give unto thee life, stability, and purity, like
Ra for ever."

It follows from this that, amongst the Egyptians, the *crux ansata* represented life, conceived
of in its widest and most abstract meaning.[2] But
is not the dispensation of life precisely one of the
essential attributes of the Great Goddess, Virgin
and Mother, destructive and prolific by turns, who
appears amongst all Semitic nations as the highest
personification of Nature under her twofold aspect,
cruel and beneficent ?

Plautus does nothing more than render the
Phœnician conception of Astarte when, in the
fourth act of *Mercator*, he defines her as :

> *Diva Astarte hominum deorumque vis, vita, salus: rursus
> eadem quæ est,*
> *Pernicies, mors, interitus, mare, tellus, cælum, sidera.*

Among the Assyro-Babylonians Nanat-Anaïta

---

[1] ÉM. COEMANS. *Manuel de langue égyptienne*, Ghent,
1887, 1st part, p. 46.

[2] Perhaps it represented symbolically the vital germ, the
spark of life ; indeed, on some monuments, it appears to be
hurled from the divine hand towards the nostrils of the dead
person, and, in a bas-relief of the New Empire, Horus and
Toth are seen to pour from a jar over the head of King
Amenophis II., Keys of Life interlaced in the form of a chain
(CHAMPOLLION. *Monuments de l'Egypte et de la Nubie*, vol. i.,
pl. xlv., fol. 1).

is called the "strength of the living;"[1] Zarpanit is termed the "generatrix;"[2] Allât guards jealously, in the world below, the Well of Life, which could revive the dead.[3] An inscription on a Mesopotamian cylinder, accompanying the image of a goddess, probably Istar, runs thus : "O thou who art adorable, who givest salvation, life, and justice, vivify my name."[4] Lastly, although Tanit, the *Virgo Cœlestis* of Carthage, assimilated to Juno by the Romans, is generally held to represent the virgin and austere side of Astarte's nature, it is probable that she combined the double character of her Semitic sisters.[5] On a *stele* of Carthage she is depicted on a triangular pediment with a child on one arm ; and the geometric figure which serves as her symbol is frequently associated with Lotuses,[6] which are flowers of Life, symbolical representations of the universal matrix.

In these circumstances the Sacred Cone must necessarily receive, among the Semites, the same import as the *crux ansata* among the Egyptians, in the capacity of a symbol of life, or even as a talisman of high power, exclusive of the phallic signification of which its triangular form admitted.[7]

---

[1] DE VOGUÉ, in the *Journal Asiatique* for 1867 (vol. x., 6th series), p. 122.

[2] G. MASPERO. *Histoire ancienne des peuples de l'Orient.* Paris, 1886, p. 141.

[3] A. H. SAYCE. *Religion of the ancient Babylonians.* London, 1887, p. 221 *et seq.*

[4] J. MENANT. *Op. cit.,* vol. i., p. 196.

[5] PH. BERGER. *Représentations figurées des stèles puniques,* in the *Gazette archéoligique* for 1876, p. 123.

[6] PH. BERGER. *Idem.,* p. 124.

[7] M. Renan has pointed out, amongst inscriptions of Gebal, and of Sidon, in the vicinity of Tyre, numbers of inverted isosceles triangles which he believes to have been connected with the worship of Astarte. It is the same image that M. Schliemann noticed on the *vulva* of the Trojan Venus (RENAN. *Mission de Phénicie.* Paris, 1864, pp. 523, 649-653.—SCHLIEMANN). *Ilios,* fig. 226.

On the other hand, as is is shown by the monuments, the *crux ansata*, together with the principal symbols of Egypt, was not long in spreading first among the Phœnicians, and then through the rest of the Semitic world. It has been found on bas-reliefs, tombs, pottery, gems, and coins in the whole region which stretches from Sardinia to Susiana, including the coast of Africa, Cyprus, Palestine, and Mesopotamia. Everywhere, seemingly, it had a religious, or prophylactic, meaning; perhaps it is a sign similar to the *tau* with which were marked, in Ezekiel's vision, the foreheads of the just who will be spared.[1] On some monuments the divine, or sacerdotal, personages hold it in one hand, as in Egypt;[2] or, again, as we have seen (pl. v., fig. *b*), it is associated with the Sacred Tree and the Lotus-flower.

Thus, between the two symbols, there was a frequent proximity; a similarity of meaning, and perhaps of use; and, lastly, the possibility of passing from one to the other without material alteration in their respective features. Is anything more needed to explain why the Phœnicians, possessing these two signs to express the idea of life as a supernatural dispensation, sought to blend the two figures in a third which preserved the essentials of its double antecedent? It would, indeed, have been singular if they had not done so.

Have we not seen, at a later period, how the Christians of Egypt in their turn adopted the *crux ansata*, not only to replace the Greek or Latin form of the Cross, but also to portray the monogram of Christ, which the Greeks had transmitted to them? The latter identification implies a much more perceptible alteration of these two signs than

[1] EZEK. ix., 4-6.
[2] RAOUL ROCHETTE. *Sur la croix ansée asiatique*, in the *Mémoires de l'Académie des inscriptions et belles-lettres*, vol. xvii., p. 375 *et seq.*, pl. xvii., 2nd part.

was the modification necessary for amalgamating the *crux ansata* with the symbol of Astarte.[1]

It is proper to mention a coincidence which, though quite accidental, may have also helped to bring together the Sacred Cone and the Key of Life. The Egyptian monuments sometimes exhibit in front of the image of the divinity invoked thereon an isosceles triangle placed above a *crux ansata* These two superposed signs, which read *ti anx*, render the prayer : "Bestow life."[2] Now it was the fulfilment of this very prayer which, among the Semites, devolved upon Astarte and her rivals.

The fact, perhaps, will be pointed out that the Phœnicians were not able to read the hieroglyphs. This assertion must not be made in too positive a manner, for, after all, it was in the Egyptian writing that the very characters of the Phœnician alphabet originated. Moreover, in this, as in similar cases, there were not wanting interpreters, sailors, traders, soldiers, and travellers of every class, to explain to the inhabitants of the Mediterranean littoral the meaning of the graphic legends which were diffused with the scarabs, gems, and amulets of Egypt throughout the whole Eastern and Semitic world. Local imagination did the rest, and in this manner popular symbolism was enriched by a new type.[3]

It is rather singular that this influence of the *crux ansata* upon the figurative representations of Sacred Cone is met with even amongst the Greeks. The great goddesses of the Asiatic littoral were early introduced into the Greek Pantheon, under their double form of divinities virgin and warlike,

---

[1] See above, fig. 86, p. 180.

[2] EUG. RÉVILLOUT, in the *Gazette archéologique* for 1888, p. 3.

[3] It is noteworthy that our astronomical sign of the planet Venus is a veritable *crux ansata*.

such as Artemis, or voluptuous and prolific like
Aphrodite. With their forms of worship came
also their symbols, particularly the Conical Stone
which already had its equivalent in the rude *cippi*
of the Pelasgic *simulacra*.[1] Under the influence
of Greek genius the Sacred Cone was not long in
developing in a direction which made it approach
the human profile. Among the terra-cottas of
Bœotia we find a species of cone with the outlines
of a head and the rudiments of arms, which represents a goddess, Aphrodite, or Harmonia.

This is unquestionably the transition from the
Sacred Cone to the human form. M. François
Lenormant, however, adduces, as more ancient, a
specimen where we merely see the Cone with its
rudiments of arms.[2] It may be questioned if these

FIG. 98. EPHESIAN ARTEMIS.
(P. DECHARME. *Mythologie de la Grèce antique*, fig. 145.)

are really arms, and even if these shapeless stumps
were not prior to any desire to recognize in this
image the human figure. I would be all the more
inclined to seek herein the trace of a modification
due to the influence of the *crux ansata*, since

[1] MAX COLLIGNON. *Mythologie figurée de la Grèce antique*,
p. 10 *et seq.*
[2] FR. LENORMANT, in the *Gazette archéologique* for 1876,
p. 68.

another type of the classic Pantheon carries us back still more directly to the image of the Egyptian symbol. This is the Ephesian Artemis who, with her head encircled by a halo, her fore-arms projecting from either side of the body, and her lower members wedged into a case, most strikingly recalls, so to speak, an anthropomorphized Key of Life (fig. 98). The resemblance, perhaps, is still stronger on some coins of Cyzicus, where the

FIG. 99. COIN OF CYZICUS.
(*Revue de Numismatique*, 1892, vol. ii., pl. ii., fig. 4.)

goddess appeared with chains hanging from the arms (fig. 99).

Strange as this comparison may appear at first sight, it finds its counterpart in an amulet belonging, to be sure, to the latter times of paganism, which was discovered amongst the ruins of the Serapeum at Alexandria.

FIG. 100.
(*The Antiquary*, 1881, p. 98.)

We have here, very probably, no longer a representation of the nourishing Artemis, modified by the intervention of the Key of Life, but a *crux ansata* altered by coming in contact with the *simulacra* of the Ephesian Artemis, or some allied goddess.[1]

The influence of the Key of Life is again visible in the following image of a Hermes consecrated

FIG. 101.

(*Mém. de l'Acad. des inscr. et bel.-let.*, vol. xvii., 2nd. part, pl. ix., fig. 12.)

to the Chthonian Mercury, god of fertility and of life.

M. Raoul Rochette draws attention to another *stele* of the same shape in an inscription of Thessaly concerning funeral games.[2]

The combination of the *crux ansata* with the Sacred Cone seems to have penetrated as far as India, if this conclusion may be drawn from an enigmatical figure to be seen amongst the symbols carved, at Amaravati, on the feet of Buddha (fig. 102 *a*).

To be sure, the Disk, or oval handle, which surmounts the Cone, is replaced, in the Buddhist symbol, by a triangular handle, or the section of a second cone inverted. But this difference is another presumption in favour of our thesis. In fact, it is precisely this substitution of a triangular

---

[1] Perhaps the influence of the Sacred Cone might also be discovered, as Herr Hugo von Lomnitz has already pointed out, in certain images of the Virgin, derived from the popular art of Spain and Sicily, where the body, enveloped in a robe which widens towards the foot, forms a veritable triangle surmounted by a head and flanked by two small arms bent horizontally.

[2] RAOUL ROCHETTE. *Sur la croix ansée asiatique. Loc. cit.*, pl. ix., fig. 11.

for an oval handle which characterizes the *crux ansata* of India, or at least the figure connected by Indian scholars with the Egyptian symbol of the

a   *b*

FIG. 102.[1]

Key of Life (fig. 102 *b*), which reached India by way of Syria and Persia.

The symbol of Astarte, thus modified by the influence of the Key of Life, seems to have continued its development amongst the Semitic nations in a twofold direction.

On the one hand, upon the *stelai* of Carthage, consecrated to Tanit, the two extremities of the cross-bar which stretches out between the handle

FIG. 103.

(*Corpus inscr. semitic*, fasc. iv. (1889), tab. lii., fig. 138.)

and the Cone are generally turned upwards at right angles.

On the other hand, it must be noted, that in Cyprus and Asia Minor the base of the triangle completely disappears (fig. 104).

We can hardly find out, in these figures, the outlines of the original Cone. Yet the most competent writers who have expressed an opinion on this subject, MM. Lenormant, Berger, Tyler,

---

[1] *a*, See frontispiece ; *b*, on a silver ingot (EDW. THOMAS, in the *Numismatic Chronicle*, vol. iv. (new series), pl. xi.).

Perrot, and others, have had no hesitation in recognizing therein the symbol of Astarte-Tanit. Here, however, there was one Egyptologist who

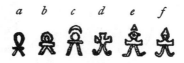

FIG. 104.[1]

lost patience. M. Eug. Revillout, the learned professor of the Ecole du Louvre, points out that these figures were merely the reproduction, more or less altered, of an Egyptian character, the sign *sa*, which means " protection " (fig. 105 *a*). Similarly, if he is to be believed, the so-called " Sacred Cone with arms and a head " would be nothing but "an Egyptian altar of a common shape," a table of offerings (fig. 105 *b*).

FIG. 105.[2]

I am of opinion that M. Revillout is not mistaken ; still those whom he accuses of being at

[1] *a*, On a coin of Cilicia (GENESIUS. *Scripturæ Phœniciae Monumenta*, tab. xxxvii.).

b, On a coin of Cyprus (DE LUYNES, *Numismatique et Inscriptions cypriotes.* Paris, 1852, p. v., fig. 12).

c, On a votive stele of Carthage (PH. BERGER, in the *Gaz. archéol.* for 1876, p. 125).

d, On a Hittite seal (PERROT et CHIPIEZ. *Op. cit.*, vol. iv., fig. 384).

e and *f*, On a Hittite cylinder (TYLER, *Babylonian and Oriental Record*, vol. i., No. 10, p. 151, London, 1887).

[2] EUG. REVILLOUT. *Sur un prétendu sceau hittite*, in the *Gazette archéologique* for 1888, p. 1 *et seq.*

fault are none the less right. It is certainly the Great Goddess who is symbolized by the ansated Cones, at least, when they appear on *stelai* with inscriptions dedicated to Tanit, when on coins, they accompany the head of Astarte, or when they combine either with the lunar Crescent, or with the Disk encircled by the Crescent (fig. 104 *c*). On a *stele* of Libya a Disk between two upright horns surmounts the Cone (fig. 107), in exactly the same manner as, in a bronze of Syria reproduced by MM. Perrot et Chipiez, it forms the head-dress of an image of Astarte.[1] On the other hand, why should we refuse to admit that the Semitic artist, when he reproduced the old *simulacrum* of the Phœnician Goddess, already altered by what it had borrowed from the Key of Life, may have clung still more closely to the imitation of symbols emanating from Egypt?

M. Revillout, observing that the figure *f* in our illustration No. 104 is placed, in the field of a Hittite cylinder, at the feet of a goddess "with prominent ears and an enormous body," does not fail to add that, "in this description every Egyptologist will at once recognize the goddess Taouer or Thoueris, with the body of a hippopotamus, with the head of the same animal, or of a lioness, and having in front of her feet—as was the prevalent custom—the sign *sa*."

Far be it from me to call this in question. Since, however, neither the Hittites nor the Phœnicians worshipped, so far as I am aware, the goddess Tauer, it is probable that the author of the cylinder wished to represent one or other of the great Asiatic goddesses—in association with their usual symbol—under forms taken from the Egyptian imagery; as in other instances, the Phœnician artists derived the features, and even the costume

---

[1] Vol. iii., fig. 26.

of their Astarte from the Egyptian type of Hathor.[1]

Thus the worshippers of Tanit were able, without the slightest misgiving, to bend upwards the two branches of their ansated triangle in order to make it resemble the image exhibited by the Egyptian altar. We must not, therefore, unreservedly accept an explanation which makes us invariably see, in the Carthaginian development of the ansated Cone, an attempt to depict Tanit under the human form. It was in this manner doubtlessly that the shapeless *simulacra* by which the Greeks were long content to symbolize their gods began to draw nearer to the human body in appearance ; and I am far from denying that the Semites did not occasionally attempt to develop the representations of their Sacred Cone in the direction of the human figure, or, on the other hand, to lend to the images of their great goddesses features which recalled the symbolic Cone. An intention of this kind is plainly disclosed in one of those singular figures engraved on the

FIG. 106.
(*Gazette archéologique* for 1879, pl. 21).

silver frontlet, found at Batna, which M. Renan has described and discussed in the *Gazette archéologique*.

This, however, is an exception, and in most existing specimens the emblem of Tanit remains a geometric figure which can in no way be likened to the human profile even when rudely outlined.

On the other hand, there is nothing to prevent

[1] *Corpus inscript. semitic,* vol. i., fasc. i. (1881), p. 2.

the Conical Stone, whilst representing Tanit, from
serving itself as an altar at the same time as a
simulacrum,—like the Phœnician *bethel* and the
Arabian *ansab.* At least, it is quite possible that
its figurative representation may have absorbed
the image of the altar on which it stood in the
sanctuary. Has it been noticed that on some
Libyan *stelai* the symbol of Tanit seems to be
made up of two distinct parts : the Cone properly

FIG. 107.
(GENESIUS. *Monumenta,* tab. 17.)

so called with its usual appendages, and a kind of
stand or pedestal ?

In most cases the sculptor will not have gone to
such a length, but will have contented himself with
turning up the two extremities of the cross-bar in
such a manner as to produce the so-called fore-arms
which recall the two vases of the Egyptian altar.
On a *stele* of Carthage these two extremities are
replaced by two Caducei, perhaps with a view to
symbolize the two male divinities who composed,
with Tanit, the great divine Triad of the Cartha-
ginians.[1]

I will also draw attention to the fact that the
symbol of the Sacred Cone, after being confounded
with the Key of Life, and then transformed into an
altar, seems to have again united with the *crux
ansata.* Indeed, on a hematite cylinder of Hittite

[1] GENESIUS, tab. 47.

origin, now in the Bibliothèque Nationale in Paris, a personage is seen who holds the object depicted below (fig. 108 *a*).

This sign is unquestionably held like a Key of Life, and we may add that it exhibits the essential features of the latter.   Moreover, it also includes

a   *b*

FIG. 108.

the outlines of what might be called the symbol of the ansated table.   Finally, it may be questioned if it is not likewise influenced by yet a third figure. In his memoir, which dates from the year 1847, M. Lajard had already grasped its resemblance to the cuneiform sign which frequently accompanies the names of the divinities in the archaic inscriptions of Mesopotamia (fig. 108 *b*).[1]

The parallel is all the more ingenious as at that time, now almost half a century ago, they did not know the exact meaning of this character, which has since been found to be an ideogram of the divinity amongst the Assyrians.   It is quite likely that, through its constant association with the names of the gods, this sign may have acquired, even beyond Mesopotamia, a general symbolic or talismanic import, and that, consequently, there was a wish to detect its likeness in the object destined to represent the Key of Life, and recall the Sacred Cone, or at least its latest modification. When engaged in investigating the pre-Hellenic

---

[1] LAJARD. *Origine et signification de la croix ansée*, in the *Mémoires de l'Académie des inscriptions et belles-lettres*, vol. xvii., 1st part, p. 361.

arts, or forms of worship, of Asia Minor we must
never forget that the recently discovered Hittite
civilization was the complex product of an inter-
mixture between the influences of Egypt and those
of Mesopotamia, engrafted perhaps on an old
Semitic stock, and, at all events, impregnated with
Phœnician elements.

It ought, however, to be remarked that a figure
identical with the cuneiform sign given above, is
found amongst the characters of Cyprian writing,
which characters are considered to be more or less
related to the Hittite hieroglyphs ; this is the letter
which renders the sound of the vowel a [1], and which,
on a coin of Cyprus, reproduced by the Duc de
Luynes, actually appears near the ansated table.

FIG. 109.

(DE LUYNES. *Numismatique cypriote*, pl. v., fig. 12.)

Lastly we have seen that Istar-Astarte had also
as a *simulacrum* an actual, or conventional, tree,
often represented between personages facing one
another. It seems as if a conical stone and a
plant, even conventional, might be indefinitely
placed in juxtaposition without their respective
representations being prompted to borrow each
other's forms. Yet this is what occurred in Syria,
if we may judge from this amulet, of recent manufacture perhaps, but certainly of a very ancient
pattern (fig. 110 *a*).

This image belongs undeniably to the symbolism
of the Sacred Tree. On the other hand the triangular shape which the central object (plant, fruit

[1] M. BRÉAL. *Déchiffrement des Inscriptions cypriotes*, in the
Journal des savants, 1877, p. 560.

or leaf) approaches in appearance, the handle or
elongated disk surmounting its top, the two
small cross-bars which give the finishing touch to
its resemblance to a cross, and especially an ansated

FIG. 110. SYRIAN AMULET.

cross,—all these features agree no less certainly
with some Phœnician representations of the *simulacrum* of Astarte (fig. 110 *b*).

That this symbol should have come down to the
Syrian of our days has nothing to surprise us,
when we hear from a recent notice sent by a
French military surgeon, Doctor Vercouvre, to the
Académie des inscriptions et belles-lettres, that a
still more authentic form of the same sign is to be
found among the modern inhabitants of Tunisia.[1]
He traces back the marks which tattoo the face
and hands of the aborigines to one and the same
type, "a doll with outstretched arms," and he adds :
"It is a reproduction of the anthropomorphic
figure with outstretched arms, which, among the
antique monuments of Phœnicia and Carthage,
represent what is called by archæologists the

---

[1] *Acad. des inscriptions et belles-lettres.* Proceedings of Dec.
9th, 1892.

symbol of the Punic trinity,"—viz., our old ansated Cone with the extremities of the cross-bar turned upwards (see fig. 103).[1]

The line separating the animal from the vegetable kingdom is not drawn so hard and fast in symbolism as it is in nature. Viewing the unceremonious manner in which such dissimilar objects as the Conical Stone, the solar Disk, the bird, the horns, the *crux ansata*, the table of offerings, the human profile, the cuneiform star, and the sacred plant come to borrow their respective forms and to blend one with another as in a transformation scene, we must perforce conclude that no hybrid combination is unacceptable to symbolism, when an amalgamation of ideas, or beliefs, is to be strengthened through blending the images by which they are expressed.

[1] Dr. Vercouvre's interpretation has been confirmed, at a subsequent meeting of the Academy, by M. Philippe Berger, who has shown, moreover, how this old symbol has become, in some cases, a flower and a cross. (Cf. *Revue de l'histoire des Religions*, 1893, t. xxvii., p. 382.)

CHAPTER VI.

THE WINGED GLOBE, THE CADUCEUS, AND THE TRISULA.

I. *The Winged Globe outside Egypt.*—The Winged Globe of the Egyptians; a combination of the Disk, the sparrow-hawk, the goat, and the serpent.—Meaning of this symbol.—Its migration into Phœnicia, Syria, Mesopotamia, and Persia.— Modification of its forms.—Its later combinations with the human image, the Sacred Bird, the Sacred Tree, and the conical *bethel.*—Its influence upon some symbolic figures of Greece and of India, the Aureole, the Thunderbolt, the *chakra,* etc.—Winged Globes of the New World. II. *The antecedents of the Caduceus.*—Homeric description of the Caduceus.—Transformations of the Greek Caduceus.— The Caduceus of the Phœnicians and the Hittites.—Assyrian ensigns, prototypes of the *labarum.*—The Caduceus in its relations with the Winged Globe and the *ashêrah.*—Hindu Caducei. III. *The transformations of the trisula.*—Definition, antiquity, and different interpretations of the *trisula.*—Its connection with the Trident and the Wheel.—Its blending with the Caduceus.—Its interchanges with the Winged Globe, the Scarab, the Lotus, the *lingam,* the idol of Jaganath, and the Tree of Buddha.—The *trisula* in the bas-reliefs of Boro-Budur. —The *trisula* in Europe.—Summing up.

I. THE WINGED GLOBE OUTSIDE EGYPT.

THERE are certainly not many features common to the different representations which the ancient Egyptians made of the sun when they depicted it, according to the locality, in the form of a radiating disk, of a goat, of a ram, of a sparrow-hawk, or of a scarab. Notwithstanding, they hit upon a means of contracting all these figures into one.

Round the Disk, now a Globe, they twisted symmetrically two *uræus* snakes, with heads erect and sometimes wearing the crown. Behind the *uræi* this Globe received the outstretched wings of the sparrow-hawk, on its top the undulating

FIG. 111. WINGED GLOBE OF EGYPT.
(LEPSIUS. *Denkmäler*, vol. iii., pl. 3 *b*.)

horns of the goat spread out; and from this fantastic mixture came those Winged Globes, which, while attaining their highest perfection under the eighteenth dynasty, formed, during the whole period of Egyptian art, so original and graceful a subject of ornamentation upon the pylons and the lintels of the temples.

It has been said, with good reason, that the Winged Globe is the Egyptian symbol *par excellence*.[1] According to an inscription at Edfu it was Toth himself who caused it to be placed above the entrances to all the temples in order to commemorate the victory won by Horus over Set, *i.e.*, by the principle of light and good over that of darkness and evil.[2]

Did the Egyptians imagine that the sun—or the soul of the sun—really assumed the form of a globe flanked by serpents, furnished with wings and surmounted by horns? Or, after having depicted the orb under its natural form, did they add *uræi* to symbolize its sovereignty, horns to

[1] PERROT et CHIPIEZ. *Histoire de l'art dans l'antiquité*, vol. i., p. 604.
[2] H. BRUGSCH. *Die Sage von der geflügelten Sonnenscheibe*, in the *Abhandlungen der königlichen Gesellschaft der Wissenschaften zu Göttingen*, 14th year (1868-1869), p. 209.

recall its strength, and wings to indicate its faculty of translation through space ?

Perhaps it is here unnecessary to choose between the two systems which divide the opinions of Egyptologists. A third interpretation, which to me seems to better account for the formation of the Winged Globe, makes it the result of a conscious and intentional combination of various personifications of the sun. M. Maspero, who is one of the most competent and persuasive defenders of the theory that the Egyptians began by believing the beast-like or fantastic creatures depicted upon their monuments to be real, admits himself that the priests may have invented composite figures with the fixed intention of expressing the union of distinct symbols and ideas.[1]

When the founding of a national monarchy in Egypt brought about the establishment of a common Pantheon, the gods, whose attributes or signification offered the greatest similarity, were related to each other, either as members of the same family, or as different forms of the same being. Is it unreasonable to assume that this movement of unification between local personifications of the same divinity found its expression in the blending of the images by which they were represented ?

It is only necessary to turn over the leaves of the handsome volumes published by MM. Perrot and Chipiez on the *Histoire de l'art dans l'antiquité*, or to cast a glance upon the first few of the plates appended by Lajard to his *Introduction à l'étude du culte de Mithra*, to be convinced that the Winged Globe was also one of the most widely spread and most venerated symbols in the whole of Western Asia.

Phœnicia exhibits it frequently on *stelai*, bas-

[1] G. MASPERO, in the *Revue de l'histoire des religions*, vol. v., p. 97.

reliefs, cylinders, gems, *pateræ*, and bowls. Frequently too, in that country, as in Egypt, the Winged Globe adorns the lintels of the temples. One of the most curious instances, quoted by M. Renan in his *Mission de Phénicie*, is furnished by the lintel of a Christian church built at Edde, near Gebal, from the materials of an ancient temple. The Globe and the *uræi* have been cut into for the reception of a red cross ; below are inscriptions which the learned Academician attributes to the worship of Adonis.[1]

The Winged Globe of the Phœnicians is found wherever their art was introduced, in Carthage, Cyprus, Sardinia, Sicily, and among different peoples of Palestine. It has even been pointed out on Israelitish seals of the oldest epoch,[2] and nothing prevents us from supposing that—like the serpent, the golden bull or calf, and the idolatrous images denounced by the prophets—it served, perhaps, to furnish a figured representation of *Yahveh.*

M. Renan, in his *Histoire du peuple d'Israël*, goes still further when he thinks he discovers the two *uræus* masses of the Egyptian symbol in the *urim-tummin*, or the two *urim*, described in Exodus, rather obscurely, as a mechanical means of consulting the divine will. "Perhaps the *uræi* of the Winged Globes," he suggests, "one meaning *yes* and the other *no*, were moved by a spring hidden behind the Disk."[3] Of course I leave to the eminent writer the whole responsibility of this theory, which is difficult to verify unless one be both an Egyptologist and a Hebraist. At all events nothing proves that the Israelites brought

---

[1] ERNEST RENAN. *Mission de Phénicie*, Paris, 1864, 1 vol., with atlas, pp. 227, 241, 857.

[2] CLERMONT-GANNEAU. *Sceaux et Cachets*, in the *Journal Asiatique*, 1883, vol. i.

[3] *Histoire du peuple d'Israël*. Paris, 1887, vol. i., p. 276.

directly from Egypt the type of their Winged
Globe ; the latter rather reproduces the forms of
Phœnician art, as is admitted, moreover, by M.
Renan.

To be sure, the Winged Globes of Phœnicia often
strive to reproduce the classic type of Egypt,
always, however, with variations which enable us
to easily distinguish them.　Sometimes the *uræi*
seem to come out from the lower part of the
Globe, so that the superior appendages may as

Fig. 112. Winged Globe of Phœnicia.
(Renan.　*Mission de Phénicie*, pl. xxxii.)

well depict serpents' tails as goats' horns, like
those of Egypt.

Sometimes these appendages are replaced by a
tuft of feathers which, perhaps, represents a sheaf

Fig. 113. Wingless Phœnician Globe with Uræi.
(Renan.　*Mission de Phénicie*, pl. lv.)

of rays, particularly when it occurs again below the
Globe in the shape of a tail.

Sometimes, again, the wings are bent downwards as in some archaic types of the Egyptian
symbol.[1]　Lastly, in some instances, the Winged
Globe assumes rather the forms which we shall
meet with in Asia Minor and in Mesopotamia.[2]

[1] Perrot et Chipiez.　Vol. iii., figs. 23, 305, 546.
[2] J. Menant.　*Les pierres gravées de la Haute-Asie.*　Paris,
1886, vol. ii., p. 223.

It is somewhat difficult, in the absence of positive documents, to determine the precise meaning which the Phœnicians ascribed to this symbol. It may be that we should see therein a solar representation. Yet, from what we know of the Phœnicians, their religion referred less to the direct worship of the orb than to the worship of the mythic personages who incarnated the principal aspects of the solar power.[1]

The Phœnicians often combined the Winged

FIG. 114. VASE OF CITIUM.
(PERROT et CHIPIEZ, vol. iii., fig. 518.)

Globe with other equivalent symbols. It is one of these combinations which I think I detect in a somewhat singular figure painted on a vase found at Citium, in the island of Cyprus, by General Cesnola (fig. 114).

With regard to this image, the learned authors of *l'Art dans l'antiquité* ask : " Should it be

[1] C. P. TIELE. *Histoire des anciennes religions des peuples semitiques.* Paris, 1882, chap. iii.

called a pillar, *stele,* or palmette ? [1]   To judge from
its most striking features—the medial leaves, the
terminal *fleuron,* the two pairs of volutes cutting the
figure in opposite directions, lastly and especially
its position between two animals facing one another
which, standing on their hind legs, appear to be
striving to reach with their mouths the extremities
of the *fleuron,*—all these details seem to manifest

FIG. 115. SACRED TREE OF PHŒNICIA.
(LAJARD.   *Mithra,* pl. liv. A, fig. 3.)

the intention of depicting the Sacred Tree of Phœnicia in its conventional form and with its characteristic accessories (fig. 115).

On the other hand, the lower half of the image
terminates in a regular pennated tail which one
would think was copied from a Winged Globe
of Western Asia ; the medial leaves may be held
to be wings ; the lower volutes suggest the oblique
appendages of the Assyrian Disk which terminates
in a loop ; finally, the upper volutes reproduce the
scroll which surmounts some specimens of the
Mesopotamian Globe.[2]

In fine, two things only are wanting in order
to make it a Winged Globe : these are the globe
and the wings.   Yet—even should it be said that
this is Hamlet with Hamlet left out—I cannot

[1] Vol. iii. (*Phénicie*), p. 706.
[2] Mr. G. Rawlinson, describing the most widely spread type
of the Sacred Tree among the Assyrians, likens the sort of
inverted Ionic capital which supports the terminal palmette to
" the scroll commonly surmounting the winged circle." (*The
five great Monarchies of the Ancient Eastern World.* London,
1862-67, vol. ii., p. 236).

help asserting that the ubiquitous influence of the Winged Globe was never revealed in a clearer manner by the brush or the chisel of an Oriental artist.

We may further instance, as an example of the same ever-present influence, the incised stone of Damascus on which I have above pointed out the amalgamation of the Winged Globe with the Sacred Cone of the Semites.[1] If this Cone represents the Great Goddess of Nature, herself considered to be the spouse of the solar Baal whom the Winged Globe symbolizes, it may be asked how far the aim of the fusion of the two symbols is not to accentuate still further the figurative representation of this mythic combination.

With greater reason the same explanation applies to the figure of Citium, if we agree to recognize therein a mutual filiation of the Winged Globe and the Sacred Tree, which we have so often seen placed one above another on the symbolic monuments of Western Asia.

North of Phœnicia, in the very middle of Asia Minor—amongst those Khetas or Hittites whose monuments disclose a complete civilization hardly dreamt of thirty years ago—the Winged Globe, once more a Disk, is noticed on seals, *stelai*, sculptured slabs and bas-reliefs, in company with

FIG. 116. WINGED DISK OF ASIA MINOR.
(LAJARD. *Mithra*, pl. i., fig. 21.)

religious subjects. Here, however, it is reproduced in a somewhat clumsy and inexact fashion, some-

---

[1] See above, fig. 94, p. 185.

times even perverted in its essential characteristics. The Globe becomes more independent of wings; the latter, in some cases, serve rather as its support than as its appendages;[1] it changes also into a Star inscribed in a circle.

I will not dwell on these variations, the meaning of which is far from evident. Perhaps they originate in attempts to adapt the foreign symbol to local forms of worship; perhaps they are merely to be ascribed to a whim, or an oversight, of the native artist when dealing with foreign models. It is indeed generally admitted that Hittite art, like the art of Phœnicia, derived its inspirations from Egypt and Assyria.

On approaching Mesopotamia we find the Winged Circle amongst the principal symbols brought into view on the bas-reliefs and cylinders

FIG. 117. WINGED CIRCLE OF ASSYRIA.
(LAYARD. *Monuments of Nineveh*, 1st series, pl. vi.)

of Assyria and Chaldæa. Sometimes it hovers above kings and priests, and again it presides at scenes of adoration and of sacrifice. The forms it assumes exhibit manifold variations, but these may be nearly all traced to two types.

One of these presents to our view a Disk surmounted by a scroll whose extremities curl upwards and thus produce the effect of two horns, not straightened out as in the Egyptian symbol,

[1] PERROT et CHIPIEZ, vol. iv., fig. 356.

but curved in the manner of an inverted Ionic
column. Below the Disk, which sometimes takes
the form of a Rosette, or a Wheel, a pennated tail
opens out like a fan between two wavy or slightly
bent appendages which fall obliquely from the
upper part of the circle.

The other type is distinguished by the presence
of an anthropoid genius inscribed in the Disk between the wings in such a manner that the horns
seem to spring from his cap and the pennated tail
forms a skirt with plaited flounces.[1] According
to the nature of the scenes where this personage
appears his right hand is sometimes uplifted in an
attitude of protection or of benediction, at other
times he holds a crown or a bow ; or again, assuming the warlike attitude especially suited to the

FIG. 118. ANTHROPOID WINGED CIRCLE.
(LAYARD. *Monuments of Nineveh*, 1st series, pl. xiii.)

divinities of Assyria, he lets fly a three-headed
arrow.[2]

Cuneiform texts elicit the fact that these Winged
Globes are no longer exclusively a solar emblem, but
that we are here in the presence of a divinity at once
more abstract and more anthropomorphic than the
sun : Assur at Nineveh, Bel or Ilu at Babylon.

[1] According to M. Léon Heuzey (*Revue archéologique*, 1887,
p. 256), these so-called plaited and goffered skirts of the
Assyrian costume, are nothing but a fringed stuff with long
locks of wool hung round the body like a shawl.

[2] G. RAWLINSON. *The Five Great Monarchies*, vol. ii., p. 235.

Perhaps this image even served to express the general idea of divinity, if we are to judge from its importance in the religious art of Mesopotamia ; sometimes, indeed, it there replaces the simple Disk, the Crescent, the Rouelle, the Cross, the Star, and the other symbols which in the field of the oldest cylinders are exhibited above divine personages, altars, pyres, the Sacred Tree, and so forth.

Yet the Winged Circles of the basin of the Euphrates, like those of Phœnicia and of Asia Minor, certainly originated in the valley of the Nile. It is there alone that they can be traced back to their simple and intelligible elements : the Disk, the sparrow-hawk, the goat, and the *uræus* serpents. Moreover—whilst in Egypt the Winged Globe is met with on monuments dating from the sixth dynasty onwards[1]—it would be vainly sought for in Mesopotamia under the first Chaldæan Empire, and even under the first Assyrian Empire.[2]

It is only from the time of the Sargonidæ that it appears on seals and bas-reliefs. The founding of Khorsabad, moreover, according to Mr. Layard, marks the epoch of the first appearance, in Assyrian art, of the Scarab, the Key of Life, the Lotus-flower, and the other symbols borrowed from Egypt.[3]

Even the discovery of the Winged Globe on older monuments of Mesopotamia would not be an argument against the Egyptian origin of the symbol. The researches of Assyriology have shown the commencement of intercourse between Egypt and Chaldæa to belong to an extremely

---

[1] LEPSIUS. *Denkmäler aus Ægypten and Æthiopien*, vol. ii., Bl. 12, figs. 116, 123, 135, 136.

[2] See the classification instituted by M. J. Menant in his valuable work on *Les pierres gravées de la Haute-Asie*.

[3] LAYARD. *Nineveh and its remains*. London, 1848-49, vol. ii., pp. 213-14.

remote period. These relations seem to date, at least, from the time of Naram-Sin, the son of Sargon, who, according to a tablet of Nabonidos, confirmed by various chronological calculations, reigned in the land of Accad in the thirty-eighth century before our era.[1] Some students even make them date from the *patesi* of Telloh, whose monuments, discovered by M. de Sarzec, are perhaps contemporary with the fourth Egyptian dynasty.[2]

If anything is surprising, it is that the principal symbols of Egypt did not sooner make their way into Chaldæan imagery. They must, in fact, have been spread abroad—long before the formation of the Assyrian Empire—with the ivories, seals, and gems brought from Egypt by the armies and caravans—witness the numerous Scarabs on the cartouches of Thothmes III. and of Amenophis III. discovered by modern explorers in the basin of the Tigris.[3]

Several experts in these matters, amongst others MM. G. Rawlinson and J. Menant, have wondered if the Winged Circle of Mesopotamia had not its prototype in the Sacred Bird with outstretched wings, which was led about in religious processions, and which already surmounts the standards sculptured at Telloh.[4] It is very certain that the Mesopotamian Disk, thanks to the presence of a pennated tail, exhibits an ornithomorphic character far more accentuated than that of the Winged Globe of Egypt. This similarity, however, provided there be any grounds for maintaining

[1] A. H. SAYCE. *Religion of the ancient Babylonians.* London, 1887, pp. 21 and 137.

[2] TERRIEN DE LA COUPERIE. *An unknown King of Lagash,* in the *Babylonian and Oriental Record* for August, 1890, p. 193 *et seq.*

[3] LAYARD. *Nineveh and Babylon.* London, 1853, chap. xii.

[4] J. MENANT. *Pierres gravées,* vol. ii., p. 17.

that equivalent symbols tend to merge into one
another, is merely a result of the importance attributed at an earlier date to the representation of the
Sacred Bird in Mesopotamia. In other places,[1]
does not M. Menant record a faint analogy between
the combination of lines which cross in the sketch
of the Winged Disk, and the group of cuneiform
characters which gives the ideogram of the supreme
Divinity as an eight-rayed star ? Here again the
general resemblance proves, not that the cuneiform sign gave rise to the symbol of the Winged
Circle, but that the latter was, so to speak, sometimes cast in the mould of the sign used to render
the conception of the divinity ; just as in Egypt it
borrowed the outlines of another solar emblem,
the flying Scarab.[2]

However this may be, the very principle of the
ornithomorphic image is undeniably of Egyptian
origin. It is Egypt alone that can have given the
Assyrians the idea of introducing the Globe,
uræi, and horns, into the representation of the
Sacred Bird. If any doubt remained in this respect, it would be dismissed by the examination
of the intermediate forms which serve as a gradual
transition between the Winged Globes of the two
countries.

In the rectilinear strokes terminating in a ball,
or hook, which form the lower appendages of certain Winged Circles of Assyria, some people have
thought they recognized an equivalent of the
claws which hold a ring in the representation of
the Egyptian vulture or sparrow-hawk.[3] There

---

[1] J. Menant. *Pierres gravées*, vol. ii., p. 18.
[2] M. Gaidoz thinks even that the Scarab may well have been
the prototype of the Winged Globe (*Le dieu gaulois du soleil et le
symbolisme de la roue*. Paris, 1886, p. 53.) To me it seems
that the resemblance of the two symbols is better accounted
for by the hypothesis of an independent origin and a subsequent
approximation.
[3] It is interesting to come across similar appendages, un-

would be nothing singular in the fact that the ornithomorphic Globe, having borrowed the wings of the Sacred Bird, had also appropriated its claws. Yet in by far the greater number of Asiatic Disks these wavy or curved lines undeniably originate in the Egyptian *uræi*, as may be proved by comparing the two figures below.

FIG. 119. EGYPTIAN GLOBE.
(LEPSIUS. *Denkmäler*, vol. ii., fig. 136.)

FIG. 120. MESOPOTAMIAN GLOBE.
(LAJARD. *Mithra*, pl. xxxvi., fig. 13.)

It remains to be explained how the Egyptian symbol of the sun became, in Mesopotamia, the figured representation of the supreme God. Mr. G. Rawlinson conjectures that the Assyrians drew a circle to designate eternity, then added wings to express omnipresence, and introduced the human figure to symbolize supreme wisdom.[1] It is possible, although indications are wanting in this respect, that a similar interpretation was applied to the Winged Globe in the sacerdotal schools of Babylon and of Tyre, during the period of metaphysical speculation, when Sanchoniathon defined, as a symbol of perpetual motion, the double pair of

deniable survivals of the Egyptian *uræi*, around Disks, Christianized by the inscription of the Cross, or Chrism, which adorn the lintel of the door in Christian tombs of Syria (LETHABY. *Architecture, Mysticism and Myth*, p. 268.)

[1] G. RAWLINSON. *The Five Great Monarchies*, vol. ii., p. 231.

wings belonging to certain divine figures derived by
Phœnicia from the art of Mesopotamia, or of Egypt.
But such subtle intentions would be sought for in
vain among the early Assyrian artists, who made
the ornithomorphic or anthropoid Disks. It is far
more likely that, under the encroaching influence
of Egyptian symbolism and art, they restricted
themselves to copying, in order to represent their
supreme god, the symbol which they knew to
express the equivalent idea in the imagery of their
neighbours.

In Egypt itself the sun appeared from remote
ages as the essential manifestation, the visible
face, the "Eye" of the One and only God. The
whole mythology of Egypt, at the period of its
complete development, had ended by becoming,
to borrow an expression of M. Paul Pierret, a
solar drama.[1] Consequently, it is easy to understand that the Winged Globe—*i.e.*, the combination of the principal images employed to
represent the sun in the valley of the Nile—was
adopted by the nations subject to the influence of
Egypt in order to symbolize their own conceptions of God in His highest manifestations.

The career of the Winged Globe was not to
cease here.

We see in its reception by the Persians how
symbols pass from one nation to another, and even
from one cult to a rival form of worship. Till
Cyrus overcame the second Babylonian Empire
in 538 B.C., Ahura Mazda, the omniscient lord,
had been perhaps exclusively represented in worship by the flame of the pyres, as was proper
for a god "similar to light in body and to truth in
spirit." Henceforth he assumes the symbol of Bel

---

[1] P. PIERRET. *Essai sur la mythologie égyptienne.* Paris,
1876, p. 15.

and of Assur : the Winged Circle under one of the
two forms given it by Assyria, but with modifications which were generally improvements. In the
anthropoid type, the Disk with its lower appendages becomes more and more of a waist-band
with loose ends. All trace of horns disappears.
The genius, inscribed in the circle, exchanges the
close-fitting tunic and the low cap of the Assyrians for the wide-sleeved dress and tiara of the
Medes. Yet his attitude remains that of Assur.
Sometimes, soaring above the royal chariot, the
god shoots an arrow at wild beasts, or against the
enemies of the sovereign ; at other times his left

FIG. 121. AHURA MAZDA.
(LAJARD. *Mithra*, pl. ii., fig. 32.)

hand is uplifted, and in his right he holds a Lotus-
flower.

The other type also exhibits more graceful and
freer forms, which may bear comparing with the
best specimens of Phœnicia or of Egypt. M.
Dieulafoy, moreover, has shown that the architecture and ornamentation of the Persians were frequently influenced by Egyptian art, taken at its
very source and not in its Assyrian imitations.[1]

In Europe I am not aware that the Winged
Globe has as yet been met with, except in the
islands of the Mediterranean, whither it was
directly introduced by the Phœnicians. Greece

[1] DIEULAFOY. *L'art antique de la Perse,* 3rd part, § iv.,
p. 33 *et seq.*

does not seem to have accorded it rights of natu-
ralization, although it adopted Asiatic symbols of
smaller importance, or less widely spread, such as
the *gammadion*, the *triscèle*, the Thunderbolt and
the Lotus. It is met with at Carthage, to be sure,
on coins whose execution reveals the plastic influence of ·Greek art.[1] But these coins are too
closely connected with the religions of Asia in
their subject, their legend, and their symbol, to
allow of our ascribing them to Hellenic civilization.

The latter was doubtlessly acquainted with the
symbol of the Disk, or of the solar Wheel. But
Greek art was too anthropomorphic to give un-
natural forms to the embodiments of its divine
ideal. It therefore reserved monstrous bodies for
monsters, and if it added wings to the shoulders
of some of its *genii*, or gods, these were mere
accessories which perverted neither the forms nor
the proportions of the human figure. When it
took from Asia symbolic combinations in which
the Winged Globe was originally represented, it
replaced it by the Thunderbolt, at once the weapon
and the symbol of its own supreme god,—as in
those capitals of the temple of Athene at Priene,
where the Thunderbolt is suspended over the
Sacred Tree and its two acolytes (see above, pl.
iv., figs. *c* and *e*).[2]

On seeing some representations of the Thunder-

[1] Duc de Luynes. *Numismatique des Satrapies.* Paris,
1846, pl. i., figs. 1, 2, 3; pl. ii., figs. 3, 4, 5.—Barclay V.
Head. *Guide to the Coins of the Ancients.* London, 1881,
pl. xi., No. 40, and pl. lix., No. 33.—A coin of Iaetia, in Sicily,
exhibits on the reverse a human face with two wings and three
legs; but this is a mere embellishment of the Asiatic *triscèle*
which, as we have seen, became the emblem of the island with
three capes.

[2] In the same plate we may follow the subsequent transformation of this symbolic detail which, on the tympanum of
the church at Marigny (pl. iv., fig. *j*) becomes a double branch
on the top of the sacred tree.

bolt which recall in a remarkable manner the outlines of the Winged Globe, it may be even asked
if it was not owing to this latter symbol that the
Greeks transformed into a Winged Spindle (fig. 122
d and *e*) the Double Trident derived from Assyria
(fig. 122 *a*). At any rate the transition, or, if it
be preferred, the combination of the two symbols
is met with in those coins of northern Africa
where Greek art was so greatly impregnated with
Phœnician types. Thus, on coins of Bocchus II.,
King of Mauritania, figures are found which M.
Lajard connected with the Winged Globe, and
M. L. Müller calls Thunderbolts, but which are
really the result of a crossing between these two
emblems (fig. 122 *b* and *c*).

a   *b*   *c*   *d*   *e*

FIG. 122. COMBINATION OF THE WINGED GLOBE AND THE
THUNDERBOLT.[1]

There is a type of *Jupiter fulmens*, which a tardy
syncretism attempted to combine, in plastic art as
in the worship, with the solar Baal of Tarsus, himself represented by the Winged Globe, or rather by
the winged god of Persian symbolism (fig. 123).

It must not be forgotten, however, that here
again we are in the very middle of Asia Minor,

[1] *a*, On a coin of Faleri (HUNTER, pl. 27, No. 16).
b and *c*, On Mauritanian coins (L. MÜLLER. *Numismatique
de l'ancienne Afrique.* Copenhagen, vol. iii., p. 95, Nos. 5
and 7).
d, On a coin of Ptolemy Soter (L. MÜLLER, *op. cit.*, vol. i.,
p. 141, No. 371).
e, On a coin of Syracuse (BARCLAY V. HEAD. *Coins in the
British Museum*, pl. 35, fig. 30).

and that this homage paid by local art to the great god of Hellenic culture did not react on the types of Europe.

Even the Winged Wheel, of which the symbolism

FIG. 123. COIN OF TARSUS.

of our industrial arts makes so frequent use, only appears by way of exception on Greek and Roman monuments, if we leave out the sort of velocipede on which Triptolemus rides; and even in these rare instances it appears merely as the abbreviation of a chariot, or as a symbol of motion, and in no case can it be connected with the Winged Circle which, on certain Asiatic monuments, originates in the Egyptian Globe.[1]

On the other hand, the plastic influence of the Winged Globe seems to have spread far further than the figures in which we find it literally reproduced. M. Gaidoz has pointed out certain representations of Ixion on the Wheel which might well have been taken from the type of the Assyrian god inscribed in the Disk.[2] Perhaps we should attribute to the same origin the halo of glory which the Christians borrowed from classic art, to surround therewith the head, or body, of their superhuman beings.

To be sure, the earliest idea of the "glory" may

[1] See, in the *Monuments inédits*, by Raoul Rochette (Paris, 1833) the scene of the judgment of Orestes (pl. xl., fig. 1), where Minerva leans on a winged wheel, which, in the author's opinion, denotes the chariot of the goddess; see also (same work, pl. xliii., fig. 2) the personage who seems to advance with the help of winged wheels placed under his feet.

[2] *Symbolisme de la roue*, p. 44.

have been directly furnished by certain aspects of
the sun. Velleius Paterculus relates, that "at
the moment when Augustus entered Rome the
arc of the sun, symmetrically curved round his
head, was seen to form a crown of the colour of
the rainbow." But it is none the less the case
that the manner in which the Aureole encircles the
bust of Assyrian divinities refers us directly to
the ring which serves Ahura Mazda or Assur as
a girdle, and which represents, as I have shown
above, the circumference of the Winged Globe,[1]—
save that the disk has here discarded its wings
and bristles with rays instead.

FIG. 124. MESOPOTAMIAN AUREOLA.
(MENANT. *Pierres gravées*, vol. ii., fig. 45.)

It should be remarked that in the Assyrian
Aureoles, the rays, instead of widening in diverging
from the centre, grow narrower as they get further
from it. It is this peculiarity, equally observable
in classic and in Christian art,[2] that permitted of
tracing their Aureoles to the analogous symbol
represented in Assyria from the fourth century
before our era.[3]

In India, although its symbolism does not seem
to have adopted the Winged Globe, we likewise

[1] Cf. the image of Assur in the cylinder reproduced above,
fig. 119.

[2] DIDRON. *Iconographie chrétienne.* Paris, 1843, p. 13.

[3] J. MENANT. *Pierres graveés*, vol. ii., pp. 55, 56.

meet with certain traditional types which may perhaps have been subjected to the influence of the old Egyptian symbol.

Thus, in a representation of Vishnu, in his *avatar* of the tortoise, I have noticed, at the Musée Guimet, a sort of wrapper, fashioned after the girdle with loose ends which characterizes the winged genius of Persia. The lower part of the body is formed of a carapace which recalls at once the tail of the Winged Disk and that of the Scarab. The wings are wanting, but their place

FIG. 125. AVATAR OF VISHNU.
(GUIGNIAUT, pl. ix., fig. 47.)

is taken by two supplementary arms, in conformity with the usual conventions of Hindu pictorial art.

Elsewhere it is the *chakra* or solar Disk whose

FIG. 126. CHAKRA OF VISHNU.
(MOOR. *Hindu Pantheon*, pl. ix., fig. 1.)

lateral appendages, representing leaves, or flames, assume the appearance, or at least take the place, of the wings in the Winged Globe. These representations are, in truth, comparatively modern, but it is probable that their type is extremely old.

It is, however, above all in the *trisula*—that Caduceus of India as it has sometimes been termed —that we will have occasion to note an evident intervention of the Winged Globe amongst the original creations of Hindu symbolism.

In the New World I hardly know of more than one figure which bears an unquestionable resemblance to the Winged Globe; this is a human face, furnished with small pennated wings and a formidable pair of moustaches, which two English travellers, Messrs. Pim and Seeman, observed cut in a rock at New Segovia in Central America.

Fig. 127.
(*Journal* of the *Roy. As. Soc.*, London, vol. xviii., (new series), p. 397.)

Mr. Robert Sewell considers that these moustaches are imitations of Assyrian scrolls, or Egyptian *uræi*.[1] But here the resemblance may well be accidental, and the choice of a globe or face, provided with wings or feathers with a view to typify the sun, is too simple a combination for it not to have been possible to occur independently in the symbolism of nations unknown to one another.

On the other hand, M. d'Eichthal thought he discovered in the ruins of a sanctuary at Ocosingo,

[1] *Early Buddhist Symbolism*, in the *Journal of the Roy. Asiat. Soc.*, vol. xviii., (new series), p. 397.

near Palenque, a fragment of the wing of a globe sculptured above a doorway.[1] But the globe is far from being depicted with such distinctness as to permit of our accepting this conclusion.

Finally, we find amongst the bas-reliefs of Uxmal, in Yucatan, a geometric design whose lower appendage suggests in a striking manner the pennated tail of certain Assyrian, Phœnician, and Persian Globes.[2] These, however, are isolated details, and it is the whole of the combination represented by the Winged Globe which must be found in all desirable conditions of authenticity ere we can deduce a case of real transmission.

Fig. 128. Solar Symbol at Uxmal.
(Publications of the *Bureau of Ethnography*, vol. ii., pl. 57, No. 5.)

II. The Origins of the Caduceus.

The Caduceus is one of the symbolic figures which have tried in the highest degree the patience of scholars. Its classic appearance of a winged rod, round which two serpents are symmetrically entwined, is very far removed from its primitive form.

Greek monuments make known to us a period when it consisted of a circle, or a disk, placed on

---

[1] *Revue archéologique* for 1865, vol. xi. (new series), p. 490.
[2] See above, figs. 117, 118, 121, 123, also 134B, and 136.

the top of a stick, and surmounted by a crescent, making thus a kind of figure 8 open at the top, ☿ .

In a still more remote age it seems to have formed a flowered bar with three leaves, τριπέταλος, as Homer says.

Through what influence were these three leaves transformed into a disk, surmounted by an incomplete circle ?

The latter form appears so often on the Phœnician monuments that we are forced to wonder, with M. Perrot, " whether the Caduceus was borrowed by the Phœnicians from Greece and its Hermes, or whether the latter did not rather

FIG. 129. GREEK
CADUCEUS.

(OVERBECK. *Kunstmythologie*,
pl. xxxvi., fig. 6.)

FIG. 130. PUNIC
CADUCEUS.

(PERROT et CHIPIEZ,
vol. iii., p. 232.)

appropriate this attribute from some eastern god, his elder by many centuries." [1]

MM. Perrot and Chipiez seem themselves to give a decisive answer to their question when, in a later volume, they show us the Caduceus on Hittite monuments of Asia Minor, where no one can dream of importations from Greece.[2]

At Carthage the Caduceus is nearly always associated with the Sacred Cone on *stelai* dedicated

---

[1] PERROT et CHIPIEZ, vol. iii., p. 463.

[2] PERROT et CHIPIEZ, vol. iv., (*Judée, Syrie*, etc., figs. 274 and 353).

either to Tanit "the face of Baal," or conjointly to
Baal Hamman and Tanit. If it is likely that
this Cone stands for the symbol of Tanit, would it
be rash to assume that the Caduceus represents
either the companion of the Great Goddess of
Carthage, the Phœnician god of the sun, or of the
solar heat, Baal Hamman—or the usual hypostasis
of Baal Hamman, his "messenger" or "angel,"
Malac Baal [1]—or, finally, the third personage of the
triad composed of Baal, Tanit, and Iol or Iolaüs,
the divine solar infant, lost and found by turns
like Atys and Adonis elsewhere ? [2]

In all these cases the Caduceus might form the
symbol of a solar divinity, and what strengthens
this assumption is the fact that on some Libyan
stelai the two Caducei which flank the Cone are
sometimes replaced by Wheels arranged in the
same manner. [3]

Does not the Caduceus of the Greeks seem likewise to have been an essentially solar emblem ?
According to the words of Homer it was a rod of
gold which alternately "charms the eyes of men
and calls them from their slumbers ;" [4] it lures the
dead to Hades, and can bring them back to the
light of day ; lastly, like a real magic wand, it
changes all it touches into gold. I in no wise
infer therefrom that Hermes was a solar god, or
even a god of the sun when below the horizon.
With the Greeks themselves, however, tradition
makes out that the Caduceus had been given him
by Apollo in return for the lyre.

Perhaps the Phœnician Caduceus passed to the
hand of Hermes amongst those Greek colonists

[1] PH. BERGER   *L'ange d'Astarté*, in the *Faculté de théologie
protestante à M. Edouard Reuss.*   Paris, 1879, pp. 52-54.
[2] FR. LENORMANT.   *Gazette archéologique*, 1876, p. 127.
[3] *Corpus inscriptionum semitic.*, fasc. iv., 1889 ; tab. liv.,
fig. 368.
[4] *Odyssey*, v., lines 47, 48.

of Cyrenaica who contributed more or less towards introducing Punic, and even Egyptian elements into the religion as into the mythology of the Hellenes.[1] Perhaps, too, the transmission was brought about on Greek soil through direct intercourse with Phœnician traders, who cannot but have diffused, with their religious and artistic products, the attributes of their own national divinities.[2]

Is it possible to retrace still further the history of the Caduceus ?

Numerous origins and manifold antecedents

[1] MAURY. *Histoire des religions de la Grèce antique.* Paris, 1859, vol. iii., p. 265 *et seq.*

[2] It is not even necessary for the Greeks to have believed in the identity of Hermes with the foreign divinity from whom they thus derived the Caduceus. It is, however, proper to point out that the analogies between Hermes and Baal Hamman were too numerous not to have struck their respective worshippers when once these gods came into contact with one another. Both are united to the goddess of love, Aphrodite-Astarte. Both have the ram as their sacred animal ; this latter feature belongs to them in common with the Ammon of the Libyans and the Ammon-Ra of the Egyptians. The divinity who patronized the business dealings of the Phœnicians must have easily passed, in the eyes of the Greeks, for the god of commerce, and we know that Hermes appropriated this function in post Homeric times.

As for Malac Baal, M. Ph. Berger reminds us that he was, like Hermes, an initiator, an intermediate agent between mankind, and the superior divinity (*L'ange d'Astarte, loc. cit.,* pp. 52-54). Both are represented and even personified by *stelai* and *hermata,* or *bethels.* Both assume, at times, the human figure with wings, save that Greek art placed the latter on the heels of its god; just as, in the Caduceus, it changed the position of the wings of the Winged Globe.

It may be added that the Greeks themselves had been impressed with this analogy between the messenger of Zeus and the hypostasis of Baal Hamman, for Pausanias (*Elis,* xv.) informs us that in the prytaneum of Olympia they rendered homage to Hera-Ammonia (probably Tanit), and to Parammon, divinities of Libya. "*Parammon,*" he adds, "*is a surname of Hermes.*"

have been attributed to it. It has alternately been considered to be an equivalent of the Thunderbolt, a form of the Sacred Tree, a contraction of the Scarab, a combination of the solar Globe and the Crescent of the moon, and so forth. All these derivations may have some foundation in fact. I once attempted to connect it with the Winged Globe, as a mere hypothesis, to be sure, but in terms perhaps too affirmative for want of having taken sufficiently into consideration the intervention of other figures in the genesis of its forms.[1]   I would now be more inclined to admit that it was first of all an instrument, a weapon, a religious, or military, ensign, gradually modified by coming into contact with other figured representations, amongst which was the Winged Globe.

Bas-reliefs of Assyria exhibit military ensigns, prototypes, perhaps, of the Constantinian *labarum*, which consist of a large ring placed on the top of a staff, and girt with two loose bandelets (fig. 131).

FIG. 131. ASSYRIAN STANDARD.

On the top of this ring—which M. Perrot has no hesitation in comparing with the circle forming the girdle of Assur in certain solar adaptations of the Winged Globe (see above, fig. 118)— place either the horns symbolical of divine power

[1] *Bulletin de l'Acad. roy. de Belgique*, vol. xvi. (1888), p. 638 *et seq.*

amongst the Mesopotamians, or the Crescent, so
frequently coupled with the Globe in the religious
imagery of the Phœnicians, and the result will be
unquestionably the image of the Punic Caduceus.

On Hittite monuments Caducei are noticed which
are terminated by a Globe in relief, surmounted by
a real pair of horns—a peculiarity which we again
meet with on a Tyrian amphora reproduced in

FIG. 132. HITTITE
CADUCEUS.

(PERROT et CHIPIEZ, vol. iv.,
fig. 353.)

FIG. 133. VARIETY OF
GREEK CADUCEUS.

(*Monuments céramogr.*, vol.
iii., pl. 36 *a*.)

De Witte and Lenormant's *Monuments céramographiques.*

The result is the same if we invert certain solar

a

b

FIG. 134.[1]

Globes of Phœnicia, which are merely an abbreviation of the Winged Globe of Egypt, as is easily seen
from the two *uræus* snakes which encircle them,

[1] *a*, See above, fig. 113; *b*, Sardinian scarab (PERROT et
CHIPIEZ, vol. iii., fig. 464).

and the tufts of feathers by which they are surmounted (fig. 134).

The very *uræi* here form the counterpart of
the loose scrolls below the Phœnician Caduceus
(fig. 135 *a* and *b*), as also underneath the Assyrian
ensign (fig. 131), and which are still noticeable in
the *stemmata* of some Greek Caducei.

We find, on a Sardinian cylinder, reproduced by
MM. Perrot et Chipiez, a curious alteration of the
Winged Globe, in which the ornithomorphic appendages are reduced to a reticular or pennated tail
(fig. 134 *b*). Putting aside the horns, which have
at the same time assumed the aspect of a fork, we
cannot but be struck by the resemblance of this
symbol to those of the Phœnician Caducei, where
the Disk seems to be supported by a conical stem
(fig. 135 *a*). In other places the horns are want-

a   *b*

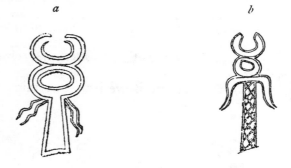

FIG. 135. CADUCÉES LIBYQUES.
(A. W. S. VAUX. *Phœnician inscript.*, pl. i., fig. 2, and
pl. vii., fig. 20.)

ing, notably in a Globe of Persepolis, which also
rests on a triangular tail ; here, however, the *uræi*
are lowered in such a manner as to form more
plainly the transition from the bandelets (fig. 136).

It is worth while remarking that the Winged
Globe was sometimes borne as a standard at the

end of a staff (figs. 138 and 139), in the manner of
the Caduceus and the Assyrian ensign.

FIG. 136. PERSEPOLITAN SCULPTURE.
(GUIGNIAUT. *Op. cit.*, t. iv., pl. xxii., fig. 117 *a.*)

Does it follow that the Caduceus was necessarily
a derivation of the Winged Globe? One might
equally admit—and it is on this point I want to
insist—that it had an independent origin, and,
at a later date, came under the influence of the
Winged Globe, or, reciprocally, that certain reproductions of the Winged Globe were modified on
coming into contact with it.[1]

It must indeed be mentioned that M. Ph.
Berger was able, with the same degree of likeli-
hood, to connect the antecedents of the Caduceus
among the Phœnicians with the *ashêrah, i.e.*, with
the stake entwined with bandelets (figs. 63, 79),
and with the other analogous *simulacra* which we
saw representing among the Syrians the goddess
of the earth, or of Nature.[2]

In support of this opinion, or rather of the
assumption that there is a transition from the
Sacred Tree surmounted by the solar Disk to the
Caduceus of the Phœnicians and the Hittites, I
have here brought together three figures taken
from cylinders found in Asia Minor.

[1] On some coins of Carthage the Caduceus alternates with
the Winged Globe above the horse. (HUNTER, tab. xv.,
No. 14, and LAJARD, pl. xlv., No. 5.)
[2] *Gazette archéologique* for 1880, p. 127.

In the first (fig. 137) the Sacred Tree is still plainly recognizable below the solar Disk; in the

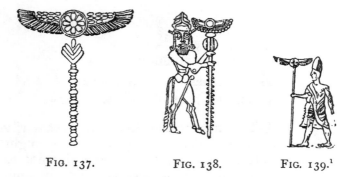

FIG. 137.   FIG. 138.   FIG. 139.[1]

second (fig. 138) it supports the latter; in the third (fig. 139) we find nothing more than a stick supporting the Winged Disk in the manner of a standard.

Let us now place side by side with these symbolic representations the following figures taken from Mesopotamian cylinders.

FIG. 140. MESOPOTAMIAN CYLINDERS.[2]

The wings of the Globe have here disappeared : on the other hand the figures *a* and *b*, which are unquestionably connected with the rudimentary forms of the Sacred Tree (cf. above, fig. 61) draw

[1] LAJARD. *Mithra*, pl. xxxiii., fig. 4.—ID., *Ibid.*, pl. lvii., fig. 5.—J. MENANT. *Pierres gravées*, fig. 112.
[2] *a, Collection de Clerq*, vol. i., pl. xxxi., fig. 330 ; *b*, PERROT et CHIPIEZ, vol. ii., p. 342 ; *c*, LAJARD. *Mithra*, pl. xxxviii., fig. 2.

nearer at the same time to the Caduceus, as this last emblem appears in fig. *c* under the form of a mace.

Whether we have here at last the prototype of the Caduceus, or whether we are once again in the presence of other figurative representations which had merely felt the influence of this mysterious emblem, is a question which the relative age of the monuments concerned can alone decide. If, however, as everything goes to prove, it is to Mesopotamia that we must go for the earliest types of the Caduceus, nothing prevents us from assuming that the latter came directly from Asia Minor to Greece, without passing through the medium of the Libyan Caduceus.

As for the latest transformation which Greek art caused the Caduceus to undergo, it may be questioned if the introduction of the serpents and wings is not here evidence of a phenomenon of symbolic atavism, a return to old, or foreign, forms ; or even of the persistency of a plastic tradition whose intermediate links have not come down to us. According to some writers the serpents of the classic Caduceus would be due to a transformation of the *stemmata* or scrolls which hang beneath the Circle. Now, as I have above shown, these latter, in the Winged Globes of Western Asia, are themselves a metamorphosis of the Egyptian *uræi*. It must be also borne in mind that the serpent twined round the end of a pole forms the symbol of Baal Hamman in the Punic imagery.[1] On the other hand, Fergusson alleges having noticed live serpents intertwined in this manner ; the Greek artist would therefore have done nothing more than adjust to the Caduceus an image provided by real life.[2]

[1] PH. BERGER. *La Trinité carthaginoise* in the *Gazette archéologique* for 1879, p. 135.
[2] *Tree and Serpent Worship.* Appendix.

At any rate, it is owing to this æsthetic transformation that the Caduceus was preserved until our own times to represent two functions of the ancient Hermes, which are more in vogue than ever with the human race, industry and commerce. Even in the matter of symbols nothing dies which deserves to live, and is capable of transformation.

In India, likewise, the Caduceus has survived to the present time under the form of two serpents intertwined. M. Guimet has found numerous specimens amongst the carvings placed as *ex voto* in the Vishnu temples of southern India.[1] It is probable that this symbol was introduced into India in the track of Alexander. It is found, indeed, on the coins of Sophytes, a native prince who copied the monetary types of the Seleucid kings, and it continued to be reproduced without interruption in the coinage of the Indo-Scythic sovereigns. But it is also met with in India under a simpler form which, like the earlier type of the Greek Caduceus, seems to be connected with the

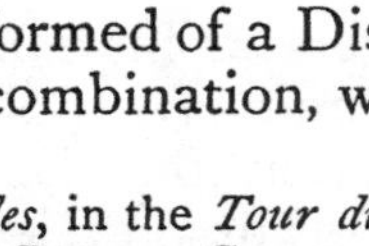

a　　b　　c

FIG. 141. VARIETIES OF INDIAN CADUCEI.[2]

Asiatic Caduceus formed of a Disk surmounted by a Crescent. This combination, which is sometimes

---

[1] *Huit jours aux Indes*, in the *Tour du Monde* for 1885, 1st part, p. 244.—See also RIVETT CARNAC. *The Snake Symbol in India*, in the *Proceedings of the Asiatic Society of Bengal* 1879, part i., pl. vi., fig. 4.

[2] *a*, PERCY GARDNER. *Coins in the British Museum. Greek and Scythic Kings of India and Bactria*, pl. xxii., fig. 9.

b, SENART. *Journal asiatique*, 1875, vol. vi., p. 137.

c, RIVETT CARNAC. *Coins of the Sunga or Mitra dynasty*, in the *Proceedings* of the *Asiatic Society of Bengal*, 1880, vol. xlix., pl. ix., fig. 19.

placed on the top of a staff, and sometimes isolated
like our astronomical sign ♉, appears to have been
confounded at an early date with the Buddhist
trisula, whose manifold transformations deserve a
chapter for themselves.

III. THE TRANSFORMATIONS OF THE TRISULA.

I have already referred to the importance of the
Trident in the symbolism of Hinduism where,
under the name *trisula* (*tri* three, and *sula* point,
spear, or pale) it occurs amongst the most important attributes of Siva. This emblem exhibits no
peculiarity of form here; it might as well figure
in the hands of Hades, or of Poseidon. This is
not the case, however, with respect to the Buddhist
trisula or, at least, the symbol which bears this
name amongst the Buddhists.

The *trisula* of the Buddhists, termed also *vardhamana*, "a crescent," may be described, in its

FIG. 142. THE TRISULA.

simplest form, as an *omicron* surmounted by an
omega.

It is, however, rarely met with under such a
simple form. The upper arc of the *omicron*, or
rather of the disk, is nearly always flanked by two
small circles, or by two horizontal strokes which
often assume the appearance of two leaves or small
wings (fig. 143 *et seq.*). The points of the *omega*
change into *fleurons;* the disk itself rests on a
staff or pedestal, and from its lower arc fall two
spires similar to serpents' tails, the ends of which
are sometimes curved upwards (fig. 143), and
sometimes downwards (fig. 154).

At times the *trisula* appears to have only an ornamentive significance. Thus we see it crowning balustrades and porticoes, adorning sword-

FIG. 143. TRISULA OF AMARAVATI.
Journal of the Royal Asiatic Society, vol. xviii. (new series), fig. 1.)

scabbards, and forming necklace-pendants and ear-rings.[1] But in most cases it unquestionably discharges the function of a symbol, and even of a religious symbol. Engraved on numerous coins by the side of religious emblems and images, it stands at the beginning and end of votive inscriptions in the caves of Western India.[2] The sculp-

FIG. 144. TRISULA ON BLAZING PILLAR.
(FERGUSSON. *Tree and Serpent Worship*, pl. lxxi.)

tures of the bas-reliefs exhibit it, in turn, on the staff of banners, on the back of an elephant, on an altar where homage is paid to it, and, lastly, on a pillar from which flames emerge (fig. 144). At

[1] A. CUNNINGHAM. *The Stupa of Barhut.* London, 1879, pl. xlix., fig. 10; pl. l., figs. 5 and 6.
[2] EUG. BURNOUF. *Le Lotus de la Bonne Loi*, p. 626.

Bharhut it occurs above the throne of Buddha. At Amaravati it is one of the signs cut on the sole of the Master's feet.[1] The oldest representations of the *trisula* are found—in conjunction with the principal symbols of Buddhism, the *swastika*, the *stupa*, the Sacred Tree, and so forth—on the coins of Krananda,[2] a native sovereign contemporary with Alexander or the earliest Seleucid kings.

FIG. 145. COIN OF KRANANDA.

Nevertheless the *trisula* was far from being solely used by the Buddhists. In caves it is sometimes placed near symbols of the solar worship, and on the coins of the Indo-Scythic princes it is not only struck beside images of the Hindu god Siva but, what at first surprises us, beside those of Greek divinities, such as Zeus;[3] it is, moreover, possible that it became a mere monetary sign, as often happens with religious symbols used in coinage.

Among the Jains, who have so many affinities

[1] A. CUNNINGHAM. *The Stupa of Bharhut,* and J. FERGUSSON. *Tree and Serpent Worship,* 1st vol., with plates. London, 1868, *passim.*—Cf. engraving of our frontispiece.

[2] Edward Thomas has maintained that Krananda was identical with the Xandrames of Diodorus (*Journal of the Royal Asiatic Society.* London, vol. i., new series, p. 477, *On the identity of Xandrames and Krananda*), which would make this coin earlier than the year 317 B.C.—Wilson, on his side, makes Xandrames to be Chandragupta, the ancestor of Asoka (Introduction to the translation of the Mûdrarakshasa. *The Theatre of the Hindus,* vol. ii., 131, 132).

[3] PERCY GARDNER. *Coins in the British Museum. Greek and Scythic Kings of India and Bactria,* pp. 106 and 107.

with Buddhism, the twenty-fourth and last of the *Tirthankaras* or legendary saints of the sect has the *vardhamana* as a symbol ; this personage even bears, according to Colebrook, the surname of *Trisula*.[1]

It may be wondered, at first sight, that the innumerable texts left by Buddhism give us no positive information with regard to the meaning and origin of the *trisula*. Few symbols have given rise, in our own times, to more varied explanations.

Some have seen therein the monogram of Buddha;[2] others the symbol of the *dharma*, the Law, which sums up the doctrine of Buddhism ;[3] others again a representation of the *tri-ratna*, the threefold jewel formed by Buddha, his Law, and his Church.[4] There are those who have discovered in the *trisula* the juxtaposition of the *dharma chakra*, the " Wheel of the Law " to the ancient letter ⅄, *y*, which itself is said to stand for the mystic formula *ye dharma*.[5] Some scholars think they recognize in it the combination of five letters symbolizing respectively intelligence (*ma*) and the four component elements of matter, air (*ya*), fire (*ra*), water (*va*), and earth (*la*).[6]

Eugene Burnouf thought he found therein the *vardhamana kaya*, "the Propitious One," one of the sixty-five signs which, according to Buddhist

---

[1] COLEBROOK. *Observations on the Jainas*, in the *Asiatic Researches*. London, 1809, vol. vii., p. 306.

[2] J. FERGUSSON. *Description of the Amaravati Tope*, in the *Journal* of the *Royal Asiatic Society*. London (vol. iii. of new series, p. 162).

[3] EDW. THOMAS, in vol. iv. (new series) of the *Numismatic Chronicle*, p. 282, foot-note.

[4] A. CUNNINGHAM. *The Stupa of Barhut*, p. 111.

[5] F. PINCOTT. *The Tri-Ratna*, in the *Journal* of the *Royal Asiatic Society*. London, vol. xix. (new series), p. 242.

[6] A. CUNNINGHAM. *The Topes of Central India*, in the *Journal* of the *Royal Asiatic Society*. London (vol. xiii., 1st series), p. 114.

tradition, adorn the impression of Buddha's foot.[1]

Finally, according to some writers, we must seek its origins amongst the less abstract images of the naturalistic forms of worship which preceded Buddhism.—M. Kern, laying stress on the actual meaning of *vardhamana*, the present participle of a verb signifying "to grow or increase," makes it the image of the "horned moon," and sees in the central protuberance of the *trisula* the nose with which we ourselves sometimes adorn the representation of the lunar crescent ☽.[2] Edward Thomas seeks therein "an ideal combination of the sun and moon;" the alteration of the primitive form would, according to him, be due to a modification in the forms of worship, or to the overthrowing of the sovereigns termed Lunar by a Solar dynasty.[3]

Mr. Burgess recognizes therein an image of the Thunderbolt;[4] Sir George Birdwood, a phallic emblem, or else the Tree of Life;[5] Mr. Monier Williams, "the Two Feet of Vishnu, with a star or embossment in the middle."[6]

Lastly, M. Beal takes it for the superposition of the Flame on the Lotus-flower, and M. Senart, of the Trident on the Wheel.[7]

---

[1] EUG. BURNOUF. *Le Lotus de la Bonne Loi.* Paris, 1852, p. 627.

[2] KERN. *Der Buddhismus*, German translation by Jacobi. Leipzig, 1884, vol. ii., pp. 241-242.

[3] EDW. THOMAS. *On the identity of Xandrames and Krananda*, in the *Journal* of the *Royal Asiatic Society.* London, vol. i. (new series), pp. 483-484.

[4] BURGESS. *Archæological Report on Elura.*

[5] SIR GEORGE BIRDWOOD, in the *Journal of the Royal Asiatic Society.* London, vol. xviii. (new series), p. 407.

[6] Quoted by Mr. Greg. *Archæologia.* London, 1885, vol. xlviii., p. 320.

[7] S. BEAL. *A Catena of Buddhist Scriptures from the East.* London, 1871, p. 11.—E. SENART. *Essai sur la légende du Bouddha* in vol. vi. of the *Journal Asiatique.* Paris, 1875, p. 184.

Among all these more or less contradictory opinions the interpretation of M. Senart is not only the simplest and moşt rational, but it is also strictly confirmed by the evidence of the monuments. There are many *trisulas* in which the upper part of the figure is separated from the Disk, some again in which it assumes distinctly angular forms ☿, instead of the rounded shape of the *omega*, ω; there are others, finally, in which it becomes beyond doubt a Trident, as amongst the sculptures of Buddha Gaya and of Boro-Budur.[1]

The Trident superposed upon the Disk is also met with upon the coins of the anonymous prince

FIG. 146. SCULPTURE OF BUDDHA GAYÂ.
(*Numismatic Chronicle*, vol. xx. (new series), pl. ii., No. 37.)

known by his title of *Basileus Sôter Megas*, and on those of several native kings.[2]

The only point on which I have some doubt is when M. Senart puts forward the Trident as the original feature, and, so to speak, the primitive nucleus of the Hindu *trisula*,—which would make it, at least in its origin, an essentially Sivait symbol, destined to represent the flash of the lightning.— As for myself, I should be more inclined to seek this nucleus in the Disk, and, consequently, to connect the *trisula* with the solar symbols.

[1] *Boro-Boedoer op het eiland Java.* Leyden, 1873, Atlas, pl. cccxvi.
[2] PERCY GARDNER. *Op. cit.*, pl. xxiv., figs. 1-6. See also SENART. *Journal Asiatique.* Paris, 1875, vol. vi., p. 185.

From the most remote times the worship of the
sun was widely spread throughout India, and, as
nearly everywhere else, the sun was first of all
represented there by a Disk, as may be seen
from the sculptures of the ancient caves, and the
ingots used for bartering before the introduction of
coins properly so-called.[1] At a later date the Disk
became a Wheel, and the Buddhists, who applied
so many solar images and symbols to their form
of worship, made it the *Wheel of the Law*, "formed
of a thousand spokes darting out a thousand
rays."

The secondary character of the *omega* (or Trident) in the *trisula* plainly follows from certain
figures brought into view by Edward Thomas in

FIG. 147. ANCIENT COIN.   FIG. 148. CAVE OF BAJA.
(*Numismatic Chronicle*, vol. xx. (new series), pl. ii.,
figs. 39 and 40.)

his valuable work on the solar symbols of India.
These are circles drawn between four *omegas*.
One of these circles exhibits four arrows radiating
from the circle between the crescents.

These figures indicate clearly the function of the
Trident in the *trisula*. Doubtlessly, in the hands
of Siva—as formerly in the hands of Neptune, and,
at a still earlier period, in those of the Assyrian
god of the air and the storm—the Trident must
symbolize the flash of the lightning. But may it not
be questioned whether, considered apart, it should

---

[1] EDWARD THOMAS. *The earliest Indian Coinage*, in vol.
iv. (new series) of the *Numismatic Chronicle*, p. 271. See also
his article in vol. xx. of same series, *The Indian Swastika*.

not be held to be, in a wider sense, the image of a Three-tongued Flame, and, consequently, when coupled with the Disk, an emblem of fire, or of solar radiation ?

Among the sculptures of Boro-Budur, in the island of Java, the Trident, which in some religious scenes is exhibited above the Disk, or Rosette, is replaced at times by a Three-pointed Flame.[1] Eug. Burnouf had already noticed, in the coloured representations of the Buddhas of Nepaul, that the headdress of the Master exhibits a ball terminating above in a kind of flame, and that on many Singhalese statues this flame takes the shape of "a kind of lyre or trident."[2] Finally, according to Mr. Beal, the *trisula* personifies, amongst the Buddhists of the north, the heaven of pure flame superposed upon the heaven of the sun.[3]

The *trisula* is then certainly a Hindu symbol. It seems, however, to have felt, at an early date, the influence of the Caduceus. Perhaps even it was in order to approach the latter in appearance that the primitive Trident of the Hindu symbol assumed the rounded forms of the *omega* and placed itself in direct contact with the Disk.

Those who have some hesitation in admitting the possibility of discovering in a complex symbol the traces of a double antecedent—as we find in a child the characteristic features of both its parents—need only cast a glance over the following picture whose contents I have taken from the coinage and figured monuments of India.

I wish to call especial attention to the figures *d* and *e*. They resemble one another so closely that writers commonly rank the former as a *trisula*

---

[1] *Boro-Boudour op het eiland Java.* Atlas, pl. cclxxx., fig. 100.

[2] E. BURNOUF. *Le Lotus de la Bonne Loi*, p. 539.

[3] S. BEAL. *A Catena of Buddhist Scriptures from the Chinese*, p. 11.

when they find it on the coins of certain Indo-Scythic princes. Yet there is no doubt but that it is directly connected with the Caduceus. More-

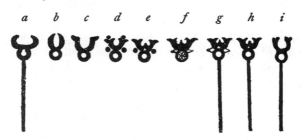

FIG. 149. CADUCEI AND TRISULAS.[1]

over, Fergusson himself has written with respect to the *trisula* :—" It bears a singular resemblance to the sign of the planet Mercury, or to the Caduceus of the god who bears this name." [2]

It is also representations of serpents intertwined, closely allied to the Caduceus, which supply us with the earliest type of the lower appendages, in the shape of spires, observed in the *trisulas* of Sanchi and Amaravati (fig. 143 and 154).

On the other hand, the most complex forms of the *trisula* exhibit an unquestionable likeness to

---

[1] *a*, Coin of Sophytes (PERCY GARDNER, pl. i., fig. 3).

b, Ancient ingot (*Numismatic Chronicle*, vol. iv., new series, pl. xi., fig. 28).

c, Old coin (*Numismatic Chronicle*, vol. iv., new series, pl. xi., fig. 16).

d, Coin of Azes (PERCY GARDNER, pl. xx., fig. 2).

e, Coin of Krananda (*Journal of the Royal Asiatic Society*, vol. i., new series, p. 475).

f, On a sculptured altar at Sanchi (FERGUSSON. *Tree and Serpent Worship*, Atlas, pl. xxv., fig. 3).

g, On the pole of a standard at Sanchi (CUNNINGHAM. *The Bhilsa Topes*, pl. xxxii., fig. 8).

h, On the pole of a standard of Sanchi (FERGUSSON. *Tree and Serpent Worship*, pl. xxxviii., fig. 1).

i, On the handle of an ivory instrument (CUNNINGHAM. *Archæological Survey of India*, vol. x., pl. ii., fig. 5).

[2] *Tree and Serpent Worship*, p. 116.

some types of the Winged Globe which have been observed in Asia Minor, Mesopotamia and Persia.

In both figures the centre is occupied by a Disk which is sometimes converted into the Wheel, or the Lotus-flower. Does not the upper part of the *trisula*, which I have termed the *omega*, recall the horns of the Mesopotamian emblem, if we only take into consideration the knob between the horns caused by the upper arc of the disk (fig.

FIG. 150. CYLINDER OF CHALCEDON.
(LAJARD. *Culte de Mithra*, pl. lii., fig. 2.)

150); or else the projection caused by the tuft of plumes which surmounts the disk of certain Winged Globes (fig. 151)?

FIG. 151. COIN OF THE SATRAPS OF TARSUS.
(LAJARD. *Culte de Mithra*, pl. lxiv.)

The shaft, frequently conical, on which some *trisulas* rest, takes the place of the fan-shaped tail, and the spires traced on both sides of this support correspond with the lines, ending in a loop, which descend on either side of the tail in the ornithomorphic Disks of Western Asia.

In order to account for this likeness, I will venture on the hypothesis that these forms of the *trisula* must have been subjected, during their development, to the plastic influence of the ancient Egyptian symbol which had come to India by way of Assyria and Persia.

The time is past when, dazzled by the sudden discovery of Vedic literature, and fascinated also by the verification of our relationship to the Aryan races of Asia, we turned towards India to seek there the universal source of symbols and dogmas, myths and gods. Since we caught a glimpse of the great antiquity of the civilizations which had reached their prime on the borders of the Euphrates and the Nile at a period when the ancestors of the Aryans were still wandering over the table-lands of Central Asia, we are far more inclined to locate in Mesopotamia, or even in Egypt, the earliest artistic centres which shed their light over the ancient world, from the Mediterranean to the Indian Ocean.

On the other hand, India, up to the Mahometan conquest, did not live in the isolated condition to which historians were long pleased to relegate it. Sir George Birdwood goes, perhaps, a little too far when he asserts, in a general manner, that nearly all the symbols of India are of Mesopotamian origin.[1] But it is none the less an established fact now, that the products of western art and symbolism must have made their way to the valley of the Indus before the appearance of the oldest stone monuments on which ancient India has left us a vestige of its beliefs.[2]

Without taking into consideration the intercourse which is supposed to have existed between the dwellers on the banks of the Indus and the most ancient empires of the Euphrates and the Nile, and without laying stress either on the factories which the Phœnicians are said to have established in southern India, I will recall to mind that Darius I

---

[1] *Journal of the Royal Asiatic Society.* London, 1886, vol. xviii. (new series), p. 407.

[2] G. RAWLINSON. *The Five, Great Monarchies of the East.* London, 1862, vol. i., p. 101.—A. H. SAYCE. *Religion of the ancient Babylonians.* London, 1887, pp. 137-138.

had annexed the valley of the Indus, and the actual province of the Punjab, about the end of the seventh century B.C.[1] Such competent authorities as James Fergusson and Géneral Cunningham have shown that India borrowed its earliest style of architecture from the Persians,[2] and in the north-east of the peninsula there have been repeatedly found products of Persian art which date back to Darius and his successors—especially cylinders and coins bearing the Winged Circle.[3] It was in one of these finds that one of the coins of Tarsus containing a Winged Circle so nearly allied to the *trisula* was found (fig. 151).

It seems to be now generally admitted that the Indian alphabets are of Semitic origin.[4] Why then should religious symbols not have followed the same paths as the symbols of language and the creations of art ?

In the centuries following the expedition of Alexander, it was Greek, or rather Græco-Asiatic art which influenced the development of Indian architecture and sculpture. Coins show us first of all sovereigns of Greek origin, who Hellenize Bactria, the Cabul country, and the valley of the Indus as far as the Ganges basin ; then Scythic and Parthian princes who maintain, until the second century of our era, the language and traditions of this civilization imported from the West.

---

[1] G. MASPERO. *Histoire ancienne des peuples de l'Orient.* Paris, 1886, p. 618.

[2] J. FERGUSSON. *Tree and Serpent Worship*, p. 94.—A. CUNNINGHAM. *Archæological Survey of India*, vol. v., Append. A.

[3] *Relics of ancient Persia*, in the *Proceedings of the Asiatic Society of Bengal.* Calcutta, 1881, 1st part, p. 151; 1883, 1st part, pp. 64 and 261.

[4] See upon this question the summing up of Mr. Cust in the *Journal of the Royal Asiatic Society.* London, 1884, vol. xvi. (new series), p. 325; also an article by M. Halévy in the *Journal Asiatique.* Paris, 1885, vol. ii.

For more than two centuries the Greek Pantheon
alone supplies images for the coins of western
India. At most a few Buddhist emblems occur
here and there ; the *Bô* tree and the *stupa* under
Agathocles, and the Wheel under Menander.
From the time of Gondophares the representation
of Siva alternates with that of Poseidon ; yet the
type of the two divinities remains so similar that
on some coins it is difficult to decide if it is the
Greek or the Hindu god.[1]

At the same time, however, there occurs in
India a veritable invasion of Iranian divinities.
Mr. Percy Gardner and M. James Darmesteter,
the former through investigating the coins of the
British Museum, and the latter through the study
of Persian traditions in the Hindu epic poem, came
simultaneously to the somewhat startling conclusion
that western India, after being Hellenised under
the Indo-Bactrians, had been largely Iranised under
the Indo-Scythians.[2] On the coins of the latter
not only do Zeus, Pallas, Helios, Selene, Poseidon,
Herakles, and Serapis alternate with Mithras,
Mao, and Atar, as well as with Siva, Lukshmi,
and even Buddha, but also the classic forms of the
Thunderbolt, the Caduceus and the Cornucopia
occur side by side with the Buddhist *trisula* and
Wheel as well as with the Sivait Trident and
bull.

India has always been the favourite home of
religious syncretism ; but at no period of its
history did it open its portals to so many different
forms of worship—even under Akbar, that great
Mogul who was willing to combine in a single religion the beliefs of the Mahometans, the Hindus,
the Parsees, the Jews and the Christians.

[1] PERCY GARDNER. *Coins of Greek and Scythic Kings in
India*, p. lviii.
[2] PERCY GARDNER. *Id.*, § iv.—J. DARMESTETER, in the
Journal Asiatique. Paris, July-August, 1887.

How could symbols have escaped an impulse which carried away the gods themselves? At any rate Buddhism would have been unfaithful to the spirit of its whole symbolism if, when acquainted with the emblems by which neighbouring religions represented their great solar divinity, or even their supreme god, it had not sought to appropriate them, either by adopting them as they stood with a new signification, or oftener by assimilating them, through slight linear alterations, with one or other of its favourite symbols.

It is, as we have seen, among the sculptures of Amaravati that the *trisula* assumes the form most closely allied to the ornithomorphic Disk. Now, nowhere else has the general influence of Græco-Asiatic art over native architecture and sculpture been verified in a more obvious manner. Already in the year 645 of our era the Chinese pilgrim Hiuen Thsang likened the sanctuary of Amaravati to the palaces of the Tahia, *i.e.*, the inhabitants of Bactria.[1] The same fact has been recorded in our own times by James Fergusson : " There is," he writes, " so much of what is Greek, or rather Bactrian, in the architectural details of Amaravati that this monument must belong to a period nearer to the Christian era than the character of the inscriptions would lead one to suppose." And the eminent archæologist adds that the study of these sculptures seems to him destined to elucidate especially the interesting question of the intercourse, and even of the exchange of thought, between east and west.[2]

The Winged Circle and the Caduceus are not,

[1] For the identification of the Tahia with the Bactrians, see PERCY GARDNER. *Op. cit.*, p. xxxi.

[2] *Description of the Amaravati Tope*, in vol. iii. (new series) of the *Journal* of the *Royal Asiatic Society*. London.—The gates of Sanchi seem to date from the first years of our era although the tope itself is older by several centuries (ROUS-SELET, *L'Inde des Rajahs*, p. 513).

moreover, the only factors which have reacted upon the genesis, or at least the development, of the *trisula*.

In an interesting paper, read in 1886 before the *Royal Asiatic Society*, Mr. Robert Sewell was perhaps the first to seek to the west of the Indus, and even in Egypt, the origins of the *trisula*, which he connects with the Scarab. The birthplace of a symbol is one thing; the origin of the figures which may have influenced its development is something very different. With this reservation, however, I must admit that there is nothing far-fetched in this parallel, especially if, following

FIG. 152.
(*Journal of the Royal Asiatic Society*, vol. xviii. (new series), fig. 13.)

Mr. Sewell's example, we interpose between the two figures the type of the Scarab with raised wings and bent legs which surmounts certain Assyrian columns.

But in Egypt itself, as M. Perrot shows, the flying Scarab borrowed the outlines of the Winged Globe,[1] by which fact, according to our theory, its resemblance to the *trisula* is sufficiently explained. It must be observed, moreover, that several of

[1] See PERROT et CHIPIEZ. *Histoire de l'Art dans l'antiquité*, vol. i., p. 811.

these Assyrian Scarabs hold between their fore-legs the Disk adorned with the *uræi*.[1]

It may be noticed, by the way, that among the Egyptians the Trident already occurs in conjunction with the Winged Globe, at least in the texts. The inscription of Edfu, which relates how Horus was transformed into a Winged Globe in order to fight the armies of Set, gives him as a weapon a three-pointed spear.[2]

On a number of monuments the Disk of the *trisula* changes into a Rosette, imitating an expanded lotus-blossom, as on the gate of Sanchi. The same monument further exhibits Lotuses at the ends of two stalks which spring from the basis of the central *fleuron;* finally, the two extreme points of the *omega* take a shape which suggests the calyx of a flower. We have already shown the solar character of the Lotus in the symbolism of the Hindus.[3] In the *trisula* the transformation of the Disk into a Lotus is therefore the equivalent, the plastic rendering of the transformation which, among the Buddhists, substituted the *padma mani*, or "Jewel of the Lotus," for the *sûra mani*, or "Jewel of the Sun"; whence the well-known formula:—*Om! mani padme,* "Oh! the Jewel in the Lotus!"[4]

Elsewhere the *trisula* seems to reproduce the Sivait emblem of the *lingam* between two serpents standing erect. This figure, which when superposed upon the Disk has perhaps a doubly phallic

---

[1] See PERROT et CHIPIEZ. *Histoire de l'Art dans l'antiquité,* vol. ii., p. 399.

[2] H. BRUGSCH. *Die Sage von der geflügelten Sonnenscheibe,* in the *Abhandlungen der königlichen Gesellschaft der Wissenschaften zu Göttingen,* vol. xiv. (1868-1869), p. 201.

[3] S. BEAL. *A Catena of Buddhist Scriptures,* p. 11.

[4] It must be observed, however, that the Disk is already found closely associated with the Lotus-flower in the symbolism of Asia Minor. (See the *Histoire de l'Art dans l'antiquité,* by MM. Perrot and Chipiez, vol. iii., fig. 509.)

import, certainly seems quite foreign to the original doctrine of Buddhism. Yet here again the Buddhists have shown themselves to be masters in the art of adapting the symbols of other religions. M. Gustave Lebon, in his *Voyage au Népaul*, quotes a characteristic instance of the fanciful interpretations with the help of which Buddhism brings about or justifies these adaptations. "The *linga*," he writes, "is likewise adopted by the Buddhists of Nepaul as an emblem of the Lotus in which Adi-Buddha manifested himself, in the shape of a flame, at the beginning of the world."[1]

It ought to be mentioned that, in the opinion of some writers, such as Ch. Lenormant and Baron de Witte, the Caduceus among the Greeks symbolized the combination of the two sexes in the

FIG. 153. CADUCEUS ON AN AMPHORA.[2]

(From the *Elite des monuments céramographiques*, vol. iii., pl. xci.)

same individual, hermaphrodism in fact,[3]—and in the valuable publication of those two archæologists upon the *Elite des monuments céramographiques de la Grèce* we find a variety of the Caduceus where a vertical projection, similar to the representation of the *phallus*, springs from the centre of the Crescent, which in this case is somewhat separated from the Disk.

[1] In the *Tour du Monde* for 1886 (vol. li., p. 266)—At Bôrô-Boudour the Sivait *linga* has become a representation of the *dâgoba* (C. LEEMANS, *Boro-Boedoer*, p. 452).

[2] Cf. the form of the *trisula* on the pillar of the sun at Buddha Gaya (our illustration, fig. 146).

[3] *Elite des monuments céramographiques de la Grèce*. Paris, 1868, vol. iii., p. 197.

On the coins of the Sunga dynasty the *lingam* placed between the serpents becomes the head-dress of Buddha ; the Disk stands for the Master's head, and the lateral appendages of the *trisula* are represented by two projections which stretch out horizontally on either side of this head.[1]

The *trisula* is thus seen to be converted into an anthropoid figure. A transformation of the same kind, but still more accentuated, is observable in the three famous idols of Puri which General Cunningham long ago proved to be three ancient *trisulas* (figs. 154 and 155).[2]

FIG. 154. TRISULA OF SANCHI.
(*Musée des moulages*, Brussels.)

These emblems were doubtlessly a great object of popular veneration at the period when Puri was a Buddhist sanctuary. When Brahminism came to establish itself there it contented itself with changing them, by means of a few slight alterations, into the image of Vishnu, or rather Jaganath, and his brother and sister. In thus appropriating the old solar symbol, still discernible in

[1] A. RIVETT CARNAC. *Coins of the Sunga or Mitra dynasty*, in the *Proceedings* of the *Asiatic Society of Bengal*, vol. xliv., 1st part, pl. vii. and viii.

[2] *The Topes of Central India*, in the *Journal of the Royal Asiatic Society*. London (vol. iii. of 1st series). General Cunningham adds that these rude figures are likewise used in native calendars to represent Vishnu in his avatar of Buddha.

spite of its successive alterations, Vishnu, moreover, did nothing but recover what belonged to
him, since he is, in Hinduism, pre-eminently the
solar divinity.

Finally, the *trisula*, whose plasticity is only
equalled by its power of absorption, borrows forms
from the vegetable kingdom with the same freedom as from the human physiognomy. M. Rous-
selet points out the resemblance of the mystic
symbol of the Buddhists to the *kalpavriksh* or
Tree of Knowledge which the Jainas represented

FIG. 155. IDOL OF JAGANNATH.
(ROUSSELET. *L'Inde des Rajahs*, p. 517.)

by a stem with three branches on the mitre of the
Tîrthankaras sculptured on the caves of Gwalior.[1]
A similar combination is observable on coins of
the Sunga dynasty, where the upper part of the
trisula, forming the head-dress of Buddha, is transformed into a regular crown of branches.[2] On
other monuments the stem on which the *trisula*
rests becomes the trunk of a tree whose branches
are laden with conventional fruits and interlaced
with necklaces of jewels.[3]

This vegetalization of the *trisula*, or, properly

[1] ROUSSELET. *L'Inde des Rajahs*, p. 370.
[2] RIVETT CARNAC. *Loc. cit.* ʼ
[3] F. PINCOTT. *The Tri-Ratna*, vol. xix. (new series) of the
Journal of the Royal Asiatic Society. London, p. 243.

speaking, of the Trident which surmounts it, is nowhere more evident than among the sculptures of Boro-Budur, where it literally merges into the *Bô* tree through a series of gradual transformations. " The shape of the points of the *trisula*," M. Ch. Leemans writes in his able commentary upon the *Atlas* published under the patronage of the Dutch government, " may some-

FIG. 156. TRIDENT OF SIVA.
(MOOR. *Hindu Pantheon*, pl. xlii.)

times have been derived from that of a flame, or else from the calyx of a flower, or again from a symbolic tree."[1] The same observation applies

FIG. 157. EGYPTIAN LOTUS.

moreover to the Trident of Siva, which at times exhibits the forms of a lotus calyx depicted in the Egyptian manner (fig. 157).

Perhaps other transformations of the *trisula* might still be found at Boro-Budur. I will restrict myself to pointing out a detail which is not without interest : the same Disk which, when transformed into a most complicated ornament, is

---

[1] *Boro-Boedoer*, p. 455 of commentary.

sometimes crowned by a Trident, is also met with between two serpents—which brings us back to the origin of the Winged Circle—the Globe of Egypt with the *uræi*.

FIG. 158. BAS-RELIEFS OF BORO-BUDUR.[1]
(*Boro-Boedoer*, Atlas, pl. cccxvi. and ccclxx.)

Moreover this ornament, between which and certain forms of the *trisula* the transition is easily traced, commonly surmounts the entrance to the pagodas depicted in the bas-reliefs—in exactly the same manner as the Winged Globe adorns the lintel of the temples in Egypt and Phœnicia.

FIG. 159. BAS-RELIEFS OF BORO-BUDUR.
(*Boro-Boedoer*, Atlas, pl. cclxxxiii., No. 105.[1])

It is proper to point out that in the West there are some figures which exhibit an odd resemblance to the *trisula*. Such is, in the first place, the Cyprian image to which I have drawn attention (fig. 114), as presenting to our view a combi-

----

[1] See also same Atlas, pl. ccxxxvi., 11; cclxxxviii., 114; and especially ccxlviii., 36, where this subject rests on the apex of a triangle which corresponds with the pennated tail of the Mesopotamian globes.

nation of the Sacred Tree and the Winged Globe.
The upper volutes with the flowered projection
bisecting the centre of the arc recall the three
points of the *trisula* with their central *fleuron*.
The pair of volutes whose lower parts are bent
downward on both sides of the base, suggest the
ophidian appendages which, in the Buddhist
symbol, descend on either side of the pedestal.
Lastly in both cases, the middle part of the figures
shows two leaves which by their position, as well
as by their shape, suggest two small wings.

Mr. William Simpson, an English artist, well
known on account of his archæological work in
connection with the monuments of India, has

FIG. 160. THUNDERBOLT OF ELIS.

pointed out the resemblance of the *trisula* to some
representations of the Thunderbolt graven on coins
of Elis which date from the fifth century B.C.[1]

FIG. 161. SCULPTURE OF BORO-BUDUR.

This Thunderbolt especially resembles a somewhat
enigmatical figure sculptured among the bas-reliefs
of Boro-Budur, where, to all appearance, it plays
the part of a *trisula*.[2]

On the whole, there would be nothing remark-

---

[1] *The Trisula Symbol* in the *Journal* of the *Roy. As. Soc.* for
1890, vol. xxii. (new series), p. 306.
[2] *Boro-Boedoer*, vol. iii., pl. ccxlvi., fig. 35.

able in these similarities, since the Thunderbolt and
the *trisula*, as we have just seen, are both a development of the Trident.

What is more singular is to find a kind of
trisula engraved on the flank of a lamb which
adorns the serpent-shaped scroll on a pastoral
staff dating from the Middle Ages.[1]

Have we here an exchange or a mere coincidence ? This is a question which I will not
venture to decide, although nothing is wanting in
the Christian symbol to make of it a real *trisula*,
neither the Disk, nor the central point imitating a
fleur-de-lis, nor the rounded projection of the two
lateral points.

After all, if we have been able to find the antecedents, and, so to speak, the factors of the *trisula*,
and even its probable signification in the creeds
which preceded Buddhism, we have not learned
much as to the meaning of this symbol in the
religion which made most use of it. The fact is,
that here the plastic figures cannot make up for
the silence of the written monuments. So long as
symbols remain images and are applicable to concrete objects, or physical phenomena, it is not impossible to discover the meaning which they in all
probability bore. But when, having entered upon
what may be called their derived or secondary
phase, they become signs and express abstract
ideas—which is nearly always the case in Buddhism—the field of interpretation becomes, so to
speak, unlimited for critics, as sometimes also for
the faithful.

The proper signification of the *trisula* remains
then in the suppositive stage, although the purpose of its transformations does not always escape
us. The issue of some hitherto unpublished text

[1] Cf. CAHIER et MARTIN. *Mélanges d'archéologie*, vol. iv.
fig. 58.

can alone reveal to us the general and authentic
meaning of this symbol, before which millions of
our fellow-creatures have bowed down, but whose
name we do not even know with any degree of
certainty.

My purpose, moreover, was less to solve a problem whose solution has so far escaped the most
competent minds, than to trace the transformations
of the *trisula* in the course of its plastic development, and to show once again with what ease
symbols of most dissimilar origin merge into one
another as soon as, in their form, or in their meaning, there occur points of contact which are sufficient to facilitate this transition.

CONCLUSION.

IN most of the instances which I have here quoted
it is easy to discover through what ways the speci-
fied symbol was transmitted from one nation to
another. In this respect the migration of symbols
proceeds directly in conformity with what may be
called the history of commercial intercourse. Whatever the similarity of form, and even of meaning,
may be between two symbolic figures of different
origin, it is proper, ere we assert their relationship, to
show the probability, or at least the possibility, of
international relations which would have served as
a vehicle of transport. This point once set at
rest, it remains to be seen who was the giver and
who the receiver.

It may be asked, for instance, why it is not the
Greeks who communicated the Thunderbolt to
Mesopotamia, or the Hindus who transmitted the

Lotus to the Egyptians? It is here especially that
the advantages we possess over preceding generations come into play. There was a time when the
origin of the gods, myths, and symbols spread
over the whole surface of the Old World could be
vaguely located in India; and another, when it
would have been rash not to ascribe to Greece the
honour of all intellectual and religious creations
possessing any moral or artistic value. But the
researches carried on for the last half century
have henceforth placed on a definite basis the
ancient history of the East, and the latter, in its
turn, has enabled us to assign their relative distance to the principal centres of artistic culture
which have reacted upon one another since the
beginnings of civilization.

We may differ in opinion as to whether the
Ionic column borrowed its volutes from the horns
of the ibex, or the half-closed petals of the lotus.
We may even argue whether Ionia received it
directly from Golgos by the ships of the Phœnicians, or from Pterium, by the caravans of Asia
Minor. But whoever has noted its presence on
the monuments of Khorsabad, or of Kouyunjik,
will not refuse to locate in Mesopotamia its start-
ing-place on its journey to the Ægean Sea. This
is only one example of those types and motives
whose development doubtlessly owed its importance to the independent inspirations of Greek
genius, but whose origins must nevertheless be
sought for in Phrygia, in Lycia, in Phœnicia, and
even beyond these countries, in the valleys of the
Tigris, the Euphrates, and the Nile. In India
likewise the most ancient products of sculpture
and of carving, when they do not bear witness to
the direct influence of Greek art—as in the Buddhist bas-reliefs of Yusufzai, and the Bacchanalian
scenes of Mathura—are connected with the monuments of Persia through the adoption of what

might be called classic motives in Persepolitan architecture : such are those capitals formed by animals, sometimes face to face, sometimes back to back, which are, as it were, a plastic signature, in the former case of Assyria, in the latter of Egypt.

I am far from denying that there arose among some nations independent and self-governing centres of artistic creation. In this respect it will be. sufficient to make mention of China and pre-Columbian America. But it must be admitted that art in the extreme East was profoundly modified through the influence of the Buddhist types which proceeded directly from India. We might even take into account a still older element which would directly connect the art, as also the religion, of the Chinese empire with the development of Mesopotamian civilization, if, as is assumed by M. Terrien de la Couperie, who has brought together a considerable amount of presumptive evidence in support of this theory, the ancestors of the Chinese were descended from the nation which occupied Chaldæa and Elam some three and twenty centuries before our era.[1] At anyrate, it would be astonishing if, in the course of so many centuries, infiltrations had not occurred between the civilizations which were developing in this parallel manner on the Asiatic continent.

As for ancient America, Gustave d'Eichthal had already called attention to the similarities which are met with on the monuments of Central America and of Buddhist Asia. For myself, I am more and more inclined to admit, not the Asiatic origin of the inhabitants of America, which is quite another question, but the intervention of certain artistic influences radiated from China,

[1] *Origin from Babylonia and Elam of the early Chinese Civilization*, in the *Babylonian and Oriental Record*, vol. iii., No. 3 *et seq.*

Japan, or the Indian Archipelago, to the shores of the New World, long before the Spanish conquest.

In short, whether we start from Japan, from Greece, from India, or even from Libya, from Etruria, or from Gaul, we always arrive, after many halting-places, at two great centres of artistic diffusion, partially irreducible as regards one another, Egypt and Chaldæa—with this difference, that, towards the eighth century before our era, Mesopotamia took lessons from Egypt, whilst Egypt learnt little of any country. Now, as we have noted more than once in the present volume, not only did symbols follow the same paths as purely ornamental schemes, but they were also transmitted in the same manner, at the same periods, and in nearly the same proportion. Concerning symbols as well as artistic products we everywhere find, by the side of aboriginal types, the deposit of a powerful current which has its more or less distant origin in the symbolism of the banks of the Euphrates, or the Nile. In a word, the two classes of importations are joined together to such a degree, that in writing the history of art we write to a great extent the history of symbols, or at least, of their migrations.

The knowledge of these migrations, in its turn, throws quite a new light not only upon the presence of the same emblems among nations who never professed the same creed, but also upon the formation of certain complex images which cannot be accounted for save as the result of a reciprocal action between symbols often differing greatly in origin and in meaning. Through thus always finding, often among nations far apart, either the same symbolic combinations, or the same features in different combinations, we might be tempted to believe that symbolism had at its disposal only an extremely limited number of signs and figures to provide for the plastic requirements of the religious sentiment.

Need I add that this is 'not so ? The variety of symbolic representations has no more limits than the spirit of analogy. But certain figures, when once formed, have so captivated the eye and the imagination that they have become the common-places of figurative language, and the artist's hand could not free itself from their influence when engaged in producing new symbols. It is equally easy to understand that, having forgotten, or having never known, the meaning to be attached to a foreign pattern, the copyist should have attempted to connect his productions with some other known and popular type. At other times, again, the symbolic syncretism is intentional and premeditated; whether it be in the desire to unite, for the sake of greater efficacy, the attributes of several divinities in a single figure, as is shown in certain pantheistic figures of Gnostic origin; or a wish to state, by the fusion of symbols, the unity of the gods and the identity of creeds, as in the mystic monogram wherein the Brahmaists of contemporary India have testified to their religious eclecticism by interweaving the *Om* of the Hindus with the Trident, the Crescent, and the Cross.[1]

Sometimes, too, the sacerdotal interest must have tended towards accentuating the analogies rather than the dissimilarities of symbols, in order to assist the absorption or unification of the doctrines which they represented. Finally, we must take into consideration the popular tendency towards syncretism which, when not held in check by a rigorous orthodoxy, acts upon symbols, as well as upon creeds, by introducing into the new form of worship the images consecrated by a long

[1] PROTAP CHUNDER MOZOUMDAR. *Life and Teaching of Keshub Chunder Sen.* Calcutta, 1887, p. 501.

veneration. Or else it is the innovators themselves who take advantage of symbolism in order
to disguise, through borrowing from antique forms,
the newness of their doctrine and, if need be, to
transform into allies the emblems, or traditions,
which they are unable to boldly extirpate.

Need I recall to mind Constantine choosing as
a standard that *labarum* which might be claimed
both by the religion of Christ and the worship of
the sun ? It is singular to find the same policy
attributed to the first Christian king of Norway.
According to an old song of the Shetland Islands,
Hakon Adalsteinfostri, obliged to drink to Odin
at an official banquet, traced quickly upon the
bowl the sign of the Cross ; and when his companions reproached him for doing so, he told
them that it was the sign of Thor's Hammer.[1]
We know, indeed, that in Germanic and Scandinavian countries the Cross of Christ more than once
drew near in appearance to the Two-headed
Hammer of Thor, as in Egypt it assumed, in more
than one inscription, the aspect of the Key of Life.[2]

Buddhism was even less scrupulous. In some
of its sanctuaries it did not hesitate to preserve
the images of the worship paid by the natives of
India to the sun, to fire, or to serpents, whilst
ascribing these rites to its own traditions. The
solar Wheel thus became easily the Wheel of the
Law ; the Cosmic Tree represented the Tree of
Knowledge, under which Sakya Muni attained the
perfect illumination ; the Seven-headed Serpent

---

[1] KARL BLIND. *Odinic Songs in Shetland*, in the *Nineteenth Century*, 1879, p. 1098.

[2] The Abbe Ansault has shown, without any difficulty, in his *Mémoire sur le culte de la croix avant Jesus-Christ* (Paris, 1891, p. 68 *et seq.*), first of all, that heathen nations used as religious emblems Greek, Latin, Maltese, *pattées*, *gammées*, *potencées*, *ansées*, *tréflées*, and other crosses ; and, secondly, that the Christian Church has always accepted these different forms of the Cross as the representation of its own symbol.

Naga was transformed into the guardian of the impression left by the Feet of Vishnu, itself to be attributed henceforth, to Buddha, and so on. Some years ago there were discovered at Bharhut the remains of a Buddhist sanctuary whose bas-reliefs exhibited emblems and religious scenes with inscriptions which served as their legends, or rather as their labels. Great was the joy of Anglo-Indian archæologists at the receipt of this intelligence. We were to have at last an interpretation of Buddhist rites and symbols, formulated by the Buddhists themselves one or two centuries before our era. We had unfortunately to lower our expectations when a minute investigation showed that it was merely an ancient temple of the sun taken possession of by the Buddhists at a later date. They had contented themselves with placing on the figured representations of the solar worship inscriptions which connected them with their own creed.[1]

Some have gone as far as to say that religions changed, but that the form of worship remained always the same. Thus formulated the proposition is too absolute. But it is certain that each religion preserves, in its rites and symbols, survivals of the whole series of former religions. And no complaint need be made of this. It is not the vessel that is important, but the wine which we pour into it ; not the form, but the ideas which animate and transcend that form.

When the Christians and the Buddhists concentrated on the image of their respective Masters the principal attributes of the sun—beginning with that halo of glory whose prototype dates back to the Aureoles carved upon the Chaldæan monuments —did they mean to do homage to the orb of day ?

[1] EDW. THOMAS. *Numismatic Chronicle*, vol. xx. (new series), p. 27.

In reality, they only claimed to refer to the venerated physiognomy of their founder the symbol
which has not only formed from time immemorial
the most radiant expression of celestial glory, but
which also characterized, in an especial manner,
the highest personification of the Divinity in contemporary creeds. We must call to mind the
reply of a Father of the Church to those who
accused the Christians of celebrating the festival
of the sun :—" We solemnize this day, not, like the
heathen, on account of the sun, but on account of
Him who made the sun." [1] Constantine went
further still when he composed, to be recited on
Sundays by his legions, a prayer which, according
to M. V. Duruy, could at once satisfy the worshippers of Mithras, of Serapis, of the sun, and of
Christ.[2]

Symbolism may combine with the most mystical tendencies, but, like mysticism itself, it is a
powerful ally of the religious sentiment against
the immobility of dogma, and the tyranny of the
written Word. M. Anatole Leroy-Beaulieu has
shown, in his valuable researches into religion
in Russia, how, thanks to the symbolic interpretation of texts and ceremonies, the conservative
ritualism of the Old Believers has managed to
arrive at the liberty of doctrines, and even, in some
instances, at a complete rationalism, without break-
ing with the traditional symbols of Christianity, and
even of the Eastern Church.[3]

There comes a time when religions which deal
largely with the supernatural come into collision
with the progress of the different branches of
knowledge, and above all with the growing belief

---

[1] S. AUGUSTIN. *In natale Domini*, sermon 190, MIGNE
edition, vol. v., 1st part, p. 1007.
[2] V. DURUY. *Histoire des Romains*. Paris, 1885, vol. vii.,
p. 54.
[3] *L'Empire des Tzars*, vol. iii., p. 451.

in a rational order of the universe. Symbolism
then offers them a means of safety, of which they
have more than once taken advantage, in order to
keep abreast of the times. If we take nations in
a lower stage of development, we find among
them *fetiches*—*i.e.*, beings and objects invested at
pleasure with superhuman faculties—then idols,
which are *fetiches* carved to resemble a human
being or animal. But we do not find any
symbols as long as there is neither the desire to
depict what is abstract by what is concrete, nor
the consciousness that there is no identity between
the symbol and the reality thus represented. When
the mind opens itself to the conception of abstract
or invisible gods, it may preserve its veneration
for its ancient *fetiches*, but under the condition of
looking upon them henceforth as but representative signs of the divinities. Lastly, when people can
conceive of a supreme God of whom the ancient
divinities are simply the ministers, or the hypostases,
these antique representations may yet have a part
to play, provided however that they be referred to
the perfections and attributes of the superior
Being in whom the Divine World is resolved.

Such is the evolution observable in the midst of
all the ancient worships, and which still continues,
often unconsciously, in many a contemporary religion. It implies, as a last conclusion, the belief
in the equivalence of symbols, that is to say, the
conviction that symbolic representations are all
inadequate, inasmuch as they attempt to explain
the inexplicable, but that they are all justifiable,
inasmuch as they aim at bringing us closer to
the Supreme Reality ; and, moreover, that they are
all beneficial in so far as they contribute to awaken
ideas of the Good and of the Beautiful. In this
respect the functions of symbolism cannot but increase ; for, in religion, as in art and literature, it

corresponds with a necessity of the human mind, which, very fortunately for our æsthetic development, has never been able to content itself with pure abstractions, nor remain at the surface of things. Here, indeed, is the secret of the impulse which increasingly moves the new generations to break with the commonplace conventions of superannuated traditions, as also with the superficial platitudes of a false realism.

ADDENDA.

CHAP. II. § 1.—The slab found at Huy on the Meuse representing a priest whose vestments are adorned with *gammadions* has an equivalent in the Musée de Cluny, at Paris, where an Abbot of Cluny, who died in 1394, is figured on his tombstone as wearing sacerdotal robes ornamented with *gammadions* in the same manner.

CHAP. III.—In the *Correspondenzblatt der Westdeutschen Zeitschrift*, 1892, p. 179 *seq.*, Mr. Ohlenschläger speaks of a bas-relief in the cathedral of Spires which recalls the group of Sampson killing the lion in the cathedral of Nivelles, with the same Mithraic affinities.

CHAP. IV. and *seq.*—I have received, too late to take advantage of it, Dr. Bonavia's recent book, *The Flora of the Assyrian Monuments and its Outcome* (1 vol., London, Archibald Constable and Co., 1894), which deals with many questions treated in this volume. Ingenious and suggestive as his views are, I see nothing in them to alter my general conclusions.

For instance, he insists, still more than I do, on the importance of the Horn symbol in Assyrian worship—going so far as to qualify their whole religion by the picturesque term of *hornism !* He has made a strong case, when he looked to this symbol as an antecedent to the Caduceus, the *fleur-de-lys*, the *anthemion* or palmette, the Ionian

volutes, the Horseshoe, the Crescent, the Thunderbolt, the *trisula*, certain Keys of Life and so forth.
I am ready to admit that in shaping the fork or
Trident of their storm gods the Assyrians have
been influenced by their habitual way of representing conventionally the Sacred Tree adorned
with the symbolical Horns. But does not the
learned author go too far, when he infers that this
weapon in the hands of the god is meant for a
pair of horns mounted on a stem and, therefore,
that the thunderbolt originally represented only a
double pair of horns with the sacred stem in the
middle ?

There would be nothing surprising if the
Assyrians had symbolized lightning by a pair of
horns, although this remains a supposition so long
as not confirmed by some text. One could understand a description or representation of the storm
god as a mighty bull, or even as a horned man
striking his victims with the head. But when we
see this supernatural being, whether horned or
not, holding in his hand a bident or a trident,
there is no need to go further and to take this
weapon for anything else than what it appears to
be—a spear or javelin with several points.

But Dr. Bonavia goes still further and contends
that it may not be at all a representation of lightning, simply a *hornstick*, a charm against the evil
eye in the hands of a protecting deity. To this,
without entering into details, I shall answer, firstly,
that according to all Assyriologists, this kind of
Trident is essentially the attribute of Rammanu,
the god of the atmosphere and therefore of the
storm; secondly, that there is a text where lightning
is described as a weapon with several heads
(W. A. I., ii., 19, trad. Sayce); thirdly, that there
exists on Assyrian monuments a gradual and un-
mistakable transition—as shown in this book and
by Dr. Bonavia's own illustrations—between his

"horned stick" and what became the Thunderbolt of the Greeks, without any apparent break of continuity in the meaning of the symbol. If somebody alleges that such break remains possible, with him lies the *onus probandi*.

G. D'A.

INDEX.

A CATALOG OF SELECTED DOVER
BOOKS IN ALL FIELDS OF INTEREST

CONCERNING THE SPIRITUAL IN ART, Wassily Kandinsky. Pioneering work by father of abstract art. Thoughts on color theory, nature of art. Analysis of earlier masters. 12 illustrations. 80pp. of text. 5⅜ x 8½. 23411-8 Pa. $4.95

ANIMALS: 1,419 Copyright-Free Illustrations of Mammals, Birds, Fish, Insects, etc., Jim Harter (ed.). Clear wood engravings present, in extremely lifelike poses, over 1,000 species of animals. One of the most extensive pictorial sourcebooks of its kind. Captions. Index. 284pp. 9 x 12. 23766-4 Pa. $14.95

CELTIC ART: The Methods of Construction, George Bain. Simple geometric techniques for making Celtic interlacements, spirals, Kells-type initials, animals, humans, etc. Over 500 illustrations. 160pp. 9 x 12. (Available in U.S. only.) 22923-8 Pa. $9.95

AN ATLAS OF ANATOMY FOR ARTISTS, Fritz Schider. Most thorough reference work on art anatomy in the world. Hundreds of illustrations, including selections from works by Vesalius, Leonardo, Goya, Ingres, Michelangelo, others. 593 illustrations. 192pp. 7⅛ x 10¼. 20241-0 Pa. $9.95

CELTIC HAND STROKE-BY-STROKE (Irish Half-Uncial from "The Book of Kells"): An Arthur Baker Calligraphy Manual, Arthur Baker. Complete guide to creating each letter of the alphabet in distinctive Celtic manner. Covers hand position, strokes, pens, inks, paper, more. Illustrated. 48pp. 8¼ x 11. 24336-2 Pa. $3.95

EASY ORIGAMI, John Montroll. Charming collection of 32 projects (hat, cup, pelican, piano, swan, many more) specially designed for the novice origami hobbyist. Clearly illustrated easy-to-follow instructions insure that even beginning papercrafters will achieve successful results. 48pp. 8¼ x 11. 27298-2 Pa. $3.50

THE COMPLETE BOOK OF BIRDHOUSE CONSTRUCTION FOR WOODWORKERS, Scott D. Campbell. Detailed instructions, illustrations, tables. Also data on bird habitat and instinct patterns. Bibliography. 3 tables. 63 illustrations in 15 figures. 48pp. 5¼ x 8½. 24407-5 Pa. $2.50

BLOOMINGDALE'S ILLUSTRATED 1886 CATALOG: Fashions, Dry Goods and Housewares, Bloomingdale Brothers. Famed merchants' extremely rare catalog depicting about 1,700 products: clothing, housewares, firearms, dry goods, jewelry, more. Invaluable for dating, identifying vintage items. Also, copyright-free graphics for artists, designers. Co-published with Henry Ford Museum & Greenfield Village. 160pp. 8¼ x 11. 25780-0 Pa. $10.95

HISTORIC COSTUME IN PICTURES, Braun & Schneider. Over 1,450 costumed figures in clearly detailed engravings—from dawn of civilization to end of 19th century. Captions. Many folk costumes. 256pp. 8⅜ x 11¾. 23150-X Pa. $12.95

STICKLEY CRAFTSMAN FURNITURE CATALOGS, Gustav Stickley and L. & J. G. Stickley. Beautiful, functional furniture in two authentic catalogs from 1910. 594 illustrations, including 277 photos, show settles, rockers, armchairs, reclining chairs, bookcases, desks, tables. 183pp. 6½ x 9¼.   23838-5 Pa. $11.95

AMERICAN LOCOMOTIVES IN HISTORIC PHOTOGRAPHS: 1858 to 1949, Ron Ziel (ed.). A rare collection of 126 meticulously detailed official photographs, called "builder portraits," of American locomotives that majestically chronicle the rise of steam locomotive power in America. Introduction. Detailed captions. xi+ 129pp. 9 x 12.   27393-8 Pa. $13.95

AMERICA'S LIGHTHOUSES: An Illustrated History, Francis Ross Holland, Jr. Delightfully written, profusely illustrated fact-filled survey of over 200 American lighthouses since 1716. History, anecdotes, technological advances, more. 240pp. 8 x 10¾.
                                25576-X Pa. $12.95

TOWARDS A NEW ARCHITECTURE, Le Corbusier. Pioneering manifesto by founder of "International School." Technical and aesthetic theories, views of industry, economics, relation of form to function, "mass-production split" and much more. Profusely illustrated. 320pp. 6⅛ x 9¼. (Available in U.S. only.)   25023-7 Pa. $9.95

HOW THE OTHER HALF LIVES, Jacob Riis. Famous journalistic record, exposing poverty and degradation of New York slums around 1900, by major social reformer. 100 striking and influential photographs. 233pp. 10 x 7⅞.
                                22012-5 Pa. $11.95

FRUIT KEY AND TWIG KEY TO TREES AND SHRUBS, William M. Harlow. One of the handiest and most widely used identification aids. Fruit key covers 120 deciduous and evergreen species; twig key 160 deciduous species. Easily used. Over 300 photographs. 126pp. 5⅜ x 8½.   20511-8 Pa. $3.95

COMMON BIRD SONGS, Dr. Donald J. Borror. Songs of 60 most common U.S. birds: robins, sparrows, cardinals, bluejays, finches, more—arranged in order of increasing complexity. Up to 9 variations of songs of each species.
                                Cassette and manual 99911-4 $8.95

ORCHIDS AS HOUSE PLANTS, Rebecca Tyson Northen. Grow cattleyas and many other kinds of orchids—in a window, in a case, or under artificial light. 63 illustrations. 148pp. 5⅜ x 8½.   23261-1 Pa. $5.95

MONSTER MAZES, Dave Phillips. Masterful mazes at four levels of difficulty. Avoid deadly perils and evil creatures to find magical treasures. Solutions for all 32 exciting illustrated puzzles. 48pp. 8¼ x 11.   26005-4 Pa. $2.95

MOZART'S DON GIOVANNI (DOVER OPERA LIBRETTO SERIES), Wolfgang Amadeus Mozart. Introduced and translated by Ellen H. Bleiler. Standard Italian libretto, with complete English translation. Convenient and thoroughly portable—an ideal companion for reading along with a recording or the performance itself. Introduction. List of characters. Plot summary. 121pp. 5¼ x 8½.
                                24944-1 Pa. $3.95

TECHNICAL MANUAL AND DICTIONARY OF CLASSICAL BALLET, Gail Grant. Defines, explains, comments on steps, movements, poses and concepts. 15-page pictorial section. Basic book for student, viewer. 127pp. 5⅜ x 8½.
                                21843-0 Pa. $4.95

THE CLARINET AND CLARINET PLAYING, David Pino. Lively, comprehensive work features suggestions about technique, musicianship, and musical interpretation, as well as guidelines for teaching, making your own reeds, and preparing for public performance. Includes an intriguing look at clarinet history. "A godsend," *The Clarinet,* Journal of the International Clarinet Society. Appendixes. 7 illus. 320pp. 5⅜ x 8½. 40270-3 Pa. $9.95

HOLLYWOOD GLAMOR PORTRAITS, John Kobal (ed.). 145 photos from 1926-49. Harlow, Gable, Bogart, Bacall; 94 stars in all. Full background on photographers, technical aspects. 160pp. 8⅜ x 11¼. 23352-9 Pa. $12.95

THE ANNOTATED CASEY AT THE BAT: A Collection of Ballads about the Mighty Casey/Third, Revised Edition, Martin Gardner (ed.). Amusing sequels and parodies of one of America's best-loved poems: Casey's Revenge, Why Casey Whiffed, Casey's Sister at the Bat, others. 256pp. 5⅜ x 8½. 28598-7 Pa. $8.95

THE RAVEN AND OTHER FAVORITE POEMS, Edgar Allan Poe. Over 40 of the author's most memorable poems: "The Bells," "Ulalume," "Israfel," "To Helen," "The Conqueror Worm," "Eldorado," "Annabel Lee," many more. Alphabetic lists of titles and first lines. 64pp. 5 3/16 x 8¼. 26685-0 Pa. $1.00

PERSONAL MEMOIRS OF U. S. GRANT, Ulysses Simpson Grant. Intelligent, deeply moving firsthand account of Civil War campaigns, considered by many the finest military memoirs ever written. Includes letters, historic photographs, maps and more. 528pp. 6⅛ x 9¼. 28587-1 Pa. $12.95

ANCIENT EGYPTIAN MATERIALS AND INDUSTRIES, A. Lucas and J. Harris. Fascinating, comprehensive, thoroughly documented text describes this ancient civilization's vast resources and the processes that incorporated them in daily life, including the use of animal products, building materials, cosmetics, perfumes and incense, fibers, glazed ware, glass and its manufacture, materials used in the mummification process, and much more. 544pp. 6⅛ x 9¼. (Available in U.S. only.) 40446-3 Pa. $16.95

RUSSIAN STORIES/PYCCKNE PACCKA3bl: A Dual-Language Book, edited by Gleb Struve. Twelve tales by such masters as Chekhov, Tolstoy, Dostoevsky, Pushkin, others. Excellent word-for-word English translations on facing pages, plus teaching and study aids, Russian/English vocabulary, biographical/critical introductions, more. 416pp. 5⅜ x 8½. 26244-8 Pa. $9.95

PHILADELPHIA THEN AND NOW: 60 Sites Photographed in the Past and Present, Kenneth Finkel and Susan Oyama. Rare photographs of City Hall, Logan Square, Independence Hall, Betsy Ross House, other landmarks juxtaposed with contemporary views. Captures changing face of historic city. Introduction. Captions. 128pp. 8¼ x 11. 25790-8 Pa. $9.95

AIA ARCHITECTURAL GUIDE TO NASSAU AND SUFFOLK COUNTIES, LONG ISLAND, The American Institute of Architects, Long Island Chapter, and the Society for the Preservation of Long Island Antiquities. Comprehensive, well-researched and generously illustrated volume brings to life over three centuries of Long Island's great architectural heritage. More than 240 photographs with authoritative, extensively detailed captions. 176pp. 8¼ x 11. 26946-9 Pa. $14.95

NORTH AMERICAN INDIAN LIFE: Customs and Traditions of 23 Tribes, Elsie Clews Parsons (ed.). 27 fictionalized essays by noted anthropologists examine religion, customs, government, additional facets of life among the Winnebago, Crow, Zuni, Eskimo, other tribes. 480pp. 6⅛ x 9¼. 27377-6 Pa. $10.95

FRANK LLOYD WRIGHT'S DANA HOUSE, Donald Hoffmann. Pictorial essay of residential masterpiece with over 160 interior and exterior photos, plans, elevations, sketches and studies. 128pp. 9¼ x 10¾. 29120-0 Pa. $12.95

THE MALE AND FEMALE FIGURE IN MOTION: 60 Classic Photographic Sequences, Eadweard Muybridge. 60 true-action photographs of men and women walking, running, climbing, bending, turning, etc., reproduced from rare 19th-century masterpiece. vi + 121pp. 9 x 12. 24745-7 Pa. $12.95

1001 QUESTIONS ANSWERED ABOUT THE SEASHORE, N. J. Berrill and Jacquelyn Berrill. Queries answered about dolphins, sea snails, sponges, starfish, fishes, shore birds, many others. Covers appearance, breeding, growth, feeding, much more. 305pp. 5¼ x 8¼. 23366-9 Pa. $9.95

ATTRACTING BIRDS TO YOUR YARD, William J. Weber. Easy-to-follow guide offers advice on how to attract the greatest diversity of birds: birdhouses, feeders, water and waterers, much more. 96pp. 5³⁄₁₆ x 8¼. 28927-3 Pa. $2.50

MEDICINAL AND OTHER USES OF NORTH AMERICAN PLANTS: A Historical Survey with Special Reference to the Eastern Indian Tribes, Charlotte Erichsen-Brown. Chronological historical citations document 500 years of usage of plants, trees, shrubs native to eastern Canada, northeastern U.S. Also complete identifying information. 343 illustrations. 544pp. 6½ x 9¼. 25951-X Pa. $12.95

STORYBOOK MAZES, Dave Phillips. 23 stories and mazes on two-page spreads: Wizard of Oz, Treasure Island, Robin Hood, etc. Solutions. 64pp. 8¼ x 11. 23628-5 Pa. $2.95

AMERICAN NEGRO SONGS: 230 Folk Songs and Spirituals, Religious and Secular, John W. Work. This authoritative study traces the African influences of songs sung and played by black Americans at work, in church, and as entertainment. The author discusses the lyric significance of such songs as "Swing Low, Sweet Chariot," "John Henry," and others and offers the words and music for 230 songs. Bibliography. Index of Song Titles. 272pp. 6½ x 9¼. 40271-1 Pa. $9.95

MOVIE-STAR PORTRAITS OF THE FORTIES, John Kobal (ed.). 163 glamor, studio photos of 106 stars of the 1940s: Rita Hayworth, Ava Gardner, Marlon Brando, Clark Gable, many more. 176pp. 8⅜ x 11¼. 23546-7 Pa. $14.95

BENCHLEY LOST AND FOUND, Robert Benchley. Finest humor from early 30s, about pet peeves, child psychologists, post office and others. Mostly unavailable elsewhere. 73 illustrations by Peter Arno and others. 183pp. 5⅜ x 8½. 22410-4 Pa. $6.95

YEKL and THE IMPORTED BRIDEGROOM AND OTHER STORIES OF YIDDISH NEW YORK, Abraham Cahan. Film Hester Street based on *Yekl* (1896). Novel, other stories among first about Jewish immigrants on N.Y.'s East Side. 240pp. 5⅜ x 8½. 22427-9 Pa. $7.95

SELECTED POEMS, Walt Whitman. Generous sampling from *Leaves of Grass*. Twenty-four poems include "I Hear America Singing," "Song of the Open Road," "I Sing the Body Electric," "When Lilacs Last in the Dooryard Bloom'd," "O Captain! My Captain!"—all reprinted from an authoritative edition. Lists of titles and first lines. 128pp. 5³⁄₁₆ x 8¼. 26878-0 Pa. $1.00

THE BEST TALES OF HOFFMANN, E. T. A. Hoffmann. 10 of Hoffmann's most important stories: "Nutcracker and the King of Mice," "The Golden Flowerpot," etc. 458pp. 5⅜ x 8½.   21793-0 Pa. $9.95

FROM FETISH TO GOD IN ANCIENT EGYPT, E. A. Wallis Budge. Rich detailed survey of Egyptian conception of "God" and gods, magic, cult of animals, Osiris, more. Also, superb English translations of hymns and legends. 240 illustrations. 545pp. 5⅜ x 8½.   25803-3 Pa. $13.95

FRENCH STORIES/CONTES FRANÇAIS: A Dual-Language Book, Wallace Fowlie. Ten stories by French masters, Voltaire to Camus: "Micromegas" by Voltaire; "The Atheist's Mass" by Balzac; "Minuet" by de Maupassant; "The Guest" by Camus, six more. Excellent English translations on facing pages. Also French-English vocabulary list, exercises, more. 352pp. 5⅜ x 8½.   26443-2 Pa. $9.95

CHICAGO AT THE TURN OF THE CENTURY IN PHOTOGRAPHS: 122 Historic Views from the Collections of the Chicago Historical Society, Larry A. Viskochil. Rare large-format prints offer detailed views of City Hall, State Street, the Loop, Hull House, Union Station, many other landmarks, circa 1904-1913. Introduction. Captions. Maps. 144pp. 9⅜ x 12¼.   24656-6 Pa. $12.95

OLD BROOKLYN IN EARLY PHOTOGRAPHS, 1865-1929, William Lee Younger. Luna Park, Gravesend race track, construction of Grand Army Plaza, moving of Hotel Brighton, etc. 157 previously unpublished photographs. 165pp. 8⅞ x 11¾.
                                                                      23587-4 Pa. $13.95

THE MYTHS OF THE NORTH AMERICAN INDIANS, Lewis Spence. Rich anthology of the myths and legends of the Algonquins, Iroquois, Pawnees and Sioux, prefaced by an extensive historical and ethnological commentary. 36 illustrations. 480pp. 5⅜ x 8½.   25967-6 Pa. $10.95

AN ENCYCLOPEDIA OF BATTLES: Accounts of Over 1,560 Battles from 1479 B.C. to the Present, David Eggenberger. Essential details of every major battle in recorded history from the first battle of Megiddo in 1479 B.C. to Grenada in 1984. List of Battle Maps. New Appendix covering the years 1967-1984. Index. 99 illustrations. 544pp. 6½ x 9¼.   24913-1 Pa. $16.95

SAILING ALONE AROUND THE WORLD, Captain Joshua Slocum. First man to sail around the world, alone, in small boat. One of great feats of seamanship told in delightful manner. 67 illustrations. 294pp. 5⅜ x 8½.   20326-3 Pa. $6.95

ANARCHISM AND OTHER ESSAYS, Emma Goldman. Powerful, penetrating, prophetic essays on direct action, role of minorities, prison reform, puritan hypocrisy, violence, etc. 271pp. 5⅜ x 8½.   22484-8 Pa. $7.95

MYTHS OF THE HINDUS AND BUDDHISTS, Ananda K. Coomaraswamy and Sister Nivedita. Great stories of the epics; deeds of Krishna, Shiva, taken from puranas, Vedas, folk tales; etc. 32 illustrations. 400pp. 5⅜ x 8½.   21759-0 Pa. $12.95

THE TRAUMA OF BIRTH, Otto Rank. Rank's controversial thesis that anxiety neurosis is caused by profound psychological trauma which occurs at birth. 256pp. 5⅜ x 8½.   27974-X Pa. $7.95

A THEOLOGICO-POLITICAL TREATISE, Benedict Spinoza. Also contains unfinished Political Treatise. Great classic on religious liberty, theory of government on common consent. R. Elwes translation. Total of 421pp. 5⅜ x 8½. 20249-6 Pa. $10.95

MY BONDAGE AND MY FREEDOM, Frederick Douglass. Born a slave, Douglass became outspoken force in antislavery movement. The best of Douglass' autobiographies. Graphic description of slave life. 464pp. 5⅜ x 8½. 22457-0 Pa. $8.95

FOLLOWING THE EQUATOR: A Journey Around the World, Mark Twain. Fascinating humorous account of 1897 voyage to Hawaii, Australia, India, New Zealand, etc. Ironic, bemused reports on peoples, customs, climate, flora and fauna, politics, much more. 197 illustrations. 720pp. 5⅜ x 8½. 26113-1 Pa. $15.95

THE PEOPLE CALLED SHAKERS, Edward D. Andrews. Definitive study of Shakers: origins, beliefs, practices, dances, social organization, furniture and crafts, etc. 33 illustrations. 351pp. 5⅜ x 8½. 21081-2 Pa. $10.95

THE MYTHS OF GREECE AND ROME, H. A. Guerber. A classic of mythology, generously illustrated, long prized for its simple, graphic, accurate retelling of the principal myths of Greece and Rome, and for its commentary on their origins and significance. With 64 illustrations by Michelangelo, Raphael, Titian, Rubens, Canova, Bernini and others. 480pp. 5⅜ x 8½. 27584-1 Pa. $9.95

PSYCHOLOGY OF MUSIC, Carl E. Seashore. Classic work discusses music as a medium from psychological viewpoint. Clear treatment of physical acoustics, auditory apparatus, sound perception, development of musical skills, nature of musical feeling, host of other topics. 88 figures. 408pp. 5⅜ x 8½. 21851-1 Pa. $11.95

THE PHILOSOPHY OF HISTORY, Georg W. Hegel. Great classic of Western thought develops concept that history is not chance but rational process, the evolution of freedom. 457pp. 5⅜ x 8½. 20112-0 Pa. $9.95

THE BOOK OF TEA, Kakuzo Okakura. Minor classic of the Orient: entertaining, charming explanation, interpretation of traditional Japanese culture in terms of tea ceremony. 94pp. 5⅜ x 8½. 20070-1 Pa. $3.95

LIFE IN ANCIENT EGYPT, Adolf Erman. Fullest, most thorough, detailed older account with much not in more recent books, domestic life, religion, magic, medicine, commerce, much more. Many illustrations reproduce tomb paintings, carvings, hieroglyphs, etc. 597pp. 5⅜ x 8½. 22632-8 Pa. $12.95

SUNDIALS, Their Theory and Construction, Albert Waugh. Far and away the best, most thorough coverage of ideas, mathematics concerned, types, construction, adjusting anywhere. Simple, nontechnical treatment allows even children to build several of these dials. Over 100 illustrations. 230pp. 5⅜ x 8½. 22947-5 Pa. $8.95

THEORETICAL HYDRODYNAMICS, L. M. Milne-Thomson. Classic exposition of the mathematical theory of fluid motion, applicable to both hydrodynamics and aerodynamics. Over 600 exercises. 768pp. 6⅛ x 9¼. 68970-0 Pa. $20.95

SONGS OF EXPERIENCE: Facsimile Reproduction with 26 Plates in Full Color, William Blake. 26 full-color plates from a rare 1826 edition. Includes "TheTyger," "London," "Holy Thursday," and other poems. Printed text of poems. 48pp. 5¼ x 7. 24636-1 Pa. $4.95

OLD-TIME VIGNETTES IN FULL COLOR, Carol Belanger Grafton (ed.). Over 390 charming, often sentimental illustrations, selected from archives of Victorian graphics—pretty women posing, children playing, food, flowers, kittens and puppies, smiling cherubs, birds and butterflies, much more. All copyright-free. 48pp. 9¼ x 12¼. 27269-9 Pa. $7.95

PERSPECTIVE FOR ARTISTS, Rex Vicat Cole. Depth, perspective of sky and sea, shadows, much more, not usually covered. 391 diagrams, 81 reproductions of drawings and paintings. 279pp. 5⅜ x 8½. 22487-2 Pa. $9.95

DRAWING THE LIVING FIGURE, Joseph Sheppard. Innovative approach to artistic anatomy focuses on specifics of surface anatomy, rather than muscles and bones. Over 170 drawings of live models in front, back and side views, and in widely varying poses. Accompanying diagrams. 177 illustrations. Introduction. Index. 144pp. 8⅜ x11¼. 26723-7 Pa. $9.95

GOTHIC AND OLD ENGLISH ALPHABETS: 100 Complete Fonts, Dan X. Solo. Add power, elegance to posters, signs, other graphics with 100 stunning copyright-free alphabets: Blackstone, Dolbey, Germania, 97 more—including many lower-case, numerals, punctuation marks. 104pp. 8⅛ x 11. 24695-7 Pa. $8.95

HOW TO DO BEADWORK, Mary White. Fundamental book on craft from simple projects to five-bead chains and woven works. 106 illustrations. 142pp. 5⅜ x 8. 20697-1 Pa. $5.95

THE BOOK OF WOOD CARVING, Charles Marshall Sayers. Finest book for beginners discusses fundamentals and offers 34 designs. "Absolutely first rate . . . well thought out and well executed."–E. J. Tangerman. 118pp. 7¾ x 10⅝. 23654-4 Pa. $7.95

ILLUSTRATED CATALOG OF CIVIL WAR MILITARY GOODS: Union Army Weapons, Insignia, Uniform Accessories, and Other Equipment, Schuyler, Hartley, and Graham. Rare, profusely illustrated 1846 catalog includes Union Army uniform and dress regulations, arms and ammunition, coats, insignia, flags, swords, rifles, etc. 226 illustrations. 160pp. 9 x 12. 24939-5 Pa. $10.95

WOMEN'S FASHIONS OF THE EARLY 1900s: An Unabridged Republication of "New York Fashions, 1909," National Cloak & Suit Co. Rare catalog of mail-order fashions documents women's and children's clothing styles shortly after the turn of the century. Captions offer full descriptions, prices. Invaluable resource for fashion, costume historians. Approximately 725 illustrations. 128pp. 8⅜ x 11¼. 27276-1 Pa. $11.95

THE 1912 AND 1915 GUSTAV STICKLEY FURNITURE CATALOGS, Gustav Stickley. With over 200 detailed illustrations and descriptions, these two catalogs are essential reading and reference materials and identification guides for Stickley furniture. Captions cite materials, dimensions and prices. 112pp. 6½ x 9¼. 26676-1 Pa. $9.95

EARLY AMERICAN LOCOMOTIVES, John H. White, Jr. Finest locomotive engravings from early 19th century: historical (1804–74), main-line (after 1870), special, foreign, etc. 147 plates. 142pp. 11⅜ x 8¼. 22772-3 Pa. $12.95

THE TALL SHIPS OF TODAY IN PHOTOGRAPHS, Frank O. Braynard. Lavishly illustrated tribute to nearly 100 majestic contemporary sailing vessels: Amerigo Vespucci, Clearwater, Constitution, Eagle, Mayflower, Sea Cloud, Victory, many more. Authoritative captions provide statistics, background on each ship. 190 black-and-white photographs and illustrations. Introduction. 128pp. 8⅞ x 11¾. 27163-3 Pa. $14.95

LITTLE BOOK OF EARLY AMERICAN CRAFTS AND TRADES, Peter Stockham (ed.). 1807 children's book explains crafts and trades: baker, hatter, cooper, potter, and many others. 23 copperplate illustrations. 140pp. 4⅝ x 6.
23336-7 Pa. $4.95

VICTORIAN FASHIONS AND COSTUMES FROM HARPER'S BAZAR, 1867–1898, Stella Blum (ed.). Day costumes, evening wear, sports clothes, shoes, hats, other accessories in over 1,000 detailed engravings. 320pp. 9⅜ x 12¼.
22990-4 Pa. $16.95

GUSTAV STICKLEY, THE CRAFTSMAN, Mary Ann Smith. Superb study surveys broad scope of Stickley's achievement, especially in architecture. Design philosophy, rise and fall of the Craftsman empire, descriptions and floor plans for many Craftsman houses, more. 86 black-and-white halftones. 31 line illustrations. Introduction 208pp. 6½ x 9¼. 27210-9 Pa. $9.95

THE LONG ISLAND RAIL ROAD IN EARLY PHOTOGRAPHS, Ron Ziel. Over 220 rare photos, informative text document origin (1844) and development of rail service on Long Island. Vintage views of early trains, locomotives, stations, passengers, crews, much more. Captions. 8⅞ x 11¾. 26301-0 Pa. $14.95

VOYAGE OF THE LIBERDADE, Joshua Slocum. Great 19th-century mariner's thrilling, first-hand account of the wreck of his ship off South America, the 35-foot boat he built from the wreckage, and its remarkable voyage home. 128pp. 5⅜ x 8½.
40022-0 Pa. $5.95

TEN BOOKS ON ARCHITECTURE, Vitruvius. The most important book ever written on architecture. Early Roman aesthetics, technology, classical orders, site selection, all other aspects. Morgan translation. 331pp. 5⅜ x 8½. 20645-9 Pa. $8.95

THE HUMAN FIGURE IN MOTION, Eadweard Muybridge. More than 4,500 stopped-action photos, in action series, showing undraped men, women, children jumping, lying down, throwing, sitting, wrestling, carrying, etc. 390pp. 7⅞ x 10⅝.
20204-6 Clothbd. $27.95

TREES OF THE EASTERN AND CENTRAL UNITED STATES AND CANADA, William M. Harlow. Best one-volume guide to 140 trees. Full descriptions, woodlore, range, etc. Over 600 illustrations. Handy size. 288pp. 4½ x 6⅜.
20395-6 Pa. $6.95

SONGS OF WESTERN BIRDS, Dr. Donald J. Borror. Complete song and call repertoire of 60 western species, including flycatchers, juncoes, cactus wrens, many more–includes fully illustrated booklet. Cassette and manual 99913-0 $8.95

GROWING AND USING HERBS AND SPICES, Milo Miloradovich. Versatile handbook provides all the information needed for cultivation and use of all the herbs and spices available in North America. 4 illustrations. Index. Glossary. 236pp. 5⅜ x 8½.
25058-X Pa. $7.95

BIG BOOK OF MAZES AND LABYRINTHS, Walter Shepherd. 50 mazes and labyrinths in all–classical, solid, ripple, and more–in one great volume. Perfect inexpensive puzzler for clever youngsters. Full solutions. 112pp. 8⅛ x 11.
22951-3 Pa. $5.95

PIANO TUNING, J. Cree Fischer. Clearest, best book for beginner, amateur. Simple repairs, raising dropped notes, tuning by easy method of flattened fifths. No previous skills needed. 4 illustrations. 201pp. 5⅜ x 8½. 23267-0 Pa. $6.95

HINTS TO SINGERS, Lillian Nordica. Selecting the right teacher, developing confidence, overcoming stage fright, and many other important skills receive thoughtful discussion in this indispensible guide, written by a world-famous diva of four decades' experience. 96pp. 5⅜ x 8½. 40094-8 Pa. $4.95

THE COMPLETE NONSENSE OF EDWARD LEAR, Edward Lear. All nonsense limericks, zany alphabets, Owl and Pussycat, songs, nonsense botany, etc., illustrated by Lear. Total of 320pp. 5⅜ x 8½. (AVAILABLE IN U.S. ONLY.) 20167-8 Pa. $7.95

VICTORIAN PARLOUR POETRY: An Annotated Anthology, Michael R. Turner. 117 gems by Longfellow, Tennyson, Browning, many lesser-known poets. "The Village Blacksmith," "Curfew Must Not Ring Tonight," "Only a Baby Small," dozens more, often difficult to find elsewhere. Index of poets, titles, first lines. xxiii + 325pp. 5⅝ x 8¼. 27044-0 Pa. $8.95

DUBLINERS, James Joyce. Fifteen stories offer vivid, tightly focused observations of the lives of Dublin's poorer classes. At least one, "The Dead," is considered a masterpiece. Reprinted complete and unabridged from standard edition. 160pp. 5 3/16 x 8¼. 26870-5 Pa. $1.00

GREAT WEIRD TALES: 14 Stories by Lovecraft, Blackwood, Machen and Others, S. T. Joshi (ed.). 14 spellbinding tales, including "The Sin Eater," by Fiona McLeod, "The Eye Above the Mantel," by Frank Belknap Long, as well as renowned works by R. H. Barlow, Lord Dunsany, Arthur Machen, W. C. Morrow and eight other masters of the genre. 256pp. 5⅜ x 8½. (Available in U.S. only.) 40436-6 Pa. $8.95

THE BOOK OF THE SACRED MAGIC OF ABRAMELIN THE MAGE, translated by S. MacGregor Mathers. Medieval manuscript of ceremonial magic. Basic document in Aleister Crowley, Golden Dawn groups. 268pp. 5⅜ x 8½. 23211-5 Pa. $9.95

NEW RUSSIAN-ENGLISH AND ENGLISH-RUSSIAN DICTIONARY, M. A. O'Brien. This is a remarkably handy Russian dictionary, containing a surprising amount of information, including over 70,000 entries. 366pp. 4½ x 6⅛. 20208-9 Pa. $10.95

HISTORIC HOMES OF THE AMERICAN PRESIDENTS, Second, Revised Edition, Irvin Haas. A traveler's guide to American Presidential homes, most open to the public, depicting and describing homes occupied by every American President from George Washington to George Bush. With visiting hours, admission charges, travel routes. 175 photographs. Index. 160pp. 8¼ x 11. 26751-2 Pa. $11.95

NEW YORK IN THE FORTIES, Andreas Feininger. 162 brilliant photographs by the well-known photographer, formerly with *Life* magazine. Commuters, shoppers, Times Square at night, much else from city at its peak. Captions by John von Hartz. 181pp. 9¼ x 10¾. 23585-8 Pa. $13.95

INDIAN SIGN LANGUAGE, William Tomkins. Over 525 signs developed by Sioux and other tribes. Written instructions and diagrams. Also 290 pictographs. 111pp. 6⅛ x 9¼. 22029-X Pa. $3.95

ANATOMY: A Complete Guide for Artists, Joseph Sheppard. A master of figure drawing shows artists how to render human anatomy convincingly. Over 460 illustrations. 224pp. 8⅜ x 11¼.   27279-6 Pa. $11.95

MEDIEVAL CALLIGRAPHY: Its History and Technique, Marc Drogin. Spirited history, comprehensive instruction manual covers 13 styles (ca. 4th century through 15th). Excellent photographs; directions for duplicating medieval techniques with modern tools. 224pp. 8⅜ x 11¼.   26142-5 Pa. $12.95

DRIED FLOWERS: How to Prepare Them, Sarah Whitlock and Martha Rankin. Complete instructions on how to use silica gel, meal and borax, perlite aggregate, sand and borax, glycerine and water to create attractive permanent flower arrangements. 12 illustrations. 32pp. 5⅜ x 8½.   21802-3 Pa. $1.00

EASY-TO-MAKE BIRD FEEDERS FOR WOODWORKERS, Scott D. Campbell. Detailed, simple-to-use guide for designing, constructing, caring for and using feeders. Text, illustrations for 12 classic and contemporary designs. 96pp. 5⅜ x 8½.
25847-5 Pa. $3.95

SCOTTISH WONDER TALES FROM MYTH AND LEGEND, Donald A. Mackenzie. 16 lively tales tell of giants rumbling down mountainsides, of a magic wand that turns stone pillars into warriors, of gods and goddesses, evil hags, powerful forces and more. 240pp. 5⅜ x 8½.   29677-6 Pa. $6.95

THE HISTORY OF UNDERCLOTHES, C. Willett Cunnington and Phyllis Cunnington. Fascinating, well-documented survey covering six centuries of English undergarments, enhanced with over 100 illustrations: 12th-century laced-up bodice, footed long drawers (1795), 19th-century bustles, l9th-century corsets for men, Victorian "bust improvers," much more. 272pp. 5⅜ x 8¼.   27124-2 Pa. $9.95

ARTS AND CRAFTS FURNITURE: The Complete Brooks Catalog of 1912, Brooks Manufacturing Co. Photos and detailed descriptions of more than 150 now very collectible furniture designs from the Arts and Crafts movement depict davenports, settees, buffets, desks, tables, chairs, bedsteads, dressers and more, all built of solid, quarter-sawed oak. Invaluable for students and enthusiasts of antiques, Americana and the decorative arts. 80pp. 6½ x 9¼.   27471-3 Pa. $8.95

WILBUR AND ORVILLE: A Biography of the Wright Brothers, Fred Howard. Definitive, crisply written study tells the full story of the brothers' lives and work. A vividly written biography, unparalleled in scope and color, that also captures the spirit of an extraordinary era. 560pp. 6¹/₈ x 9¹/₄.   40297-5 Pa. $17.95

THE ARTS OF THE SAILOR: Knotting, Splicing and Ropework, Hervey Garrett Smith. Indispensable shipboard reference covers tools, basic knots and useful hitches; handsewing and canvas work, more. Over 100 illustrations. Delightful reading for sea lovers. 256pp. 5⅜ x 8½.   26440-8 Pa. $8.95

FRANK LLOYD WRIGHT'S FALLINGWATER: The House and Its History, Second, Revised Edition, Donald Hoffmann. A total revision—both in text and illustrations—of the standard document on Fallingwater, the boldest, most personal architectural statement of Wright's mature years, updated with valuable new material from the recently opened Frank Lloyd Wright Archives. "Fascinating"—*The New York Times*. 116 illustrations. 128pp. 9¼ x 10¾.   27430-6 Pa. $12.95

PHOTOGRAPHIC SKETCHBOOK OF THE CIVIL WAR, Alexander Gardner. 100 photos taken on field during the Civil War. Famous shots of Manassas Harper's Ferry, Lincoln, Richmond, slave pens, etc. 244pp. 10⅝ x 8¼. 22731-6 Pa. $10.95

FIVE ACRES AND INDEPENDENCE, Maurice G. Kains. Great back-to-the-land classic explains basics of self-sufficient farming. The one book to get. 95 illustrations. 397pp. 5⅜ x 8½. 20974-1 Pa. $7.95

SONGS OF EASTERN BIRDS, Dr. Donald J. Borror. Songs and calls of 60 species most common to eastern U.S.: warblers, woodpeckers, flycatchers, thrushes, larks, many more in high-quality recording. Cassette and manual 99912-2 $9.95

A MODERN HERBAL, Margaret Grieve. Much the fullest, most exact, most useful compilation of herbal material. Gigantic alphabetical encyclopedia, from aconite to zedoary, gives botanical information, medical properties, folklore, economic uses, much else. Indispensable to serious reader. 161 illustrations. 888pp. 6½ x 9¼. 2-vol. set. (Available in U.S. only.) Vol. I: 22798-7 Pa. $9.95
Vol. II: 22799-5 Pa. $9.95

HIDDEN TREASURE MAZE BOOK, Dave Phillips. Solve 34 challenging mazes accompanied by heroic tales of adventure. Evil dragons, people-eating plants, bloodthirsty giants, many more dangerous adversaries lurk at every twist and turn. 34 mazes, stories, solutions. 48pp. 8¼ x 11. 24566-7 Pa. $2.95

LETTERS OF W. A. MOZART, Wolfgang A. Mozart. Remarkable letters show bawdy wit, humor, imagination, musical insights, contemporary musical world; includes some letters from Leopold Mozart. 276pp. 5⅜ x 8½. 22859-2 Pa. $7.95

BASIC PRINCIPLES OF CLASSICAL BALLET, Agrippina Vaganova. Great Russian theoretician, teacher explains methods for teaching classical ballet. 118 illustrations. 175pp. 5⅜ x 8½. 22036-2 Pa. $6.95

THE JUMPING FROG, Mark Twain. Revenge edition. The original story of The Celebrated Jumping Frog of Calaveras County, a hapless French translation, and Twain's hilarious "retranslation" from the French. 12 illustrations. 66pp. 5⅜ x 8½. 22686-7 Pa. $3.95

BEST REMEMBERED POEMS, Martin Gardner (ed.). The 126 poems in this superb collection of 19th- and 20th-century British and American verse range from Shelley's "To a Skylark" to the impassioned "Renascence" of Edna St. Vincent Millay and to Edward Lear's whimsical "The Owl and the Pussycat." 224pp. 5⅜ x 8½. 27165-X Pa. $5.95

COMPLETE SONNETS, William Shakespeare. Over 150 exquisite poems deal with love, friendship, the tyranny of time, beauty's evanescence, death and other themes in language of remarkable power, precision and beauty. Glossary of archaic terms. 80pp. 5³⁄₁₆ x 8¼. 26686-9 Pa. $1.00

BODIES IN A BOOKSHOP, R. T. Campbell. Challenging mystery of blackmail and murder with ingenious plot and superbly drawn characters. In the best tradition of British suspense fiction. 192pp. 5⅜ x 8½. 24720-1 Pa. $6.95

THE WIT AND HUMOR OF OSCAR WILDE, Alvin Redman (ed.). More than 1,000 ripostes, paradoxes, wisecracks: Work is the curse of the drinking classes; I can resist everything except temptation; etc. 258pp. 5⅜ x 8½. 20602-5 Pa. $6.95

SHAKESPEARE LEXICON AND QUOTATION DICTIONARY, Alexander Schmidt. Full definitions, locations, shades of meaning in every word in plays and poems. More than 50,000 exact quotations. 1,485pp. 6½ x 9¼. 2-vol. set.
Vol. 1: 22726-X Pa. $17.95
Vol. 2: 22727-8 Pa. $17.95

SELECTED POEMS, Emily Dickinson. Over 100 best-known, best-loved poems by one of America's foremost poets, reprinted from authoritative early editions. No comparable edition at this price. Index of first lines. 64pp. 5³⁄₁₆ x 8¼.
26466-1 Pa. $1.00

THE INSIDIOUS DR. FU-MANCHU, Sax Rohmer. The first of the popular mystery series introduces a pair of English detectives to their archnemesis, the diabolical Dr. Fu-Manchu. Flavorful atmosphere, fast-paced action, and colorful characters enliven this classic of the genre. 208pp. 5³⁄₁₆ x 8¼. 29898-1 Pa. $2.00

THE MALLEUS MALEFICARUM OF KRAMER AND SPRENGER, translated by Montague Summers. Full text of most important witchhunter's "bible," used by both Catholics and Protestants. 278pp. 6⅝ x 10. 22802-9 Pa. $12.95

SPANISH STORIES/CUENTOS ESPAÑOLES: A Dual-Language Book, Angel Flores (ed.). Unique format offers 13 great stories in Spanish by Cervantes, Borges, others. Faithful English translations on facing pages. 352pp. 5⅜ x 8½.
25399-6 Pa. $8.95

GARDEN CITY, LONG ISLAND, IN EARLY PHOTOGRAPHS, 1869–1919, Mildred H. Smith. Handsome treasury of 118 vintage pictures, accompanied by carefully researched captions, document the Garden City Hotel fire (1899), the Vanderbilt Cup Race (1908), the first airmail flight departing from the Nassau Boulevard Aerodrome (1911), and much more. 96pp. 8⅞ x 11¾. 40669-5 Pa. $12.95

OLD QUEENS, N.Y., IN EARLY PHOTOGRAPHS, Vincent F. Seyfried and William Asadorian. Over 160 rare photographs of Maspeth, Jamaica, Jackson Heights, and other areas. Vintage views of DeWitt Clinton mansion, 1939 World's Fair and more. Captions. 192pp. 8⅞ x 11. 26358-4 Pa. $12.95

CAPTURED BY THE INDIANS: 15 Firsthand Accounts, 1750-1870, Frederick Drimmer. Astounding true historical accounts of grisly torture, bloody conflicts, relentless pursuits, miraculous escapes and more, by people who lived to tell the tale. 384pp. 5⅜ x 8½. 24901-8 Pa. $8.95

THE WORLD'S GREAT SPEECHES (Fourth Enlarged Edition), Lewis Copeland, Lawrence W. Lamm, and Stephen J. McKenna. Nearly 300 speeches provide public speakers with a wealth of updated quotes and inspiration–from Pericles' funeral oration and William Jennings Bryan's "Cross of Gold Speech" to Malcolm X's powerful words on the Black Revolution and Earl of Spenser's tribute to his sister, Diana, Princess of Wales. 944pp. 5⅜ x 8⅜. 40903-1 Pa. $15.95

THE BOOK OF THE SWORD, Sir Richard F. Burton. Great Victorian scholar/adventurer's eloquent, erudite history of the "queen of weapons"–from prehistory to early Roman Empire. Evolution and development of early swords, variations (sabre, broadsword, cutlass, scimitar, etc.), much more. 336pp. 6⅛ x 9¼.
25434-8 Pa. $9.95

AUTOBIOGRAPHY: The Story of My Experiments with Truth, Mohandas K. Gandhi. Boyhood, legal studies, purification, the growth of the Satyagraha (nonviolent protest) movement. Critical, inspiring work of the man responsible for the freedom of India. 480pp. 5⅜ x 8½. (Available in U.S. only.) 24593-4 Pa. $8.95

CELTIC MYTHS AND LEGENDS, T. W. Rolleston. Masterful retelling of Irish and Welsh stories and tales. Cuchulain, King Arthur, Deirdre, the Grail, many more. First paperback edition. 58 full-page illustrations. 512pp. 5⅜ x 8½. 26507-2 Pa. $9.95

THE PRINCIPLES OF PSYCHOLOGY, William James. Famous long course complete, unabridged. Stream of thought, time perception, memory, experimental methods; great work decades ahead of its time. 94 figures. 1,391pp. 5⅜ x 8½. 2-vol. set.
Vol. I: 20381-6 Pa. $14.95
Vol. II: 20382-4 Pa. $14.95

THE WORLD AS WILL AND REPRESENTATION, Arthur Schopenhauer. Definitive English translation of Schopenhauer's life work, correcting more than 1,000 errors, omissions in earlier translations. Translated by E. F. J. Payne. Total of 1,269pp. 5⅜ x 8½. 2-vol. set. Vol. 1: 21761-2 Pa. $12.95
Vol. 2: 21762-0 Pa. $12.95

MAGIC AND MYSTERY IN TIBET, Madame Alexandra David-Neel. Experiences among lamas, magicians, sages, sorcerers, Bonpa wizards. A true psychic discovery. 32 illustrations. 321pp. 5⅜ x 8½. (Available in U.S. only.) 22682-4 Pa. $9.95

THE EGYPTIAN BOOK OF THE DEAD, E. A. Wallis Budge. Complete reproduction of Ani's papyrus, finest ever found. Full hieroglyphic text, interlinear transliteration, word-for-word translation, smooth translation. 533pp. 6½ x 9¼.
21866-X Pa. $12.95

MATHEMATICS FOR THE NONMATHEMATICIAN, Morris Kline. Detailed, college-level treatment of mathematics in cultural and historical context, with numerous exercises. Recommended Reading Lists. Tables. Numerous figures. 641pp. 5⅜ x 8½.
24823-2 Pa. $11.95

PROBABILISTIC METHODS IN THE THEORY OF STRUCTURES, Isaac Elishakoff. Well-written introduction covers the elements of the theory of probability from two or more random variables, the reliability of such multivariable structures, the theory of random function, Monte Carlo methods of treating problems incapable of exact solution, and more. Examples. 502pp. 5³/₈ x 8¹/₂. 40691-1 Pa. $16.95

THE RIME OF THE ANCIENT MARINER, Gustave Doré, S. T. Coleridge. Doré's finest work; 34 plates capture moods, subtleties of poem. Flawless full-size reproductions printed on facing pages with authoritative text of poem. "Beautiful. Simply beautiful."–*Publisher's Weekly.* 77pp. 9¼ x 12. 22305-1 Pa. $7.95

NORTH AMERICAN INDIAN DESIGNS FOR ARTISTS AND CRAFTSPEOPLE, Eva Wilson. Over 360 authentic copyright-free designs adapted from Navajo blankets, Hopi pottery, Sioux buffalo hides, more. Geometrics, symbolic figures, plant and animal motifs, etc. 128pp. 8⅜ x 11. (Not for sale in the United Kingdom.) 25341-4 Pa. $9.95

SCULPTURE: Principles and Practice, Louis Slobodkin. Step-by-step approach to clay, plaster, metals, stone; classical and modern. 253 drawings, photos. 255pp. 8⅛ x 11.
22960-2 Pa. $11.95

THE INFLUENCE OF SEA POWER UPON HISTORY, 1660–1783, A. T. Mahan. Influential classic of naval history and tactics still used as text in war colleges. First paperback edition. 4 maps. 24 battle plans. 640pp. 5⅜ x 8½. 25509-3 Pa. $14.95

THE STORY OF THE TITANIC AS TOLD BY ITS SURVIVORS, Jack Winocour (ed.). What it was really like. Panic, despair, shocking inefficiency, and a little heroism. More thrilling than any fictional account. 26 illustrations. 320pp. 5⅜ x 8½. 20610-6 Pa. $8.95

FAIRY AND FOLK TALES OF THE IRISH PEASANTRY, William Butler Yeats (ed.). Treasury of 64 tales from the twilight world of Celtic myth and legend: "The Soul Cages," "The Kildare Pooka," "King O'Toole and his Goose," many more. Introduction and Notes by W. B. Yeats. 352pp. 5⅜ x 8½. 26941-8 Pa. $8.95

BUDDHIST MAHAYANA TEXTS, E. B. Cowell and others (eds.). Superb, accurate translations of basic documents in Mahayana Buddhism, highly important in history of religions. The Buddha-karita of Asvaghosha, Larger Sukhavativyuha, more. 448pp. 5⅜ x 8½. 25552-2 Pa. $12.95

ONE TWO THREE . . . INFINITY: Facts and Speculations of Science, George Gamow. Great physicist's fascinating, readable overview of contemporary science: number theory, relativity, fourth dimension, entropy, genes, atomic structure, much more. 128 illustrations. Index. 352pp. 5⅜ x 8½. 25664-2 Pa. $9.95

EXPERIMENTATION AND MEASUREMENT, W. J. Youden. Introductory manual explains laws of measurement in simple terms and offers tips for achieving accuracy and minimizing errors. Mathematics of measurement, use of instruments, experimenting with machines. 1994 edition. Foreword. Preface. Introduction. Epilogue. Selected Readings. Glossary. Index. Tables and figures. 128pp. 5³/₈ x 8¹/₂. 40451-X Pa. $6.95

DALÍ ON MODERN ART: The Cuckolds of Antiquated Modern Art, Salvador Dalí. Influential painter skewers modern art and its practitioners. Outrageous evaluations of Picasso, Cézanne, Turner, more. 15 renderings of paintings discussed. 44 calligraphic decorations by Dalí. 96pp. 5⅜ x 8½. (Available in U.S. only.) 29220-7 Pa. $5.95

ANTIQUE PLAYING CARDS: A Pictorial History, Henry René D'Allemagne. Over 900 elaborate, decorative images from rare playing cards (14th–20th centuries): Bacchus, death, dancing dogs, hunting scenes, royal coats of arms, players cheating, much more. 96pp. 9¼ x 12¼. 29265-7 Pa. $12.95

MAKING FURNITURE MASTERPIECES: 30 Projects with Measured Drawings, Franklin H. Gottshall. Step-by-step instructions, illustrations for constructing handsome, useful pieces, among them a Sheraton desk, Chippendale chair, Spanish desk, Queen Anne table and a William and Mary dressing mirror. 224pp. 8⅛ x 11¼. 29338-6 Pa. $13.95

THE FOSSIL BOOK: A Record of Prehistoric Life, Patricia V. Rich et al. Profusely illustrated definitive guide covers everything from single-celled organisms and dinosaurs to birds and mammals and the interplay between climate and man. Over 1,500 illustrations. 760pp. 7½ x 10⅛. 29371-8 Pa. $29.95

Prices subject to change without notice.

Available at your book dealer or write for free catalog to Dept. GI, Dover Publications, Inc., 31 East 2nd St., Mineola, N.Y. 11501. Dover publishes more than 500 books each year on science, elementary and advanced mathematics, biology, music, art, literary history, social sciences and other areas.